THE BEST WE CAN BE

The Story of
the Ithaca High School
Band, 1955-67

FRANK L. BATTISTI AND
R. BRUCE MUSGRAVE

Published by
Meredith Music Publications
a division of G.W. Music, Inc.
4899 Lerch Creek Ct., Galesville, MD 20765
http://www.meredithmusic.com

MEREDITH MUSIC PUBLICATIONS and its stylized double M logo are trademarks of
MEREDITH MUSIC PUBLICATIONS, a division of G.W. Music, Inc.

International Standard Book Number: 978-1-57463-159-3
Cataloging-in-Publication Data is on file with the Library of Congress.
Library of Congress Control Number: 2010932307
Printed and bound in U.S.A.

To the students in the 1955–67 Ithaca High School Band

"A joy to teach—energetic, creative, committed, dedicated, passionate—
everything a teacher could hope for."

Frank Battisti (Reunion Banquet, June 24, 2006)

"The future of music may not be with music itself, but rather....
in the way it makes itself a part of the finer things
humanity does and dreams of."

Charles Ives

CONTENTS

Acknowledgements ix

A Word from the Publisher x

A Word from the Authors xi

Time Line: Ithaca High School Band, 1953–67 xiii

Introduction xvii

PART I	**Frank Battisti Arrives at Ithaca High School (1953–55)** . . . 1	
CHAPTER 1	The Apprenticeship: Teaching at Ithaca High School, 1953–54 3	
CHAPTER 2	The Torch is Passed: John W. Graves's Final Year as IHS Band Director, 1954–55 5	

PART II	**Building a Program—Foundations for Pursuing Individual and Group Excellence (1955–60)** 7	
CHAPTER 3	Traction and Momentum: Band Grows in Size and Quality of Performance, 1955–56 9	
	Recollection by Peter Farrow, Class of 1960 . . . . 15 Weekly Lessons with Mr. B	
CHAPTER 4	Looking Good—Sounding Great—Receiving Public Recognition—Program Expanded, 1956–57 16	
	Recollection by Peter Farrow, Class of 1960 . . . . 19 Brass Choir Rehearsing in Mr. B's Office at Old IHS	

CHAPTER 5   Elation and "That Funny Music"—Concert in Canada—
Commissioning of First Piece, 1957–58 21

Recollection by Peter Farrow, Class of 1960 27
Marching Band Rehearsal at Old IHS

CHAPTER 6   Premier Premiere: First World Premiere Performance—
More Travel—Bach Honor Society, 1958–59. 28

Recollections by Lois Lounsbery, Class of 1960 37
Band and Washington Park
First Rehearsal
Theory Class

CHAPTER 7   Off to First Band Camp—Band Parents' Night—
Trips to Rochester, NY to hear Eastman Wind Ensemble
Concerts—Maestro Fennell's First Visit to IHS, 1959–60 . . . 38

Recollections by Peter Farrow, Class of 1960. 45
First Band Camp
Going to Eastman Wind Ensemble Concerts
Fennell Visits IHS for the First Time

Recollection by Lois Lounsbery, Class of 1960 47
Fennell's Visit and Mozart *Serenade No. 10*

PART III   **Musical Experiences to Stimulate Imagination, Creativity,
and Expressive Spirit** . . . . ·49

CHAPTER 8   In the New High School: A New IHS—Persichetti
Commission—Expanded Repertoire, 1960–61 51

Reflection by Bruce Musgrave, Class of 1965. 56
Technology, Such As It Was

CHAPTER 9   In the Big House: Midwest Tour—A Second Band—Small
Ensembles Perform at Eastman School of Music, 1961–62 . . .58

Reflection by Bruce Musgrave, Class of 1965. 73
Demanding in Public, Supportive in Private

CHAPTER 10   A Gift to Remember: Special Christmas Present—
Solo and Small Ensemble Recitals—Theory and
Conducting Classes, 1962–63 74

Reflection by Bruce Musgrave, Class of 1965. 85
Outside the Music

CHAPTER 11   The Fallen Chief: New York Trip and Grief—Persichetti
Memorial Commission—Project Creativity—Severinsen—
Contemporary Music Festival—*Remembrance*, 1963–64 87

Reflection by Bruce Musgrave, Class of 1965 101
Marching Band-Concert Band: the Strange Synergy

Reflection by Bruce Musgrave, Class of 1965 111
Creativity

CHAPTER 12   A Great One: On His Own Dime—Benny Goodman Visits
IHS—ABC Performance—Composer-in-Residence—
Premieres of Three Commissioned Works, 1964–65 113

Reflection by Bruce Musgrave, Class of 1965 129
Leadership, Role Models, and Mentors

CHAPTER 13   A Program in Full Stride: Midwest Clinic Concert with
Fennell, Revelli, Beeler, Sinta, Buyse and New York Brass
Quintet—Second Contemporary Music Festival—Premieres
of Three More Commissioned Pieces, 1965–66 131

Reflection by Bruce Musgrave, Class of 1965 153
Band Director as Coach

CHAPTER 14   The Beat Goes On: Yankee Stadium Performance—Boston
MENC Concert—Mr. B's Final Concert, 1966–67 155

Reflection by Bruce Musgrave, Class of 1965 174
Competition and Cooperation

PART IV   **Departure and Reunion** 177

CHAPTER 15   Departure: Mr. B Leaves IHS, 1967 179

Reflection by Bruce Musgrave, Class of 1965 185
Why It Happened

CHAPTER 16   Returns: Ithaca High School Band Reunion—"The Best
Reunion Ever!!!," June 23–24, 2006 188

Reflection by Bruce Musgrave, Class of 1965 194
Where Are They Now?

Postscript 197

About the Authors 198

APPENDICES

APPENDIX 1   A 50th-Anniversary Concert, May 7, 2009 201

APPENDIX 2   Ithaca High School Band Commissioned Works, 1955–67. . . 207

APPENDIX 3   Ithaca High School Band Recordings, 1955–67. 208

APPENDIX 4   Resources Used in Writing This Book. 208

ACKNOWLEDGEMENTS

The authors would like to thank the following individuals for their valuable assistance in writing this book.

Charlotte Battisti
Terry (McKeegan) Davis
Jody (Meade) Earle
Peter Farrow
John W. Graves
Lois Lounsbery
David Wickstrom

A WORD FROM THE PUBLISHER

I had no intention of publishing this book. As a publisher, it is necessary to read manuscripts on a daily basis and the idea of reading another manuscript, one that I had no intention of publishing, was not high on my list of priorities. However, as a friend of Frank Battisti and the publisher of his earlier works, I agreed to review the book and give him some feedback on it. The idea for writing a history of the 1955–67 Ithaca High School Band originated at a reunion of former students in Ithaca, NY in 2006. Many who attended expressed the wish that someone would write a complete history of the band during these years. Since Battisti was the only person who had witnessed and experienced everything that happened between 1955 and 1967, it fell to him to write it. *The Best We Can Be* is an incredible story about a dedicated group of students and their teacher, Frank Battisti—a man with vision, creativity and an incredible work ethic who challenged his students and himself to be the *best they could be*—**in everything they did.**

Once I began to read this *history*, I simply couldn't put it down. I was moved by the magnitude of the Ithaca program and all that was involved; the motivation, creativity, student-centered teaching and learning, commissions, half-time shows and a myriad of other components. Like Battisti's students, I too was motivated. I was motivated to share this incredible journey with others; band directors, teachers, parents, administrators and anyone interested in creative teaching and learning.

The Best We Can Be is an inspiring, uplifting story—a powerful model of what can be achieved through the dedicated pursuit of both individual and collective excellence. It is a must read for anyone involved in the education of young people.

Garwood Whaley,
President and Founder, Meredith Music Publications
January 11, 2010

A WORD FROM THE AUTHORS

As Garwood Whaley states in his "Word from the Publisher," the idea for writing a history of the 1955–67 Ithaca High School Band originated at a reunion of former band members in Ithaca, NY in 2006. Many expressed a desire that someone would write a complete history of the band during these years. Since I was the only person who had experienced everything that happened from 1955 through 1967, it fell to me to write this history.

Brian Norcross's *One Band That Took a Chance—the Ithaca High School Band from 1955 to 1967 Directed by Frank Battisti* is an excellent book. However, it focuses primarily on the activities and accomplishments of the IHS Concert Band during those years. *The Best We Can Be* covers the entire spectrum of the band's activities (i.e., all concert and marching band performances, trips, commissioning of works, contemporary music festivals, guest composers, conductors, soloists, etc.). The book's narrative is enhanced by many photographs, letters, programs, newspaper clippings, concert reviews, magazine articles, etc. Three former band members—Peter Farrow and Lois Lounsbery, IHS Band '55–60, and Bruce Musgrave, IHS Band '62–65—add personal recollections and reflections of their IHS Band experiences.

The words "me" and "I" never appear in this book. This is intentional. The success of 1955–67 Ithaca High School Band was the result of the dedication and collaborative effort of many people, including trusting and supportive parents; sympathetic school administrators; a community that valued music and the allied arts; dedicated teachers; guest artists such as Warren Benson, Frederick Fennell, Don Sinta; my wife Charlotte and our children; and most of all, the exceptional and dedicated students of the Ithaca High School Band. It was a privilege to be a part of it.

Frank L. Battisti '49
December 23, 2009

For those of us so fortunate as to have been members of the IHS Band, the memories are indelible; the influences, endless. Working through these materials to synthesize and sequence them for others has sharpened many of those memories, resurfaced others and, decades later, deepened an already deep appreciation of the marvelous impacts the band exerted. May reading this history have a similar effect on others who were there, by reviving those precious years. For those who were not directly involved, may these pages provide insight into the elements of an activity that meant so much to so many. The director's own words carry the most weight here, and he has indeed composed the majority of the narrative. Throughout the book the story is supplemented by "recollections" and "reflections" by immensely grateful former band members. For one of them, the 2006 IHS Band Reunion provided a starkly telling realization: of the fifty or so most important people in his life, some three dozen of them came his way during his three years in the IHS band, and virtually all of them attended that reunion.

Bruce Musgrave '65
December 21, 2009

TIME LINE: ITHACA HIGH SCHOOL BAND, 1953–67

1953	Frank Battisti begins teaching instrumental music lessons at IHS, assists Band Director John W. Graves.
December 1954	IHS Band brass players start playing Christmas carols at IHS faculty homes.
1955	Frank Battisti becomes Band Director at IHS.
	IHS Band begins series of annual school assembly concerts.
	IHS Band plays concert outside of Ithaca for the first time at Owego Free Academy, Owego, New York.
1958	IHS Band travels to Cornwall, Ontario, Canada for concert at St. Lawrence Collegiate—band's first trip outside of United States.
	IHS Band commissions first piece from Warren Benson.
	Bach Honor Society established by Mr. B and IHS Band members.
April 1959	IHS Concert and Marching Bands travel to Maryland and Washington, DC to present concerts in Annapolis and Westminster, MD and perform in the National Cherry Blossom Parade.
May 20, 1959	Premiere performance of *Night Song* by Warren Benson— IHS Band's first commissioned work.
Sept. 3–7, 1959	First IHS Band Camp at Ithaca College camp in Danby Hills.
February 5, 1960	Mr. B and band members travel to Rochester, NY to hear Eastman Wind Ensemble concert. Trips to these concerts continue for the next seven years.

March. 16, 1960	First IHS Band Parents' Night
May 29, 1960	Frederick Fennell visits IHS Band for first time—visits continue through 1967.
September 1960	New Ithaca High School opens with separate Music Building.
May 19, 1961	Premiere performance of Vincent Persichetti's *Serenade for Band*, IHS Band's third commissioned work.
August 10, 1961	First IHS Band Chicken Barbecue held at Stewart Park.
Nov. 21–27, 1961	IHS Band tour to Midwest. Marching Band performs in J. L. Hudson Parade in Detroit and at Cleveland Memorial Stadium for Cleveland Browns vs. New York Giants NFL game. Concert Band performs concerts in Dayton's NCR Auditorium and at Williamsville, NY High School.
May 2, 1962	Harvey Phillips guest soloist with IHS Band on two school assembly programs. Phillips-IHS Band relationship continues through 1967.
December 1962	IHS Band members commission Warren Benson to write piece for Mr. B as a Christmas gift. The piece, *Remembrance*, premiered in 1964.
January 1962	Repertory Band (later renamed Symphony Band) formed at IHS.
May 15, 1963	Donald Sinta performs solos with IHS Band on school assembly programs—begins long relationship with Mr. B and the IHS Band.
Nov. 21–24, 1963	IHS Band trip to New York City abruptly halted by the assassination of President John F. Kennedy. Performance at Yankee Stadium cancelled.
December 1963	IHS Band commissions Vincent Persichetti to write piece in memory of John F. Kennedy (*Turn Not Thy Face*).
January 1964	"Project Creativity" started.
February 26, 1964	Carl "Doc" Severinson performs solos on band's school assembly concerts.
April 13–19, 1964	First IHS Band Contemporary Music Festival.

April 23–24, 1964	IHS Invitational Band Festival.
July 21–24, 1964	Ithaca Summer Youth Band (IHS Concert Band) performs at New York World's Fair and Rockefeller Plaza.
December 26, 1964	IHS Band performs in Buffalo, NY for Buffalo Bills–San Diego Chargers AFL Championship game.
March 12, 1965	Benny Goodman performs with IHS Jazz Ensemble at school assembly concert.
April 28, 1965	IHS Band premieres Barney Childs's *Six Events for 58 Players*—first aleatoric piece written for high school band.
December 16, 1965	IHS Concert Band performs at Midwest Band Clinic in Chicago, Illinois.
May 11, 1966	IHS Band premieres three commissioned works by Alec Wilder, Warren Benson, and Walter Hartley on Spring Concert.
1966–67	David Borden becomes Ithaca Public Schools' MENC-Ford Foundation Composer-in-residence.
October 2, 1966	IHS Band performs in New York's Yankee Stadium for New York Giants–Cleveland Browns NFL game.
February 12, 1967	IHS Band performs concert at Eastern Division MENC Conference in Boston, Massachusetts. Program includes premiere performances of two newly commissioned works and *Prisms* (for concert band and pre-recorded electronic sounds) by Herbert Bielawa.
May 4–14, 1967	Second IHS Band Contemporary Music Festival.
May 17, 1967	IHS Band premieres three commissioned works by Warren Benson, Vincent Persichetti and Robert Ward. Mr. B's final concert with the IHS Concert Band.
October 2, 1967	Mr. B informs IHS Band students he is leaving Ithaca High School.
October 15 1967	IHS Band performs in Buffalo, New York for Buffalo Bills–Oakland Raiders NFL game.
November 4, 1967	Farewell Banquet for Mr. and Mrs. B at Cornell University's Statler Hotel.

April 1997	John Philip Sousa Foundation selects Mr. B's Ithaca High School Concert Band for their Historic Roll of Honor of High School Concert Bands, 1920–1980. This Roll of Honor identifies high school concert bands whose musical excellence at the national level exerted historically significant influence on high school band programs.
June 23–24, 2006	The 1955–67 IHS Band "best-ever reunion" in Ithaca, New York.
Oct. 12 & 17, 2006	Dual premiere performances of Dana Wilson's *Day Dreams* at New England Conservatory and Ithaca College. Work commissioned by former IHS Band students as a 75th birthday gift to Mr. B.
May 5–7, 2009	50th-Anniversary Concert and Celebration in Ithaca, NY (Boynton Middle and Ithaca High School Bands) marking the May 20, 1959 premiere performance of Warren Benson's *Night Song*, the first IHS Band-commissioned work.

Prefatory Note

Frank Battisti was never addressed as Mr. Battisti by the students in the Ithaca High School Band—to them, he was "Mr. B." This is the appellation that is used throughout this book.

Overview of the Ithaca High School Band Experience, 1955–67.

Membership in the Ithaca High School Band was challenging. Mr. B expected and demanded great commitment, dedication and hard work from everyone, including himself. The constant quest for "excellence," to be "the best one could be," challenged everyone and nurtured an awareness that achieving and maintaining "excellence" required extraordinary dedication and effort.

Mr. B tried to make every lesson, rehearsal, concert and marching band performance, etc. a thrilling and exciting EUREKA-DISCOVERY experience. He developed a band program that provided students with opportunities to experience music as re-creators (players), creators (composers) and consumers (listeners).

In seeking "group excellence," students discovered the importance of the individual in attaining it. Their collaborative music-making experiences brought them closer together (common denominators were magnified, differences diminished), elevated their spirits, deepened their souls and enriched their lives. Being dedicated, committed and working hard (striving to be "the best one could be") became an exciting, joyful, and fulfilling way of life.

Ithaca City School District in the 1950s–60s.

In the 1950s and '60s Ithaca, New York was a small community in the Finger Lakes region of New York State. Its 18,000 inhabitants (plus 22,000 faculty and students at Cornell University and Ithaca College) lived in relative seclusion in semi-rural Upstate New York. It was a place where people enjoyed living and hated to leave, where imaginations were fertile, and where things seemed to happen.

The Ithaca City School District served a community of 50,000, encompassing 155 square miles. The district headquarters and secondary schools were located in the City of Ithaca at the south end of Cayuga Lake. It consisted of thirteen elementary schools, two junior high schools, and one high school. In 1963 the graduating class at Ithaca High School numbered 563, of which 14 were finalists in the National Merit Scholarship competition and 55 were New York State Regents Scholarship winners. The total district enrollment in 1966–67 was 8,196 students. The district also supported an Adult Education program with an enrollment of 2,300. A staff of 480 professional employees and 222 service personnel carried on the work of the district's educational programs.

The Philosophy of the Ithaca High School Band Program, 1955–1967.

All IHS Band experiences were directed towards helping every student find "joy and excitement in music making and creative endeavor." Students studied and performed great music in small and large ensembles, composed pieces for their instruments, and collaborated with composers in giving birth to new works written especially for them. "Development of a 'creative' way of life, as experienced through creative musical endeavors, was the desired goal of the IHS Band Program."

The policy of the Ithaca Public Schools prohibited school music ensembles from participating in contests or competitions. Music was considered an art, and teachers were challenged to educate in a manner that helped students develop excitement for the intrinsic values of music. Contests and competitions were the antithesis of this educational objective.

1955–67 Ithaca High School Band—From One to Two Interconnected Musical Organizations.

In 1955 there was one Ithaca High School Band. The same roster of students performed at all outdoor and indoor events (i.e., high school football games, school concerts, community parades [Halloween, Veterans' Day] and civic events [School Board Nominating Committee Meeting, United Fund Rallies, etc.]).

In the late 1950s this "single band structure" was altered and the "Little Red" Marching Band and Concert Band became two separate, interconnected musical organizations. The "Little Red" Marching Band existed from September through early November, and the Concert Band and its affiliated ensembles (chamber music groups, jazz ensemble, Repertory/Symphony Band) for the remainder of the school year.

Summary of Ithaca High School Band Program, 1955–67—Visiting Composers, Conductors, Soloists, Ensembles.

1. Weekly Instrumental Music Lessons
2. Concert Ensembles:

   Concert Band
   Symphony Band
   Small Ensembles
   Jazz Lab Workshop/Ensemble

3. Marching Band
4. Solo and Chamber Music Recitals
5. Ithaca High School Band Commissioned Works Project
6. Project in Creativity
7. Guest Conductors, Soloists, Composers and Ensembles

   Conductors
   Frederick Fennell
   Clyde A. Roller
   Richard Franko Goldman
   Norman Dello Joio
   William D. Revelli
   Thomas Beversdorf
   Vincent Persichetti
   Walter Beeler

   Soloists
   Benny Goodman
   "Doc" Severinsen
   Harvey Phillips
   Donald Sinta
   Robert Jaeger
   Jimmy Burke
   William Hebert

   Composers
   Vincent Persichetti
   Warren Benson
   Leslie Bassett
   Alec Wilder
   Walter Hartley
   John Huggler
   David Borden
   Robert Ward
   Norman Dello Joio

Ensembles
New York Brass Quintet
Eastman Brass Quintet
Ithaca College Woodwind Quintet
Ithaca College Brass Quintet
Eastman Wind Ensemble
University of Michigan Symphony Band
Luther College Wind Ensemble
U. S. Air Force Band
Oberlin Wind Ensemble

8. IHS Band Contemporary Music Festivals

Festival programs included recitals of original compositions by IHS Band students; recitals of contemporary music by small ensembles/chamber music groups from IHS, Ithaca College, and the Eastman School of Music; lectures by guest musicians and artists; concerts by IHS Concert Band and visiting ensembles; exhibitions of paintings and photographs by high school students.

9. Bach Honor Society
10. Composer-in-Residence Project

MENC-Ford Foundation Composer-in-Residence in 1966–68.

11. Band Awards
12. Band Camp
13. Special Performances (MENC Conference, Midwest National Band & Orchestra Clinic and NFL and AFL championship games)
14. Attending Concerts

In Ithaca, Bailey Hall concerts which featured national and international soloists and ensembles; Ithaca College and Cornell University concerts and recitals.
In Rochester, concerts by the Eastman Wind Ensemble.

15. IHS Invitational Band Festival
16. Summer Lessons/Band Program
17. Master Classes and Clinics presented by visiting guest artists.
18. Band Parents' Night

Ithaca High School "Little Red" Marching Band, 1955–67.

When Mr. B became IHS Band Director in September 1955, he was not a proponent of high school marching band activity. He envisioned a band program with little or no marching band activity. However, Dr. John W. Graves, IHS principal (and Mr. B's former band director), urged him not to eliminate or down grade the marching band. He reminded Mr. B that high school football was important in Ithaca—that on every Saturday from late September to early November, city, town and county residents came together, sat on the same side of the field, and collectively cheered for Ithaca High School (the football team **and band**). He stressed the importance of the band in this ritual of community togetherness and solidarity. Mr. B found Dr. Graves's comments persuasive and decided to keep the marching band in the IHS Band program.

The "Little Red" Marching Band functioned for eight weeks during the football season, after which it made no appearances for the rest of the school year. Membership in the group was open to all students who played a woodwind, brass or percussion instrument. Students did not have to be in the Marching Band in order to participate in the Concert or Symphony Bands.

From 1960–67 some of the band's marching routines and musical arrangements were created by students. These endeavors "…gave students creative opportunities…and helped maintain a music education focus on the marching band" (Norcross, p. 42). Also, the drum majors, section leaders and student assistants handled much of the instruction in the marching band.

In 1955 the IHS "Little Red" Marching Band numbered 79 students—in 1967, 158 students. The band performed at all home and away IHS football games and from 1961–67 at six NFL and AFL professional football games in Cleveland, Ohio (Municipal Stadium), Buffalo, New York (Memorial Stadium) and New York City (Yankee Stadium). The IHS "Little Red" Band was regarded as one of the premiere marching bands in the nation.

The music performed by the marching band ranged from Broadway show melodies (*My Fair Lady, West Side Story, The Roar of the Greasepaint—The Smell of the Crowd,* etc.) to classical concert music (Prokofiev, Holst, Stravinsky, Walton, Copland, Barber, etc.). Mr. B, assistant band director Michael Walters, and Alpha Hockett, a former member of the band, wrote most of the band's arrangements. Charlotte Battisti, Mr. B's wife, copied the parts.

Major Performances of the 1955–67 Ithaca High School "Little Red" Band.

November 26, 1961 NFL game in Cleveland, Ohio: New York vs. Cleveland (Televised by NBC and CBS).

November 25, 1963 NFL game in New York, NY: New York vs. St. Louis. Eastern Division Championship Game (Performance cancelled because of assassination of President John F. Kennedy—was scheduled to be televised by CBS).

December 26, 1964 American Football League Championship Game in Buffalo, New York: Buffalo vs. San Diego (Televised by ABC).

October 3, 1965 AFL game in Buffalo, New York: Buffalo vs. Oakland (Televised by ABC).

October 2, 1966 NFL game in New York, NY: New York vs. Cleveland (Televised by CBS).

October 15, 1967 AFL game In Buffalo, New York: Buffalo vs. Oakland (Televised by NBC).

Band Camp.

Commencing in fall 1959 every band year began with a pre-school camp located in the Danby hills, 14 miles south of Ithaca. The first band camp was four days in length. In 1960 it was expanded to a full week. In order to avoid having the students rehearse "on the field" during the hottest part of day, the camp operated on double daylight savings time (clocks were advanced two hours ahead of Eastern Standard Time). Below is a typical daily band camp schedule:

7:30 AM	Rise and shine
8:15 AM	Breakfast in the main lodge (main lodge used for meals, indoor rehearsals, and meetings)
8:45 AM	Easy calisthenics
9:00–11:00 AM	Rehearsal on the field for all band members, color guards, major-ettes, drum major, drum sergeant
12:00 noon	Lunch
12:45–2:30 PM	Sectional rehearsals
2:50–4:00 PM	Optional rehearsals and/or special help for individual members
4:00 PM	Recreational activities
5:30 PM	Dinner
6:30–9:15 PM	Full band rehearsal
9:30–11:00 PM	Evening activities
11:30 PM	Lights out

Ithaca High School Concert Band, 1955–67.

The activities and experiences of students in the 1955–67 IHS Concert Band were unique—they played great music (solo, chamber, and large ensemble), composed music, commissioned important composers to write pieces for them, performed with world-class soloists and conductors, sponsored contemporary music festivals and created a "Bach" Honor Society.

The top priority of the Concert Band program was the performance of high quality music. The literature studied and performed ranged in style from baroque to contemporary (e.g. aleatoric music; music for non-traditional instruments and/or notated in non-traditional ways; pieces that incorporated electronic sounds, etc.). Mr. B believed that the student's musical values and appreciation were profoundly affected by the music he/she studied, performed, created and consumed.

The focus of the IHS Concert Band program was on the musical growth of each student. Brain Norcross comments on this priority issue in his book, *One Band That Took a Chance*:

...success [in the Ithaca High School Band] was based upon each individual's daily growth...learning about music, listening to music, writing music,...[in]

both large and small ensembles...The [concert performance] was more of an open house presentation of what [they had] learned. The educational and musical experiences of the rehearsal were the primary focus...This does not diminish the importance of [performance], but rather puts it into perspective. [Also,] the Ithaca High School Band did not compete. Competition was not a musical experience. The only challenge was for the individual student to reach his/her potential... (Norcross, p. 109)

In 1997 the IHS Concert Band was placed on the John Philip Sousa Foundation's Historic Roll of Honor of High School Concert Bands, 1920–80 for their "important contributions to music education and the musical world."

Major Performances of the 1955–67 Ithaca High School Concert Band.

May 20, 1959	Spring Concert, Ithaca High School, Ithaca, New York. Premiere performance of *Night Song* by Warren Benson—first IHS Band-commissioned work.
May 19, 1961	Spring Concert, Ithaca High School, Ithaca, New York. Distinguished American composer Vincent Persichetti guest conducted the premiere performance of his *Serenade for Band*, the band's third commissioned work.
April 28, 1965	Spring Concert, Ithaca High School, Ithaca, New York. Premiere performances of three commissioned works: *Designs, Images and Textures* by Pulitzer Prize-winning composer Leslie Bassett; *Star-Edge* by Warren Benson with Donald Sinta, saxophone soloist; and *Six Events for 58 Players* by Barney Childs. All composers were present for the premiere performances of their pieces.
December 16, 1965	Midwest International Band Clinic Concert, Chicago, Illinois. Premiere performance of Alec Wilder's *Entertainment III*, guest conducted by Frederick Fennell. Other guest conductors on the concert were Walter Beeler and Dr. William D. Revelli. Donald Sinta, Leone Buyse, and the New York Brass Quintet were the featured guest soloists.
February 12, 1967	MENC Conference Concert, Boston, Massachusetts. Concert consisted of five IHS Band-commissioned works including the premiere performances of *Celebration* by John Huggler, composer-in-residence with the Boston Symphony Orchestra, and *Helix* by Warren Benson, with Harvey Phillips as tuba soloist. The program also included Herbert Bielawa's *Prisms*, a work for pre-recorded electronic sounds and band.

May 17, 1967   Spring Concert, Ford Hall, Ithaca College, Ithaca New York. Premiere performances of three IHS Band-commissioned works: *Turn Not Thy Face* (in memory of John F. Kennedy) by Vincent Persichetti, *Fiesta Processional* by Pulitzer Prize-winning composer Robert Ward, and *All-American; Teenage; Lovesongs* by David Borden, Ithaca Public Schools composer-in-residence. All composers were present for the premiere performances of their pieces. Frederick Fennell also guest conducted Percy Grainger's *Lincolnshire Posy*.

Music Lessons.

Every student had a weekly 30-minute lesson with Mr. B which focused on development of technical and expressive instrumental skills. These lessons also provided Mr. B with opportunities to influence student commitment, sense of responsibility and dedication.

Auditions/Challenges.

Membership in the Marching Band was open to all IHS woodwind, brass and percussion students. Placement in the Concert and Symphony Bands was by audition. Periodic "Challenges" throughout the year provided opportunities for students to advance in their section.

PART I   Frank Battisti Arrives
at Ithaca High School
(1953–55)

CHAPTER I   The Apprenticeship:
             Teaching at Ithaca High School,
             1953–54

(Note: Chapters 1 and 2 provide information about Ithaca High School Band activities during 1953–54 and 1954–55, the years Frank Battisti taught instrumental music lessons at the high school. They provide background information about the program he inherited when he became band director in September 1955.)

Frank Battisti attended Ithaca High School from 1946-1949. He played trumpet in the IHS band and orchestra and conducted a pit orchestra when students filed in and out of Foster Hall for school assembly programs. After graduating in 1949 he went to Ithaca College and earned a Bachelor's degree in Music Education in May 1953.

In September 1953 he was hired to teach instrumental music in the Ithaca Public Schools. Lessons at Ithaca High School had always been taught by the band director. However, in 1953 IHS Band Director John W. Graves was appointed acting vice-principal and could not teach them (he remained band director). Mr. B taught these lessons from September 1953 to June 1955.

⊰ ⊱

Below is a photo of the 1953-54 IHS Band performing at a football game. There were 62 students in the band (54 student musicians, 1 drum major, 1 drum sergeant and 7 majorettes).

The band's half-time shows consisted of marching up and down the field in block formation, forming stick figures, and spelling out words such as "Hello," "IHS," "USA." When football season was over the band moved indoors and began its concert activities. The photo, below, shows the band in its concert configuration—Director John W. Graves stands in front of the ensemble.

On May 21, 1954 the band presented its Annual Spring Concert. This was its only performance of the second semester (see program, below).

Suite in F for Military Band	Gustav Holst
March	
Song of the Blacksmith	
Fantasia on the "Dargason"	
Russian Sailor Dance	Gliere
River Jordan	Whitney
Italian in Algiers	Rossini
Incidental solos by Roberta Harper and Marne Sayles, flute; Peter Hedrick, oboe; Anne Ensworth, clarinet; Irving Selsley, bassoon; David Kresge and Sandra Hemming, alto sax.	
Second Cornet Solo	Andrieu
Robert Dakin, Cornet	
Roberta Harper, Piano	
Rumbalero	Lang
China Doll	Anderson
March of "The Slide Trombones"	Lang

CHAPTER **2** The Torch is Passed:
John W. Graves's Final Year as IHS
Band Director, 1954–55

Membership in the 1954-55 IHS Band increased to 75 students (63 student musicians, 1 drum major, 6 majorettes, and for the first time, a color guard section of 5 members)—see photo, below.

Band director John Graves, Mr. B and seven brass players started an IHS Band tradition in late December (1954)—playing Christmas carols at the homes of Ithaca High School faculty members. This tradition continued until Mr. B left IHS in November 1967.

Band members enjoyed three social events in 1954-55—Halloween and Christmas parties in the fall semester and a round and square dance at Mt. Pleasant Lodge in February.

The May 20, 1955 Spring Concert consisted of twelve pieces including solo works for trumpet, percussion and tuba. It was typical of programs presented by high school bands in the mid-1950s. This concert marked Director John W. Graves's final appearance with the band and Mr. B's first (he conducted Vincent Persichetti's *Pageant*) (see program below).

ITHACA HIGH SCHOOL
Concert Band
May 20, 1955

President . . . . Dorothy Willman

Vice-President . . . . Larry Bennett

Secretary-Treasurer . . . . Bill West

Librarians . . . . Roberta Harper, Marlene Hankinson

Uniform Manager . . . . Nancy Willman

Drum Major . . . . Albert Cappucci

Conductor . . . . John W. Graves

Assistant Conductor . . . . Frank Battisti

Hall of Fame—March . . . . *Olivadoti*

The Girl I Left Behind Me . . . . *Anderson*

Waltz op. No. 8 and Hungary op. No. 23 . . . . *Moskowski*
  Piano four hands—Phoebe Mason, Andrew Thomas

Pageant . . . . *Persichetti*

Soliloquy for Trumpet . . . . *Morrissey*
  Cornet Soloist—Robert Dakin

Vincent Youmans Fantasy . . . . *arr. by Yoder*

The Ninth Grade Choral Group: "Sweet Sixteen
  Directed by Vito Mason
  Grandfather's Clock . . . . *Irvin*
  Oklahoma . . . . *Rodgers*

Finale from the 1st Symphony . . . . *Saint-Saens*

Dipsy Diddle—Drum Solo . . . . *Schinstine*
  Soloist—Stewart Wallace

Suite of Old American Dances . . . . *Bennett*

Tubby the Tuba . . . . *Kleinsinger*
  Soloist—Warren Marks

Beguine for Band . . . . *Osser*
American Youth March . . . . *Gould*

Narrator—Ted Tottey

Ushers—Al Cappucci, Joan McCully, Joan VanDeman, Janice VanAlstine,
  Frances Sheppard, Joanne Bucci, Kathryn Myers.

PART **II**   Building a Program—
Foundations for
Pursuing Individual and
Group Excellence
(1955–60)

CHAPTER **3**   Traction and Momentum:
Band Grows in Size and Quality of
Performance, 1955–56

Note: Chapters 3–7 deal with history of the Ithaca High School Band from 1955-60. These years were extremely important in the band's growth and development. Everyone (the students and Mr. B) worked very hard and achieved much—the band grew in size and more importantly, in the quality of its performances. New kinds of musical activities and experiences were added to the band curriculum. It was during these years that the band's reputation for high individual and collective excellence was established.

❧ ❧

Music Department facilities at the "old" Ithaca High School were very confined and limited. They included two teaching studios, one for S. Carolyn Marsh, the orchestra director/string teacher, the other for Mr. B. Adjacent to their studios was a room where music, percussion instruments and band uniforms were stored. Band and orchestra rehearsals were held on Foster Hall stage—sectionals in Mr. B's office. There were no practice rooms.

During the fall semester the band rehearsed three times per week (Monday, Wednesday and Friday), and in the spring, twice per week (Tuesday and Thursday)—rehearsals were 52 minutes in length. Because the school's athletic fields were two miles north of IHS, the band used Washington Park (four blocks away) for their fall outdoor rehearsals. The march to and from the park limited the actual rehearsal time to 20–25 minutes.

❧ ❧

During the mid-1950s some music educators/band directors began "…experimenting with the concepts of comprehensive musicianship [; they] understood that the high school band [needed to] serve as the medium by which a large group of young Americans [could] become musically literate in every sense of the phrase" (Norcross, p. 1). Mr. B embraced this philosophy and set about creating a band program that, he hoped, would excite and challenge the students musically, intellectually, and emotionally.

He began by requiring everyone to practice "at least 30 minutes every day"—the students had to develop good technical skills in order to perform the music he wanted them to play. Each student submitted a record of their practice time at their weekly lesson and was awarded two grades, one for "effort" (amount of time practiced), the other for "accomplishment" (how well they played their lesson). Everyone was also required to practice their band music an hour and a half a week.

Marching Band

The Ithaca High School Band that greeted Mr. B in September 1955 consisted of 80 students (71 student musicians, 1 drum major, 4 color guards, and 4 majorettes). Below is a photograph of the 1955 IHS Marching Band minus the color guards and majorettes. Drum major Albert Cappucci is at the left, Mr. B at the right.

The band's football game performances became new and different. Gone were traditional marching maneuvers, stick figure formations and the spelling out of words—the band now performed innovative precision marching routines and specially arranged music. An article in the October 29, 1955 edition of *The Ithaca Journal*, **"Good Music, Marching Precision Mark Football Performances of IHS Band,"** praised the band's new marching and musical style – "…the band looks good and sounds great." On the next page is a photo from the article. It shows Mr. B discussing a precision marching routine with four members of the band.

Thousands of people saw the band perform at the IHS–Moosehart of Illinois football game which was played at Cornell University's huge Schoelkopf Field. The photo, below, shows band members in the midst of their halftime show performance.

Concert Band

In early November (1955) auditions were held for placement in Concert Band. Prior to this time, students automatically moved from the marching to the concert band. Sixty-nine students were selected for membership in the ensemble including 13 seniors, 21 juniors, 24 sophomores and 11 freshmen. Students not selected for the Concert Band played in the Preparatory Band (a non-performance, pre-Concert Band ensemble).

Traditionally the band performed only one concert during the second semester. Mr. B added two more—school assembly programs at IHS and Owego (NY) Free Academy. He was confident that more performances would stimulate student musical growth and enthusiasm for the band.

The following two photographs show Mr. B (top) rehearsing the concert band on Foster Hall stage and (bottom) directing a clarinet sectional rehearsal.

The band's school assembly concerts at Owego Free Academy on May 10, 1956, and IHS on May 16, 1956 garnered enthusiastic response from both students and faculty members. After the IHS concert, Mr. B received numerous notes from faculty colleagues (not music teachers) praising the band's performance. Below are three of them.

"Your band this morning was *superb*—the nearest thing to a professional performance I've ever heard a high school group give."

"That concert this morning was *excellent*. They performed like experts."

"The concert was *tremendous* !!!!"

The music on the May 18, 1956 Spring Concert ranged in style from Bach's *Prelude and Fugue in f minor* to Howard Hanson's *Chorale and Alleluia*. It also included pieces for trumpet and percussion trios (see program below).

Program

❖❖

Block M Concert March . . . . *Jerry H. Bilik*

❖❖

Chorale and Alleluia . . . . *Howard Hanson*

❖❖

Bright Eyes . . . . *Walter A. Finlayson*
Dana Furman, Charles Dickinson, David Foster
Trumpet Trio

❖❖

The Typewriter . . . . *Leroy Anderson*
Transcribed by F. E. Werle

❖❖

Death and Transfiguration (Finale) . . . . *Richard Strauss*
Arr. A. Austin Harding

❖❖

Ballet Parisien . . . . *Jacques Offenbach*
Arr. Merle J. Isaac
1. Galop   2. Finale

❖❖

We Kiss in the Shadow . . . . *Richard Rodgers*

❖❖

I Whistle a Happy Tune . . . . *Richard Rodgers*

❖❖

The Halls of Ivy . . . . *Russell-Knight*
Arr. Williams
The Harmonettes

❖❖

The Great Gate of Kiev . . . . *M. Moussorgsky*
Arr. Erik Leidzen

❖❖

Prelude and Fugue in F minor . . . . *Johann S. Bach*
Arr. R. L. Moehlmann

❖❖

Haskell's Rascals . . . . *Paul Yoder*
Stewart Wallace, Neil Wintermute, William Mobbs
Snare Drum Trio

❖❖

Rowdy Dance . . . . *Burnet Tuthill*

❖❖

Relax . . . . *Paul Yoder*

❖❖

The Nutmeggers . . . . *Eric Osterling*

❖❖

Ushers

Albert Cappucci, *head usher*

Deanna Histed   Connie Rotunno

Sherry Huntley   Madeline Whitted

❖❖

Ithaca Journal music critic Martin Rosenwasser, professor of Clarinet at Ithaca College, reviewed the band's 1956 Spring Concert. In his review Rosenwasser commented that the "…ensemble tone is very good" and "its execution…excellently precise…Applause was so enthusiastic at the end of the concert that the band played the Osterling march again." Rosenwasser's entire review is shown below (*The Ithaca Journal*, May 21, 1956).

Music   High School Band
Foster Hall

The Ithaca High School Band presented its annual Spring Concert in Foster Hall Friday night, and an excellent concert it was. The ensemble tone was very good and the band was well rehearsed, with consequent excellently precise execution and good intonation.

The program opened with the Bloch M Concert March by Jerry M. Billick. Mr. Billick wrote this March in 1955 for the University of Michigan Symphonic Band, of which he was first trombonist. This is a fine march, slightly on the modern side in the harmonies and rhythms. The trio strain, with dance band muted trumpet effects, is especially interesting. Next was the Chorale and Alleluia by Howard Hanson. This, in my opinion, is one of the most effective original compositions for band. The interpretation was excellent, the band's tone and rhythmic sense being of especially high caliber. The third number on the program, Bright Eyes, by Walter A. Finlayson, an Ithaca College graduate, was for three solo trumpets with band accompaniment. Trumpeters Dana Furman, Charles Dickinson and David Foster gave a fine performance. Their tone and staccato were very good. Leroy Anderson, composer of "Sleigh Ride" and other interesting novelties, was represented by a piece called "The Typewriter," written for solo typewriter with band accompaniment. Though the band played well, the typewriter was not loud enough. It should have been closer to the front of the stage.

The Finale of Richard Strauss' Death and Transfiguration was performed from a transcription by A. Austin Harding, director emeritus of bands at the University of Illinois. Although this was well played (except for a few intonation difficulties), I feel that the transcription just misses being effective. The first half of the band's part of the program came to an end with the playing of two excerpts, Gallop and Finale, from the suite, Ballet Parisien. This is a collection of Offenbach melodies and rearranged by Merle J. Isaac. It is gay, light-hearted music and was played in like manner.

While the band was given a rest our eyes and ears were given a treat by the performance of the Harmonettes, six lovely young ladies with voices to match. They sang "We Kiss in the Shadow" and "I Whistle a Happy Tune" by Russell Knight. Warmer tones and more vibrato could have been employed in "We Kiss in the Shadow," but "I Whistle a Happy Tune" was quite enjoyable and the "Halls of Ivy" was done very well.

The Band began its second half of the program with the "Great Gate of Kiev" section from Moussoigsky's Pictures at an exhibition, transcribed for band by Erik Leidzen. This is very effective band music and the performance was excellent. Special praise is due the lower brass for beauty of tone, and the fine cymbal player. The next number was also a transcription. This was by R. L. Moehlmann of a Prelude and Fugues. This was not a very effective transcription. Also the intonation between clarinet and flute sections was not at its best in this piece.

The last four numbers on the program were of a light nature. Haskells' Roscales by Paul Yoder (for Haskell Harr, famous drum instructor) features a snare drum trio of Stewart Wallace, Neil Wintermute and Bill Mobbs. Their performance was excellent. Roudy Dance by Burnet Tuthill was originally written for Fabien Sevitzky, former conductor of the Indianapolis Symphony. It ends with a wonderful climax and has some very unusual and ear-tickling effects. Paul Yoder was represented again, this time by a number called Relax. This is Latin-American in style and is very enjoyable.

The program concluded as it began, with a Concert March. This one was the "Nutmeggers," by Eric Osterling. This is a top-notch concert march with wonderful dynamic contrasts and some very interesting effects. It was played spiritedly. Applause was so enthusiastic at the end of the program that the band played the Osterling number again.

Orchids are due Mr. Frank Battisti, the conductor, for an excellent job. The band is very clean in all phases of playing and presents a good time and excellent interpretation to boot. The fine announcements of descriptions of each number also contributed to the enjoyment of the program. It is a shame that Spring comes but once a year.

MARTIN ROSENWASSER

Band members were excited and proud of their accomplishments and achievements in 1955-56. The 1956 *Annual* (IHS yearbook) described the band as being "One of the most spirited and hard working groups at IHS." By year's end two hallmark tenets of the Ithaca High School Band program were firmly in place—individual musical growth and committed student involvement.

Recollection by Peter Farrow, Class of 1960

Weekly Lessons with Mr. B

Today I was coached at my lesson with Mr. B in his office on the details of holding this instrument (euphonium), with particular attention to my embrochure. Missed notes, flubbed entrances, clumsy tonguing, hoping against hope that this high note will happen…playing this thing is a bit of a challenge. Mr. B is so focused on achievement, on doing one's best.

But that doesn't cause stress because he goes about teaching in such a supportive, even respectful, way. He's so in touch with what you're going through…I suspect he remembers his first year on trumpet. So it's off to practice an hour each day (at the expense of my parents' peaceful evenings).

Back in Mr. B's office next week, hoping to show improvement but always knowing that I'll receive support and encouragement as I strive to the next modest level of achievement.

But I'm only starting out. When I listen in band rehearsals, to the juniors and seniors, it's clear where I can go if I aspire to the standard Mr. B sets. And even while I'm striving to get there, I can be part of the band. OK, practice, and live up to Mr. B's standards.

What's amazing, when you think about it, is he does this for every kid in the band. Wow!

CHAPTER **4**   Looking Good—Sounding Great—
Receiving Public Recognition—
Program Expanded, 1956–57

Marching Band

The fall 1956 IHS Marching Band numbered 82 members including 72 student musicians, 1 drum major, 1 drum sergeant, 5 color guards and 3 majorettes. A late September article in *The Ithaca Journal* praised the band for its excellent early-season performances, "…[The band] **clicked in pre-game and half-time shows. Director Frank Battisti has applied plenty of polish to his unit. It appeared to be in mid-season form.**" The photo below shows the 1956 "Little Red" Band marching down-field at the beginning of its pre-game show.

After watching the band perform at the IHS-Auburn High School football game in Auburn, NY, New York State Senator George Metcalf wrote the following letter to the editor of *The Ithaca Journal.*

> **Perhaps your readers would like to know what a marvelous impression the band of Ithaca High School made on the people of Auburn during Friday's football game between the two high schools.**

In my experience I have seen few college bands, [that] could compare favorably in precision and quality of performance with theirs. The discipline of the musicians was excellent, and they showed clearly the result of intensive practice under capable leadership.

Through you, may I commend them highly for an outstanding job.

George R. Metcalf
34 Dill Street
Auburn

Concert Band

Seventeen IHS Band students were selected for the Sectional All-State Band, which was held at Hartwick College on November 9-10, 1956. Eleven were chosen for first-chair positions.

Two new ensembles were added to the IHS Band Program in 1956-57. One was a 12-piece dance band, the "Blue Tones" (see photo, below). It was directed by student trumpet player Charles Dickinson. The group played for several IHS dances and for the Junior-Senior Prom at Morrisville-Eaton Central School.

The second was a Brass Choir, which presented its first concert for the MENC Chapter at Ithaca College in March 1957. Celia W. Slocum, Chair of Music Education at the College, praised the ensemble's performance.

Our students are all potential teachers and they were much impressed not only by the quality of the musical performance but also by the spirit and excellent organization portrayed by the group. [Quote from letter to Mr. B]

Below is a picture of the Brass Choir.

The May 17,1957 Spring Concert featured three student soloists and a piece conducted by Warren Marks, drum major and tuba player in the band (see program, below).

Program

Proud Heritage	William P. Latham
George Washington Bridge	William Schuman
Trombographic	David Bennett
<div align="center">Larry Bennett, Trombone</div>	
Toccata	Girolamo Frescobaldi
	arr. Earl Slocum
Concerto No. 1	W. A. Mozart
Allegro vivace	arr. Lorenzo Sansone
<div align="center">Jacqueline Klune, French horn</div>	
Psalm for Band	Vincent Persichetti
Prelude and Fugue in d minor	Johann Sebastian Bach
	arr. R. L. Morehlman
Concertino for Clarinet	Carl Maria von Weber
	arr. M. L. Lake
<div align="center">Jonathan Levine, Clarinet</div>	
Charter Oak	Eric Osterling
<div align="center">Warren Marks, Student Conductor</div>	
Fandango	Frank Perkins
	arr. Floyd E. Werle

Ithaca Journal music critic Forrest Sanders, professor of cello at Ithaca College, reviewed the concert. He wrote that the band's performance was "…one of the best I have heard them do… [The band] plays very musically, with excellent ensemble, precision, balance and a fine regard for dynamic levels." (See Sanders's entire review, below.)

Music

Ithaca High School Band Concert

In Foster Hall Friday evening, the Ithaca High School Band gave their annual Spring Concert. It is an event, along with the Choral and Orchestra concerts, much looked forward to, and the Band, under the very capable direction of Frank Battisti, gave one of the Best performances I have heard them do.

The band is a large one, very well-disciplined, well-schooled, and one that plays very musically, with excellent ensemble, precision, balance and a fine regard for dynamic levels.

Three members of the organization appeared as soloists with band accompaniment. They were Larry Bennett, trombone, playing David Bennett's "Trombographic," Miss Jacqueline Klune, French horn, who played "Concerto No. 1, Op. 412, in D Major," first movement, by Mozart, and Jonathan Levine, clarinet, playing Weber's "Concertino," arranged by M. L. Lake.

All of these were handled with skill, a fine regard for the musical content, and with good taste. Ensemble and balance problems were good, the technics of the soloists well-developed and portrayed. Coming off especially well was the clarinetist whose tone and phrasing were first rate, and whose selection lent itself best to the particular medium of accompaniment.

I particularly enjoyed the band's playing of the contemporary works —Vincent Persichetti's "Psalm for Band," Frank Perkins' "Fandango," played with real spirit, fire, and with a fantastic tempo, and Eric Osterling's concert march, "Charter Oak." The latter seems a better piece than the popular "Blue Mist" by the same composer. Warren Marks, the band's drum major, did a nice job of conducting the concert march.

Also very well played were "Proud Heritage," by Latham, William Schuman's "George Washington Bridge," the Frescobaldi "Toccata" arrangement by Earl Slocum, and the Moehlmann arrangement of Bach's "Prelude and Fugue in D minor."

Ithaca may very well be proud of its high school band and its fine young director.

In pleasant contrast of medium, six young ladies styled the "Harmonettes" presented two Rodgers-Hammerstein numbers, "If I Loved You," and "June Is Bustin' Out All Over," very harmoniously indeed.

— FORREST SANDERS

Ralph W. Jones, Chairman of the IHS Health Education Department, wrote to Mr. B after the concert,

"That was the finest band concert ever !!"

Recollection by Peter Farrow, Class of 1960

Brass Choir Rehearsing in Mr. B's Office at Old IHS

Lessons with Mr. B are one thing, but rehearsing the brass choir in his office… well, that's quite another. If you want evidence that this school building was constructed around the turn of the century, just come to Mr. B's office and try to visualize it as a rehearsal room. This isn't a trio...there are nine of us, and the room can't be more than 6 × 12, with his desk taking up the last couple of feet. And while the trumpets and baritones can cram close to one another, the trombones have to aim between the players in front of them to play certain notes, which runs into the problem that the person in front may move once in a while. At least we have the sousaphone pushed to the back of the room, where Mr. B's desk looks out the window to the parking lot. And Mr. B has to conduct with his back to the door, where the adjoining closet forms a barely sufficient "podium." You really get to know your fellow players at old IHS!

CHAPTER 5   Elation and "That Funny Music"—
Concert in Canada—Commissioning
of First Piece, 1957–58

Marching Band

"Ladies and Gentlemen—for your enjoyment and entertainment, we present the 1957 Ithaca High School 'Little Red' Band." These words signaled the start of the band's first half-time performance on September 21, 1957, which featured music from the recently opened Broadway musical hit, *My Fair Lady*.

There were now 85 students in the IHS Marching Band—72 student musicians, 1 drum major, 1 drum sergeant, 6 color guards, 5 majorettes (see photo, below).

Many of the band's 1957 half-time shows were built around current events. A show in mid-October, "Say It With Music," saluted the Russians' launches of Sputnik I and II. The following week the band formed a rocket ship that exploded and dissolved into satellites as it performed "How High the Moon." For a flu epidemic that was sweeping the nation, the band formed a hypodermic syringe and performed "I've Got You Under My Skin."

The IHS football field was located 12 blocks north of the high school. On "game day" band members met at the school, marched to the field, performed at the game and then marched back to the high school—a total of over four miles! The photo, below, shows the band marching past the high school after a football game in September 1957. (*Ithaca Journal* photo)

—Wilfred Randal

HIGH SCHOOL BAND leads a happy parade down N. Cayuga St. Saturday afternoon after the Ithaca football team returned to its winning ways with a 39-0 victory over Elmira Southside. **(Story and more pictures on the game on Page 10.)**

Below, IHS Band members cheering at a late fall 1957 football game.

The following article appeared in *The Tattler*, IHS student newspaper. It is a humorous account of a fictitious freshman's experience in the 1957 IHS "Little Red" Band.

Frannie Freshman   by F. E.

I'm Frannie; I'm a freshman, a big freshman at last. Of course, all those other sophomores, juniors, and seniors don't think I'm a *big* freshman, but anyway.

You know, sometimes I think I'd rather be a freshman—those other kids are so busy being important and active and leading lights, and all we have to do is nothing, 'cause nobody expects anything of us so we don't have to do anything. Naturally, we do. We do almost everything in this school, but no one realizes it, I guess.

Take the band, for instance. I'm in the band; so are a lot of other kids, but then. I play twelfth clarinet. Probably some day I'll be eleventh clarinet, but that's a long way off. Our band leader is an awful slave driver, but we slaves don't mind too much, 'cause the high school kids like the band pretty much when we finally do get to a game. People even write to us from other cities sometimes. I would if I lived in another city.

Marching band is very confusing to people who practice very much (and of course we *all* do), because you practice sitting down, and you can't do that too much when you're marching.

I've also found that it's kind of hard to tap your foot to the rhythm when you're marching. (Maybe it's just as well, anyway, 'cause it sounds like the thunder of hoof-beats when we do.) Dad says band is good for me, though; I get very good ankle muscles—*I* don't know if that's good or not.

I have a problem: We have a small living room. You may not think this is a problem, but band members get the plans for the half-time shows about a week before we do them. We take them home and practice them and go cavorting around the house. Since we have a small living room, I wanted to practice in the back yard, but Mom had objections. She didn't think the neighbors could imagine the rest of the band prancing around with me as we do. After all, we do have our reputation to consider even if one member of the family is in the band.

Two-hour night rehearsals aren't exactly my favorite aspect of band, but I almost got to stop worrying about them, and about memorizing and about finding my raincoat, and all those other things. I wore white socks. So what? So I wore white socks? Ha! So I'll never wear white socks to band again so long as I live. What's wrong with white socks? There'll be a moment of silent reverence . . . One does *not* wear white socks to band. If you can't take my word for it, ask Mr. Battisti. He'll be more than willing to tell you, but plan to spend quite a lot of time being told.

I like band. I like it even though we freshmen have to do all the work. Nasty break. Well anyway, we get to stop all the traffic at rehearsals. That's fun.

Concert Band

By 1957 the IHS Band brass players' tradition of playing Christmas carols in Ithaca and throughout the countryside had expanded into a three-night affair. In addition to serenading school faculty members and administrators, the students now played carols for patients at the Ithaca Reconstruction Home and residents at the Odd Fellows' State Home and Home for Elderly Women. Sam Woodside, popular WHCU radio announcer, commented on the group's "caroling exploits" during his December 24, 1957 broadcast.

> **While most people depend upon the overworked mailman, or the chance meeting on the street or at holiday social events to convey their Christmas Greetings, a dozen members of the Ithaca High School Band have been delivering their sentiments in person, set to music, around the countryside these past three nights…Traveling about by car from point to point in the city and suburbs–as far away as Slaterville, Brooktondale and Trumansburg–the Brass Choir has managed to serenade about 60 institutions and households between 6:30 and 11:30 PM Sunday, Monday and last night–announcing themselves simply by sounding off with the traditional Christmas carol and moving along quickly to their next objective…**

The 1957-58 Concert Band numbered 65 students, 21 of which were seniors. In 1955-56 there were only 13 seniors in the IHS Band (Mr. B's first year as director). Students were now choosing to remain in band throughout their entire four years at IHS. Accolades from family, friends, classmates, people in the community and stories on radio/in newspapers made them proud to be members of the group.

In May 1958 the band traveled to Cornwall, Ontario, Canada to perform a joint concert with the St. Lawrence Collegiate band, orchestra and chorus. It was the group's first trip outside the United States. The band's performance garnered generous and enthusiastic applause from the audience and high praise from the local press (see excerpt from *Ithaca Journal* story, below).

Band members discovered a new and different educational environment at St. Lawrence Collegiate—everything was in French and English (classroom instruction, signs, posters, etc.). IHS Band students who were studying French were thrilled to be able to speak to their hosts in their native language. Before they left the Cornwall area, band members toured the St. Lawrence Seaway Project (a week before it was flooded). On the trip home they stopped at Alexandria Bay, NY and cruised through the Thousand Islands.

On May 21, 1958 (a week after the band returned from Cornwall, Ontario), *The Ithaca Journal* published an article on the band's Canadian trip. It contained a quote from a Canadian newspaper's review of the band's performance at St. Lawrence Collegiate.

> **The Ithaca Band–on a close level with the quality of the famous Coldstream Guards as to tone, pitch and precision–gave the whole concert a not-inconsiderable lift…The kind of music favored [by the band] is exciting, rhythmic, a great deal of dissonant material–which somehow sounds exhilarating and splendid with this band.**

The May 16, 1958 Spring Concert was, by all accounts, the best since Mr. B became band director in 1955 (see program below).

Program

Flash of Crimson ....Walter Alan Finlayson

Symphonic Suite ....Clifton Williams
      1. Intrada   3. March
      2. Chorale   4. Jubilee
This was the Oswald Award-Winning Composition—American Bandmasters Association, 1957.

Bugler's Holiday ....Leroy Anderson
   DANA FURMAN, GORDON LIGHT, WILLIAM COGGSHALL, *Trumpet Trio*

Divertimento for Band ....Vincent Persichetti
      1. Burlesque   2. March

Procession of Nobles (Cortege) from "Mlada" ......Nicholas Rimsky-Korsakov

Piano Concerto in g minor ....F. Mendelssohn, Op. 25
    First movement—Molto allegro con fuoco
      SUSAN ENSWORTH, *soloist*

Fanfare and Scenario ....John Cacavas

March to the Scaffold from "Symphonie Fantastique"....Hector Berlioz, Op. 14

Calypso Joint ....Kenneth L. Farrell

ITHACA HIGH SCHOOL BAND
Organized 1917

President ....William Mobbs
Vice-president ....Richard York
Secretary-Treasurer ....Kathryn Trapp
Librarian ....Evelyn Hall
Drum Major ....Peter Farrow
Conductor ....Frank L. Battisti

Flutes	*Second Clarinets*	*Alto Saxophones*
*Patricia Phillips	Tracy Benjamin	Carol Miller
*Virginia Klune	Carole Welker	Kathleen McKeegan
Curtis Ufford	Linda Tarbell	*Tenor Saxophone*
Seth Levine	Janet Hankinson	Evelyn Hall
Katherine Detweiler		*Baritone Saxophone*
Suzanne Colbert	*Third Clarinets*	David Sears
	Barbara Darling	*Bassoons*
Oboes	Nancy King	Jean Laux
June Smith	Lois Lounsbery	Claire Webster
Daniel Evett	Margaret Payne	Susan Ensworth
		First Cornets
First Clarinets	*Alto Clarinet*	Dana Furman
J. C. Page	Margaret Baur	Gordon Light
Kathryn Trapp		*Second Cornets*
James Hedlund	*Bass Clarinet*	*Richard Koski
Betty Allen	Linda Ervay	*Martin Thayer

Everyone was excited and thrilled by the band's performance. Among those who came backstage after the concert to congratulate Mr. B was Warren Benson, a composer and one of Mr. B's professors at Ithaca College. He praised the band's performance but then asked Mr. B a very disturbing question: "Why do you play so much funny music?" (He was referring to pieces other than those composed by Persichetti, Rimsky-Korsakov, Mendelssohn and Berlioz.) Mr. B was stunned! The question punctured the joy and elation he felt about the band's excellent performance. However, it did touch upon an issue Mr. B had been wrestling with since 1955—the lack of quality literature for high school bands. After pondering Benson's question for a week he decided to do something he hoped would improve the situation—he invited Benson to write a piece for the IHS Band. When Benson accepted, Mr. B instructed him to "compose the best piece you can and don't write down for the students. If your piece is too difficult for us to perform, we'll pay you your commission fee and find a band that can play it." (He gave this same instruction to all composers he commissioned to write pieces for the IHS Band.)

There was a marked increase in the number of students participating in small ensembles in 1957–58. These ensembles rehearsed twice per week—once with a faculty coach and once by themselves.

Recollection by Peter Farrow, Class of 1960

Marching Band Rehearsal at Old IHS

We got to stop traffic as we marched down Cayuga Street to Washington Park three times a week in the fall. The time required to get down and back within the 52-minute 7th period definitely shortened the time we had to work on the formations. However, it did give us a chance to work on the music and basic marching skills. Working on the formations sometimes seemed like ordered chaos, especially when we had to learn a new show in three short rehearsals. Mr. B was always at his visibly high-energy level, always tempered by his caring respect for us, as he worked to explain what we were supposed to do—there, see, he is stepping off the routine while we watch, as we wonder how long it will take all of us to get it. "OK, everybody, let's try that one more time."

Over time there's a sense of accomplishment; he's teaching us to work together for a common goal. It's hard to play at your best when you are concentrating on picking up your feet in a somewhat unnatural way, yet in every sense Mr. B is helping us prepare for the concert band we look forward to, even as we hold up traffic and distract the kids at Boynton Junior High School.

An amusing memory—Mr. B has the entire band lined up on the goal line, facing the sideline, and everyone is supposed to step forward on the first note. As usual, he is standing back a bit, the better to see the overall picture as it will appear to the fans in the stands at the game on Saturday. He sees that the line doesn't move the way he intends, so he strides over to demonstrate, then stands back while we try again, and it doesn't work, so he strides over and demonstrates again, then strides away, and it still doesn't work. Finally he figures out that we are too close together to be able to take a step forward on the first note; no one wants to step on the person in front of them. He makes an adjustment and it works. Hopefully we'll get the rest of the kinks out at Saturday morning's rehearsal.

CHAPTER **6** Premier Premiere:
First World Premiere Performance—
More Travel—Bach Honor Society,
1958–59

Marching Band

There were 87 students in the 1958 IHS "Little Red" Band (72 student musicians, 1 drum major, 1 drum sergeant, 7 color guards, 6 majorettes). Below is the band's Fall 1958 performance schedule:

September 20	Elmira Free Academy	Home
September 27	Band Day	Cornell University
September 28	Dedication of U. S. Army Reserve Center	Ithaca
October 4	Elmira Southside	Elmira
October 11	Binghamton North	Home
October 18	Vestal High School	Home
October 25	Binghamton Central	Binghamton
October 30	Halloween Parade	Ithaca
November 1	Auburn	Auburn
November 8	Johnson City	Home
November 11	Veterans' Day Parade	Ithaca

Rehearsals for the new year began the week before school opened. They were held in the evenings at the high school. On the next page is a photo of the 1958 IHS Marching Band.

The theme of the band's first halftime performance on September 20, 1958 was "American Firsts." The show included a precision dance routine to "The Birth of the Blues" and a precision marching routine to "Don't Give Up the Ship."

The following photo shows the band performing a precision marching routine during a halftime performance.

Concert Band

Twelve members of the Concert Band were selected to perform in the Sectional All-State Band at Syracuse University on November 21-22, 1958. French horn player Freemont Shepherd was also selected to perform in the New York All-State Band at the Eastman School of Music in Rochester, NY in December 1958.

In April (1959) the IHS Band traveled to Maryland and Washington, DC to perform concerts at Annapolis and Westminster, Maryland High Schools and march in the National Cherry Blossom Parade. The money needed to finance the trip was raised through cookie and candy sales, selling magazine subscriptions, a bottle drive, and band dinners and dances.

The band left for Annapolis on Thursday April 9. Traffic problems encountered en route delayed the band's arrival by four hours (arrived at 12:15 AM !!). Unfortunately, this prevented band members from attending a party arranged for them by the Annapolis Band. IHS Band students spent the night (actually Friday morning) in the homes of Annapolis band members. The next morning the band performed a school assembly program at Annapolis High School. Following the concert the students toured the United States Naval Academy, ate lunch and then left for their performance at Westminster (MD) High School. The concert there, like the one in Annapolis, was very well received by the student audience.

During the drive into Washington DC a Maryland state trooper stopped and ticketed the two band buses for going 58 mph in a 30 mph speed zone. Each was fined $11.45.

Unfortunately, it rained during the National Cherry Blossom Parade (April 10). However, the wet weather did not dampen the band members' spirit and enthusiasm. Hundreds of spectators cheered their energetic performance along the parade route.

On the next page is a *Washington Post* article about the parade.

8000 Blossom Fete Paraders Watched by Crowd of 135,000

Eight thousand marchers and 135,000 watchers cheerfully bore an intermittent rain last night as one of the largest annual Cherry Blossom Festival parades streamed along K st. nw.

Officials had predicted 60,000 attendance after only 1500 showed up for crowning of the queen, which was shifted from the Tidal Basin to the National Guard Armory because of rain

for the first time in the history of the event.

But the parade crowd grew as the rain slackened.

The 52 princesses on their floats and in cars wore mostly b a c k l e s s, off - the - shoulder gowns. One or two drew a fur cape around them against the chill.

Participating in the big parade were more than two hundred units hailing from Alaska to Texas. There were a score of floats.

Alaska, marching for the first time as a state, had a float with its princess, Carla

Pictures on Page B1.

Carter, seated in the 49th star. The float from Texas, no longer the largest state, maintained that it had the biggest heart.

Festival Queen C a r o l y n Marie Harris, the daughter of Rep. Oren Harris (D-Ark) smiled and waved from her limousine in the vanguard of the parade.

She received her $100,000 crown during the afternoon in ceremonies on a hastily-built stage at the Armory from Secretary of the Interior Fred A. Seaton.

The crowning ceremonies will be repeated today at 2 p. m.

at the Jefferson Memorial. In case of rain, they will be switched again to the Armory.

More than 500 Metropolitan policemen kept the cheerful parade crowd in order. Fifty automobiles were r e m o v e d from illegal parking spaces to keep the parade route clear.

Twelve students had a hair-raising experience during the band's stay at the Ambassador Hotel. After jamming themselves into an elevator, they started their descent to the lobby. Suddenly the elevator stopped between floors. The students panicked and began pushing every button they could find. Their frantic calls were answered when an over-head trap door popped open and everyone climbed to safety.

While in Washington the students visited many of the capital's historic sites and, on their trip home, the historic battlefield in Gettysburg, Pennsylvania.

Rehearsals of the band's first commissioned work, Warren Benson's *Night Song,* began on February 3, 1959. Mr. B told *The Ithaca Journal* he considered the Benson commission the most worthwhile musical project undertaken by the band since he became band director. "[This is]…a new…musical experience for both the band members and myself and we look forward to [rehearsing] and premiering *Night Song.*"

The premiere performance of *Night Song* took place on the band's May 20, 1959 Spring Concert. See program on the next page.

Band

The Showman	Howard E. Akers
The Marriage of Figaro	W. A. Mozart
	Arr. Earl Slocum
Canzona	Peter Mennin
Commissioned by Edwin Franko Goldman through The League of Composers (1951)	
Bell Symphony	Henry Purcell
	Arr. L. Johnston
Night Song	Warren Benson
Commissioned by the Ithaca High School Band. This is a first performance.	
Second Suite in F	Gustav Holst

    I.   March
   III. Song of the Blacksmith

In Thee Is Gladness	J. S. Bach
	Arr. Maurice Whitney
Military Symphony in F	Francois Gossec
	Edited by R. F. Goldman and R. L. Leist

    I.   Allegro Maestoso
   III. Allegro

Ides of March	Donald I. Moore
Onward, Ye Peoples!	Jean Sibelius

Band and Choir

. . . . . . strive for the light! . . . . Forward, where faith
revealeth the way! For God is our guide, and He
will never fail.

ITHACA HIGH SCHOOL BAND
Organized in 1917

President	Donald Sherwood
Vice President	James Hedlund
Secretary-Treasurer	Evelyn Hall
Drum Major	Peter Farrow
Drum Sergeant	Donald Dickinson
Narrator	Robert Smith
Conductor	Frank L. Battisti

Flutes
Virginia Klune
Curtis Ufford
Seth Levine
Joyce Catalfano
Carolyn Wright
Barbara Child
Linda Stump
Oboes
Dan Evett
Beth Brann
Clarinets
James Hedlund
Ben Tracy
Barbara Darling
Lois Lounsbery
Janet Hankinson
Abigail Mohn
Janice Murphy
Julie Christensen
Margaret Payne
David Corson

Lonnie Poole
Nancy Cladel
Paul Wolfowitz
Alto Clarinets
Rosemary Gates
Dorothy Rosa
Bass Clarinet
Linda Ervay
Alto Saxophones
Kathleen McKeegan
Virginia Mai
Tenor Saxophone
Evelyn Hall
Baritone Saxophone
David Sears
Bassoons
Margaret Musgrave
Jean Laux
Mickey Campbell
Cornets
Richard Koski
Gerald Kleeman

Richard Komarmi
Carol Thompson
Carl Koski
Eldon Baldwin
Marilyn Trapp
Trumpets
Martin Thayer
Alan Kellogg
Judy Jackson
French Horns
Freemont Shepherd
Rosalind Srb
Sally Henderson
Judy Watson
Charles Sweet
Trombones
Donald Sherwood
Dorothy Griffith
Stephen Judson
Dean Winkelblech
John Snow

Baritones
Peter Farrow
Jean de Forest
Roger Gee
Richard Page
Sousaphones
Donald Dickinson
George Kent
Stephen Wade
String Bass
Barbara Hartman
Tympani
Kenneth Shulman
Percussion
George Padar
Tim Craig
Stephen Stutz
Victor Newhart
Bells, Chimes
Edwenna Rosser
Charlotte Sweet

Night Song is a slow, lyrical and thinly orchestrated work with important solo passages for flute, oboe, clarinet, French horn, and baritone. These solos were performed by Virginia Klune, Dan Evett, James Hedlund, Freemont Shepherd, and Peter Farrow, respectively.

Harold Weaver, in his *Ithaca Journal* review of the concert, wrote the following about *Night Song*.

> [*Night Song*] in contrast to so many contemporary band pieces is quite thinly scored and thus more difficult to perform since one section or soloist after another feels the pressure of individual performance. The work was very well received and it was apparent the boys and girls of the Band enjoyed both working with the piece and performing it.

Weaver praised the band's entire concert performance.

> The band played with skill and conviction…[Peter Mennin's] *Canzona* is a difficult work with much rhythmic complexity and modern harmonic structure, [and] the Band showed their thorough training, high level of individual instrumental competence and the sensitive and musically intelligent leadership of their conductor. *The Bell Symphony* … was excellently performed. Intonation, balance, phrasing and rhythmic precision were of the highest order…Not many high school bands have the opportunity to premiere a work by a recognized composer. Mr. Battisti deserves special commendation for his selection of music of artistic worth since unfortunately the concert band literature abounds with musical trash and it requires considerable effort and research to find music for band which is aesthetically significant and within the technical grasp of high school musicians.

Night Song was rejected for publication by a number of music publishers. They deemed it "too risky because of the solos for euphonium, French horn and the important oboe parts." It was finally accepted and published by Chappell & Co in 1961. The score's dedication reads, "Commissioned by the Ithaca High School Band, Frank L. Battisti, conductor."

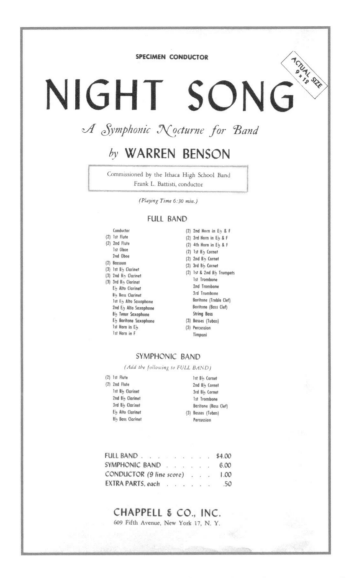

Brian Norcross in his book, *One Band That Took a Chance*, writes the following about the commissioning of *Night Song*.

> Commissioning composers to write music for bands was not a new idea in 1958 ... What was inventive was that a high school was embarking on this project, that a ... composer who had not written for band or specifically for high school band, was composing for the band, and that this new piece did not fit the mold of "traditional" band music.

The personal interaction band members had with Benson, and later with all the composers who wrote pieces for them, expanded and deepened their appreciation for the creator and the creative act. Norcross comments on the significance of this interaction:

> **The students had a direct human connection with…the commissioned composers. The name of the composer had personal meaning to them because generally, they knew the composer…This personal interaction gave significant meaning to these experiences. Because of these experiences, students wanted to perform the commissioned works well to please the composer. They came to know the creative process in an intimate and personal manner, and this affected many of their lives.** (Norcross, p. 97)

Band students raised all the money needed to commission works—they wanted every composer to know that the commission and commission fee came **directly from them** and not from an outside source (i.e., Ithaca City School District, band parent association, art foundation, etc.).

꽃 꽃

The band's Bach Honor Society was started in 1958–59. Its objectives were to:

1. recognize superior musicianship
2. manifest interest in all music and especially contemporary music and musicians
3. promote the art of music and generate a spirit of cooperation among musicians
4. foster appreciation of the fine arts
5. motivate earnest study and encourage superior attainment
6. provide opportunities for the free exchange of ideas
7. stimulate a desire to do and achieve good things throughout life

The society sponsored IHS student recitals, lectures, clinics, guest artists and visiting ensembles. Students earned points to qualify for membership through practice, listening to music, academic achievement, reading books, visiting museums, going to concerts, etc. (see chart, on the next page).

```
                        I. H. S. BAND BACH SOCIETY

                    Honor Members of the I. H. S. Band


        The earning and losing of points:


           Points are earned by:

             1.  first chair position in band                      100
             2.  for each chair advanced in section                 50
             3.  playing scale perfectly in rehearsal                10
             4.  for each 30 minutes of sight reading (over minimum)  15 per week
             5.  for each 30 minutes of strobotuner work (over minimum) 15 per week
             6.  for each 30 minutes of practice on band, ensemble
                    music 9(over minimum)                            20 per week
             7.  for each 60 minutes of practice on lesson           35
             8.  for each concert attended                           50
             9.  for each concert, opera listed to completely (2hrs.) 15
            10.  for each book on music or art read                 100
            11.  attendance at small ensemble rehearsal              20
            12.  studying of another instrument                     100
            13.  for each 60 minutes of practice on second instrument 35
            14.  for each public performance representing an
                         I. H. S. wind organization                 150
            15.  instrument inspection                               75
            16.  sectional all state selection                       25
            17.  all NYS band selection                              50
            18.  for each 30minutes of project work                  15
            19.  Bach Recital and Band Solo Recital        Solo       50
                                                        Ensemble      25
            20.  scholastic ranking         for every "1"            15
                                            for every "2"            10
                                            for every "3"             5


           Points are deducted for:


             1.  scholastic ranking         for every "4"             5
                                            for every "5"            10
             2.  tardiness to regular rehearsal                      10
             3.  failure to bring instrument or music to rehearsal   50
             4.  talking or otherwise disturbing a rehearsal         25
             5.  tardiness in reporting for public performance      100
             6.  smoking while in uniform; at any band function     300
             7.  tardiness to sectional, small ensemble rehearsal    15
             8.  playing someone else's instrument without permission 100
             9.  not ready to play at start of scheduled rehearsal   25
            10.  not knowing, playing scales                         20
            11.  not getting in 25 minutes per week on strobotuner   10
            12.  not getting in 75 minutes per week of reading       10


        MINIMUM REQUIREMENTS:  For Sight Reading...........15 minutes per day (75 min. per week)
                               For Strobotuner.............25 minutes per wk.
                               For Band Music..............90 minutes per wk.
```

The point totals needed to qualify for membership in the Bach Honor Society were: Sophomore—8,000, Junior—8,000, Senior—5,000.

The 1959 *Annual* described the IHS Band as "one of the most active and hardest working organizations at Ithaca High School…Our band stimulates interest in good musicianship and presents high caliber music to the public…"

Recollections by Lois Lounsbery, Class of 1960

Band and Washington Park

In 1980, twenty years after graduating from Ithaca High School in the last class to graduate from the old building on Cayuga Street, I returned to the area and moved into a downtown house that faced Washington Park. I had lived there a few months before I remembered that this was the park where we used to practice our marching routines. Weather permitting, at the beginning of 7th period during football season, we would quickly take our places out on Buffalo Street and march four blocks down to the park. At the time, I never gave a thought as to how we could do this so easily. Mr. B must have had an arrangement with the city. But back then, it seemed perfectly normal that traffic in all directions should stop for the IHS Band wherever we happened to be.

First Rehearsal

The first piece I remember reading through in my first year in band (after a year in the Prep Band) was the finale of Tchaikovsky's *Fourth Symphony*. It seemed as though we began right up to tempo, and keeping up with the other clarinetists playing those rapid sixteenth-note violin parts was both a struggle and a thrill. Shortly afterwards, perhaps the same day, I went to Lent's Music Store and bought a recording by the Philadelphia Orchestra. Lent's was a great place. You could pull out any record (LP) and listen to it, then put it back in its jacket and either buy it or return it to the shelf. This was before everything was hygienically wrapped in cellophane.

Theory Class

In the summer of 1958 or 1959, Mr. B began theory classes for anyone who was interested. The dozen or so of us who attended met in his little office one evening a week. We covered several aspects of music theory, using Walter Piston's *Harmony* as our text. The class provided my first experience with ear training. Is it a major 6th? If you're hearing the first two notes of the NBC theme, yes it is. An augmented 4th? If it's the opening of *Maria* from *West Side Story*, definitely. But my most memorable moments from those theory classes were when Mr. B read several passages from J. W. N. Sullivan's *Beethoven: His Spiritual Development*. He read from the chapter about the last string quartets, then played the Budapest's recording of the great *Quartet No. 14 in C# minor*. The combination of the unearthly beauty of the music following Sullivan's words was a transcendent experience. Recently, I looked through the book to see if I could pinpoint any particular passages. Nothing was marked, but the following could very likely have been included: "Those faint and troubling intimations we sometimes have of a vision different from and yet including our own, of a way of apprehending life, passionless, perfect and complete, that resolves all our discords, are here presented with the reality they had glimpsed."

CHAPTER 7   Off to First Band Camp—
Band Parents' Night—Trips to
Rochester, NY to hear Eastman Wind
Ensemble Concerts—Maestro Fennell's
First Visit to IHS, 1959–60

Marching Band

By fall 1959 the "separate but interconnected structure" of the IHS Marching and Concert Bands was fully in place. There were 87 students in the 1959 Marching Band (72 student musicians, 1 drum major, 1 drum sergeant, 7 color guards, 6 majorettes) including six sousaphones. This allowed "ITHACA" to be displayed on the bells of the sousaphones across the last rank in the band.

For the first time in its history the band began its year with a four-day pre-school camp held at Ithaca College's Summer Camp facility, located 14 miles south of Ithaca in the Danby Hills. Each student paid $13.50 to attend. From September 3–7, 1959, band members rehearsed music and practiced marching routines in preparation for their forthcoming fall performances. Mr. B told *Ithaca Journal* reporter Jerry Langdon that the camp was " . . . very successful. We accomplished in [four days] what would normally take about three weeks to do." However, band camp was not all work and no play. Between rehearsals, band members participated in recreational activities such as swimming, outdoor games, and interesting social events (ex. skit night, dancing, cabin decoration contest, etc.). Cabin #10 won the best skit contest in 1959. It featured drummer David "Satchmo" Mobbs and his "sun-baked" All-Stars.

The Sol Goldberg *Ithaca Journal* photo on the next page shows sousaphone players (left to right) Robert Smith, Steven Wade and William Sullivan playing their instruments while percussionist James Craig serves as a "floating music stand" in the camp's Jewel Pond

The band's busiest day of the fall season was on Saturday, October 10.· Band members spent the morning rehearsing and, in the afternoon, performing at Cornell University's Band Day. After the game they boarded buses and traveled to Elmira, NY where they performed at the IHS—Elmira Free Academy football game that evening.

In an interview, published later that month in *The Ithaca Journal* (**"High School Band Wins Plaudits for School, City, Director"**), Mr. B commented that the "esprit de corps" of the 1959 band was especially high—"This is the most enthusiastic and hardest working group of band members we have had at IHS since I came here in 1953." (Note:

Mr. B made this comment about all his IHS Bands. However, he was **very** impressed with the extraordinary dedication, commitment and work ethic of the 1959 Marching Band students.)

In the same *Ithaca Journal* article, reporter Jerry Langdon wrote,

Twenty people approached the director [Mr. B] in a restaurant near Elmira two Saturday nights ago to compliment him and his group.

A man in the same profession as the director said to a member of his cast out of a clear blue sky: "You certainly live up to the reputation you have."

The praise? It came from (1) several Elmira football fans following the EFA-Ithaca High game, (2) Jonathan Elkus, director of the Lehigh University Band . . .

The photo, below, shows the band performing at a fall 1959 IHS football game.

The "themes" of the four 1959 half-time shows were:

1. "Bands of the Land." Highlighted the big bands of Glenn Miller and Benny Goodman and the marching bands of Michigan and Duke Universities.
2. "I've Got Rhythm." Celebrated various styles of popular music (ex. "South Rampart Street Parade," "Mambo Jambo," "Shake, Rattle and Roll," etc.).
3. "You're a Grand Old Flag." Saluted the newest state in the union, Hawaii ("Hawaiian War Chant"), the Mississippi River ("Old Man River") and square dancing ("Skip to my Lou").
4. "Roaring Twenties." Featured "flapper-era" music (a precision marching routine to "Avalon" and a dance routine to "Five Foot Two.")

In October the "Little Red" Band participated in Ithaca's first remote telecast—a kick-off rally for the Tompkins County United Fund Drive from Ithaca High School's Foster Hall. It was televised over WICB-TV, Ithaca's community television station.

Percussion student David Mobbs organized two IHS Pep Bands, one Red and one Gold (sponsored by the IHS athletic department). These two bands alternated playing at IHS home basketball games.

Concert Band

The 1960 IHS Concert Band performance/events schedule:

January 25, 1960	Board of Education Concert	Ithaca
February 5, 1960	Eastman School Band Concert	Rochester
March 1-3, 1960	Guest Clinician, Walter Beeler	Ithaca
March 11, 1060	Eastman Wind Ensemble Concert	Rochester
March 16, 1960	Band Parents' Night	Ithaca
March 25, 1960	University of Michigan Symphony Band	Union-Endicott
April 8, 1960	Eastman School Band Concert	Rochester
April 20, 1960	Eastman Wind Ensemble Concert	Rochester
April 27, 1960	Small Ensembles performances	Ithaca College WICB-TV
May 3, 1960	MENC Student Chapter Program	Ithaca College
May 6, 1960	Onondaga Central High School	Syracuse
May 10, 1960	Double Assembly Concerts at IHS Jimmy Burke, Cornet Soloist	Ithaca
May 15, 1960	IHS Brass Choir and Ithaca College Brass Ensemble Joint Concert	Cornell Sage Chapel
May 18, 1960	Annual Spring Concert	Ithaca
May 24, 1960	Joint Concert IHS and IC Brass Choirs	Ithaca College
May 27, 1960	Dr. Frederick Fennell, Guest Conductor	Ithaca
May 29, 1960	IHS Band and Ithaca College Concert Band Joint Concert at DeWitt Park	Ithaca
June 2, 1960	Boynton Junior High School Concert	Ithaca

Mr. B began taking band members to Eastman Wind Ensemble concerts in Rochester, NY in February 1960. About 30-35 students attended each concert through April 1967. Students paid $1.00 to cover the cost of bus transportation—Ithaca City School District buses were used. Not many people attended Eastman Wind Ensemble concerts in the huge Eastman Theatre—IHS Band students made up the majority of the audience at most of these concerts. After the concert Maestro Fennell would often come out to the bus and thank the students for coming.

Eastman Wind Ensemble concerts stimulated and motivated Mr. B and the students. They were inspired and excited by the ensemble's performance and the pieces they heard. Soon many of them were included in the band's repertoire (e.g. Howard Hanson's *Chorale and Alleluia*, H. Owen Reed's *La Fiesta Mexicana*, Vincent Persichetti's *Symphony for Band, Op. 69*, etc.).

Small ensemble participation continued to expand in 1960—there were now numerous trios, quartets and quintets. A special *"harmoniemusik"* ensemble of 13 students rehearsed and performed selected movements from Mozart's *Serenade No 10 in B-flat, K. 361*. These ensembles performed on Bach Honor Society recitals and at various community functions.

Mr. B added a "Music and Art History" component to the IHS Band rehearsal curriculum in 1960. Its purpose was to help students better understand the relationships between music and the other arts. In an interview with a reporter from the *Tattler*, Mr. B stated that " . . . high school students don't receive enough education in the Arts, they're unaware of the relationships that exist between them."

Starting in January 1960 Mr. B devoted the first ten minutes of every rehearsal to reading pieces in chronological order starting with Gregorian chant and progressing to mid-20th century contemporary works. As the students read these pieces they also viewed prints of paintings, sculpture, architecture, etc. created concurrently with them. These prints were mounted on corridor walls leading to the rehearsal stage. Students also received supplemental written information on the composers, artists and works.

The first of what became annual IHS Band Parents' Nights was held on March 16, 1960. The objective of these "Nights" was to acquaint parents with the goals and activities of the IHS Band program. Each year hundreds of band parents, siblings, relatives and guests attended this event. The evening began with a dish-to-pass supper in the school cafeteria followed by a short talk by a guest speaker. Afterwards everyone, except parents playing in the Band Parents' Band, went to the Music Building where they viewed exhibits, attended demonstrations and listened to a student recital program. Parents playing in the Parents' Band went to a 45-minute rehearsal with Mr. B.

The selection of the Band Parents' Band began a month prior to the event. Band members were asked to submit names of parents who played/had played band instruments. These parents received a letter from Mr. B congratulating them on their selection to the Band Parents' Band and a set of parts to practice and prepare. Participation in this band always generated much excitement among the participants. Their performance (labeled "the blast from the past") always received a standing ovation. The final event of the evening was a 30-minute "Super Band" reading session—everyone who played an instrument participated—IHS Band members, moms, dads, brothers, sisters, uncles, aunts, grandparents and guests.

Below is the 1960 IHS Band Parents' Night program (this format was used for all future Band Parents' Nights).

1960 Band Parents' Night Program

6:00 PM	Dish-to-pass dinner in IHS cafeteria
6:30 PM	After dinner address
	Topic: Music in the High School
	Dr. Craig McHenry, Dean, School of Music
	Ithaca College
7:00 PM to	Rehearsal of Band Parents' Band
8:30 PM	Visit to Exhibits and Demonstrations Student Recital Performance of Student Compositions
	Marching Band movies
	Band Photo Gallery
8:30 PM	Concert
	Band Parents' Band
	("the blast from the past")
	Frank Battisti, Conductor
9:00 PM	Super Band conducted by Mr. B.
	Reading of music by band students, parents, brothers, sisters, uncles, aunts, grandparents, guests.

On April 26, 1960 five small ensembles—the Brass Choir, Clarinet Choir, Flute Choir, Woodwind Quintet and Percussion Ensemble—presented a concert on WICB-TV. Forty IHS Band students participated in this telecast performing music by Palestrina, Fox, Tcherepnin, Haydn and Siwe.

May (1960) was a very busy month for the band. On May 6 it performed concerts in schools in central and western New York State (Onondaga and Cheektowaga Central Schools). The following week (May 10, 1960) Jimmy Burke, cornet soloist with the world-famous Goldman Band and principal trumpet of the Baltimore and Radio City Music Hall symphony orchestras, performed two solos on the band's school assembly concerts—*The Bugler* by Edwin Franko Goldman and *A Trumpeter's Lullaby* by Leroy

Anderson. IHS Band trumpet players Jerry Kleeman and Richard Koski joined Burke for his encore—*The Magic Trumpet*, one of his own compositions.

The band's brass players premiered Warren Benson's *Nocturne and Rhumba* on a joint concert with the Ithaca College Brass Ensemble at Cornell University's Sage Chapel on May 5. *Nocturne and Rhumba* was the band's 1959-60 commissioned work (limited financial resources prevented the commissioning of a full-ensemble piece). The piece received a second performance on May 24, 1960 at Ithaca College.

The May 18, 1960 Spring Concert was performed in a "damaged" Foster Hall. Two weeks prior to the concert, the stage curtain caught fire and caused extensive damage to the stage area. Quick renovation work—the damaged floor was covered with plywood—made it usable for the concert. Below is a copy of the program.

Program

Totem Pole ....Eric Osterling

Chorale and Alleluia ....Howard Hanson

Chorale Preludes ....William P. Latham
    O Sacred Head Now Wounded
    Now Thank We All Our God

Concerto for Trumpet ....Joseph Haydn
    Allegro
                Peter Farrow, soloist

Toccata for Band ....Frank Erickson

West Side Story Selection ....Leonard Bernstein

Symphonic Songs for Band ....Robert Russell Bennett
    Spiritual
    Celebration

Carnival of Venice ....Giulio Briccialdi
          Virginia Klune, soloist

Symphony for Band ....Vincent Persichetti
    Vivace

Hands Across the Sea ....John Philip Sousa

Band members were excused from their regular classes on May 27 so they could spend the entire day rehearsing with Dr. Frederick Fennell (his annual visits continued through 1967). Fennell was a very dynamic and energetic conductor (he traveled to Ithaca in a red Corvette sports car, license plate A-440). During the day Fennell conducted exciting rehearsals of pieces by Grainger, Persichetti, Robert Russell Bennett, Bernstein and Sousa. His infectious enthusiasm and expressive conducting captivated and thrilled the students. He immediately became their favorite guest conductor.

In a letter to Mr. B following his visit, Fennell wrote,

The day that I had with you is one that I shall not soon forget and it was a great and deep inspiration to me. I look forward to the time when I might come back and spend more time with those wonderful young people and with you ... Congratulations to you on remarkable work, wonderfully done ... [the IHS Band is] one of the finest high school bands I have ever conducted and certainly the finest in the last 4 or 5 years.

All of Fennell's visits ended with a banquet at the Lehigh Valley House. Friends such as Warren Benson and Donald Sinta often joined Fennell, Mr. B and band members for these affairs. The after-dinner festivities were always the same and included the reading of the Band Poem (usually written by a committee of students), viewing of band slides and movies, and the presentation of a gift to Dr. Fennell. The one he received in the early 1960s was unique. Band members knew of Fennell's great interest in Civil War history. At the moment he was greatly concerned about the threat posed by real estate developers who hoped to purchase part of the Gettysburg battlefield and use it for commercial development. The U. S. Department of the Interior, in an attempt to keep this from happening, launched a campaign to get people/organizations who wanted to keep the battlefield as it was, to buy parcels of this land to prevent its acquisition by real estate developers. IHS Band members purchased the deed to a 10 × 10 foot plot of this "hallowed ground" and presented it to Fennell at the banquet—he was "floored," overwhelmed and speechless.

The Concert Band's final performance of the year was a joint concert with the Ithaca College Concert and Repertory Bands in DeWitt Park on May 29, 1960.

Senior band members graduating in June 1960 were the only students ever to be Ithaca High School Band members for four years (September 1956 to June 1960). Prior to these years IHS was (and continues to be) a three-year high school (grades 10 through 12).

Recollections by Peter Farrow, Class of 1960

First Band Camp

What a change from last year, when we had to squeeze major rehearsal requirements into a limited number of relatively short pre-school rehearsals at the high school in preparation for the first game that wasn't that far off. It felt like Mr. B always cut us some slack for the first few games as we kept working to reach high standards by mid-season.

Now, we'll have the time to meet the standard which Mr. B sets, and to which we eagerly strive . . . four days of rehearsals, morning and afternoon, and in such a wonderful setting, with the opportunity to get to know other band members in a new way and build the entire group's sense of relationship and shared goals. What a wonderful idea Mr. B has had in creating this opportunity for our adolescent striving. Of course, there are downsides, like the boys all sleep in the cabins over here and the girls all sleep in the cabins over there, but if that makes the adults more comfortable, then OK (and most of us aren't dating anyhow, just thinking about it). Meanwhile we have the opportunity to let the IHS marching band absorb our entire day, as we absorb the enriching experience of striving for attainable achievements that we'll remember with pride, probably for the rest of our lives.

Going to Eastman Wind Ensemble Concerts

Going to Rochester to hear the Eastman Wind Ensemble gives us a new perspective. For starters, it's not every concert hall that allows one to hear a wind ensemble instead of an orchestra, string quartet or solo piano. Our only other exposure to wind ensemble playing is when we are playing, and it sounds different sitting in the hall than it does sitting on stage. And there's something about watching the individual musicians, who after all aren't that much older than we are. In fact, there's Jonathan Levine, who was one of our clarinetists just a couple of years ago, and here he is in this magnificent concert hall playing with one of the finest wind ensembles in the country . . . Mr. B knows how to help us see possible horizons.

One evening there was even a humorous moment that gave comfort to student musicians, whose journey to better performance necessarily travels along a path marked by missed notes, entrances on the wrong beat or in the wrong measure, or other miseries to be feared as your fellow musicians hear them. It was on the last piece of the concert, a march. Marches often end with an exclamation point . . . like "Stars and Stripes Forever," where the melody ends, going from D to C to B flat, and then after a rest, the final chord repeats on a single beat. Frederick Fennell, presumably caught up in the music, conducts that exclamation point with his signature flamboyant gesture but this march doesn't have an exclamation point, so the performers look at him, as they should, but don't play the note, also as they should. Silence, followed by applause spiced by some polite chuckling. What a wonderful moment for aspiring student performers, to know that even the best performers make mistakes once in a while . . . now that takes some of the pressure off as you strive to do your best.

Fennell Visits IHS for the First Time

May 1960—the band is going to have a rehearsal. What's new about that? Well, "new" hardly describes it. Dr. Fennell, who has been conducting the Eastman Wind Ensemble concerts we've been going to this winter, is leading the rehearsal. This is "big," more than "big," it's awesome. We're just a bunch of high school kids, and he's going to give us his full attention for most of the day with a perspective that we'll be hearing for the first time. What an opportunity! It turns out he has his own moment of awe . . . "a sousaphone, what's it doing here, I'm used to seeing a tuba" his facial expression tells us. But George Kent [sousaphone player] does OK and the rest of us work just as hard. This exposure to a musician of major skill and reputation helps us better understand and appreciate the wonderful music our instruments allow us to explore.

Recollection by Lois Lounsbery, Class of 1960

Fennell's Visit and Mozart *Serenade No. 10*

The day Frederick Fennell visited was much anticipated. The Eastman Wind Ensemble was the wind group against which all other wind groups were compared, and here was the Founder-Director amongst us. At the end of the day, he [conducted] some of the small ensembles, and the Mozart *Serenade No. 10* group was one of them. The opening Largo features some brief clarinet solos. My heart stood still when Mr. B asked us to play the movement for Fennell. He listened and then asked me to "ease" the tempo where the notes rose. We tried it a couple of times. I knew exactly what he wanted, but couldn't quite bring it off. I had learned it a certain way and was not flexible enough at that point to do it differently on the spur of the moment. I think of that sometimes when I'm explaining to piano students how they need to take into account the tendency to speed up as the music ascends.

PART III Musical Experiences to
Stimulate Imagination,
Creativity, and
Expressive Spirit

CHAPTER **8**   In the New High School:
A New IHS—Persichetti
Commission—Expanded Repertoire,
1960–61

Marching Band

The "new" Ithaca High School opened in September 1960. It was a campus-type school located in the Fall Creek section of Ithaca (see picture, below). The *Annual* described the nine-building complex as "spacious and bright," offering "untold advantages and opportunities."

The music building (located in the lower right section of the photo, above) contained a 1,000-seat auditorium (Claude L. Kulp Auditorium), a large rehearsal room, four practice rooms, three teaching studios and library, uniform and storage rooms. These facilities were a huge improvement over those at the old high school. A unique feature of the building was the large floor-to-ceiling bulletin boards that lined the corridor walls. Mr. B posted hundreds of photographs of IHS Band members rehearsing, performing and socializing on these bulletin boards (they proved to be a great attraction and drew many students to the music building). One of the "non-building" improvements was the location of the athletic fields. Their placement, near the music building, eliminated the need for band members to march four blocks to and from rehearsals during the football season.

The 1960 IHS "Little Red" Band consisted of 87 student members (72 student musicians, 1 drum major, 1 drum sergeant, 7 color guards, 6 majorettes). The two photographs, below, show the band performing at Bredbenner Field.

Below is a photo of the 1960 "Little Red" Band trumpet and trombone sections.

A marching band newspaper, the "IHS Band SNOOP," was published twice a week during the fall. Below is the front page of the November 4, 1960 issue of the paper.

Concert Band

In the summer of 1960 Mr. B decided to commission a non-local composer. His choice was Vincent Persichetti, a distinguished, nationally-recognized American composer, and a faculty member at the Juilliard School of Music in New York City. Persichetti was a prolific composer, who had written over 80 works, including seven symphonies, three string quartets, ten piano sonatas, concertos, song cycles, serenades and a variety of miscellaneous works. Mr. B offered him a commission fee of $500, which Persichetti promptly rejected as being too low (his normal fee for a 6-7 minute piece was $1,000). Persichetti asked if the fee could be increased—Mr. B told him that the band's financial resources made this impossible. His negative response, however, did not discourage Mr. B, who continued to write and urge him to accept the commission. His persistence paid off—Persichetti suddenly changed his mind and accepted the commission. In a letter to Mr. B, dated September 30, 1960, Persichetti indicated he intended to write either a Chorale-Prelude or a Suite for band. When the score and parts arrived on February 3, 1961 it was a six-minute divertimento-type piece in five short movements entitled, *Serenade for Band*.

Mr. B invited Persichetti to come to Ithaca and conduct the premiere performance of his new piece. Persichetti accepted and arrived in Ithaca on May 17, 1961 He rehearsed with the band twice, on Thursday and Friday afternoons, May 18 and 19, respectively. Persichetti's visit generated a great deal of attention and publicity for the band. When William Austin, Chair of Cornell University's Department of Music, heard that Persichetti was coming to IHS, he immediately contacted Mr. B and invited him to visit Cornell University. Persichetti spent Friday morning May 19 meeting with Cornell music department faculty members and graduate composition students.

Below is a copy of the May 19, 1961 Spring Concert program, which featured the premiere performance of Persichetti's *Serenade for Band*, the band's third commissioned work.

Program

Star Pageant ....Walter Finlayson

Armenian Dances ....Aram Khachaturian
                          Arranged and edited by Ralph Satz

Trumpet Concerto ....Johann N. Hummel
                          Edited by Armando Ghitalla
                          Band score by John Corley
    Rondo
            Richard Koski, Trumpet Soloist

Suite Francaise ....Darius Milhaud
        Normandie
        Ile de France
        Alsace-Lorraine

Seranade for Band, Op. 85 ....Vincent Persichetti
        Pastorale
        Humoreske
        Nocturne
        Intermezzo
        Capriccio
            This will be the premiere performance of "Serenade for
        Band" which was commissioned by the Ithaca High School
        Band. Mr. Persichetti will conduct this first performance.

Lincolnshire Posy ....Percy Grainger
        "The brisk young Sailor" (returned to wed his True Love)
        "Lord Melbourne" (War Song)

Suite of Old American Dances ....Robert Russell Bennett
        Schottische
        Wallflower Waltz
        Rag

Barnum and Bailey's Favorite ....Karl King

The concert was a huge success, and everyone, including Vincent Persichetti, was extremely pleased and happy. In a letter to Mr. B following the concert he wrote,

My Ithaca visit was a delightful experience for me. You have made a first rate band at the school and helped build wonderful people. As you know, I was very pleased with the premiere ...

Persichetti also wrote a note to the band students.

The *Serenade* premiere was a delightful one. I was particularly pleased with the projection of the musical line and the shaping of the phrases. This is so important when bringing a new work to the listener.

The personal warmth, musical enthusiasm and high quality of playing was a joy. I hope we can meet again soon.

The music performed by the band in 1961 testifies to the ensemble's musical growth and development. Many band members were now taking private lessons with faculty members at the Ithaca College School of Music—some even traveled to Rochester, NY and studied with Eastman School of Music teachers. Collectively, the students possessed the technical skills, musical knowledge and maturity needed to perform important (and challenging) wind band/ensemble works such as Grainger's *Lincolnshire Posy*, Milhaud's *Suite Francaise*, and Robert Russell Bennett's *Suite of Old American Dances*.

In May (1961) two previous guest artists returned to IHS. On May 3, Jimmy Burke performed *Danze Allegro* (one of his own compositions) with the band on their school assembly concerts. Four weeks later (May 30) Frederick Fennell returned for another day of terrific music making with the band. This time he conducted full ensemble works by Khatchaturian, Persichetti, Milhaud and Grainger plus selected movements from Mozart's *Serenades No. 11* and *12* and Richard Strauss's *Suite, Op. 4* and *Serenade, Op. 7*.

In a letter to students following his visit Fennell wrote,

... [I'm] SO impressed with the playing and the high caliber of citizenry in your parts ... I think you should play in the Eastman Theatre sometime.

Brian Norcross provides the following comment on Frederick Fennell's annual end-of-the-year rehearsals with the IHS Band,

There were often small ensemble rehearsals that Fennell would direct followed by an extended band rehearsal ... Fennell found himself free to work on musical growth rather than [getting the band ready for a performance in the evening]. (Norcross, p. 52)

On June 2, 1961 the band performed a concert at Boynton Junior High School. This was the first in a series of annual concerts presented, on alternating years, at one of the district's two junior high schools (the other was DeWitt Junior High School). The concerts continued until Mr. B left IHS in 1967.

Reflection by Bruce Musgrave, Class of 1965

Technology, Such As It Was

From the not-all-that-lofty technological platform of 2009, the technology of the IHS Band some fifty years earlier appears quaint, if not downright primitive. As the words of this piece dance to life across the screen of the laptop, a second laptop sits on a table to the writer's left. On the table to the writer's right sit not only a wireless remote phone from the writer's landline, but also a Blackberry—yielding in all access to two phone accounts, and three e-mail accounts, all open, wirelessly. Resting in his shirt pocket are two flash drives and a smart disc the size of a postage stamp, each with a capacity of several volumes of the *Encyclopedia Britannica*. Back in the late '50s during the writer's junior high school years, when he was so jealous of his two older sisters who had just completed their joyous years in the IHS Band, a phone call would come, via the Caroline Farmers' Exchange, on a wall-mounted, crank telephone, with a party line of eight (the neighbors' kids, also in the band, had a ring of three longs and three shorts, while the writer's ring was three longs—the customized ring tones of that era). To call anyone "out of party" required cranking one long ring for the operator: "Hello, Jenny? This is Timmy. Can I speak to Lassie?"

Things weren't all that much better, technologically speaking, during most of Frank Battisti's tenure with the IHS band. He had been at it for several years already, for instance, when a new Smith-Corona electric typewriter replaced his old manual Underwood for generating all the band correspondence and typescript. When it came time to distribute memos or other mass-produced documents, A. B. Dick spirit master ditto copies were all we knew; photocopying and the Xerox machine wouldn't come along for almost a decade. Widespread word processing emerged after that. Recording of rehearsals was a key aspect of the program, but virtually all of that recording was done on a clanking, decidedly low-fidelity Wollensack reel-to-reel tape deck. Communicating over distance by voice with the band members was also essential, but in an era of no pagers, and no cell phones—much less any text-messaging or Blue Tooth devices—all of that phone contact occurred via a phone tree consisting of nothing but land lines. Many of the great moments of the bands were recorded on film, by still or Super-8 movie cameras, but with at best a one-week turnaround time from the developer's, on processed celluloid, the digital image being a thing unheard of at that point. Equally unknown was the videocassette recorder. A few of us thought we were very with-it when we began carrying transistorized radios the size of cigarette packs in our shirt pockets. It was sometimes possible to tune in either WTKO or WHCU, but little else. Up the hill at Cornell, they were starting to experiment with an IBM 1401 computer; it was the size of Mr. B's office, was programmed with punch cards, and had about one third the computing power of a decent contemporary laptop. We thought of it as very high-tech when we finally acquired an oscillating Strobotuner for checking individual pitches electronically. "Igor," the sweep-second hand machine that conducted us in Barney Childs's *Six Events for 58 Players*, seemed nearly otherworldly as a technological innovation at the time.

Yet with what we had, we never felt the lack of any of those devices. Mr. B's daily reminders and other messages on the bulletin board in front of his office were as precious to us as any blast e-mail or streaming video could be, and most of us had read that bulletin board religiously before 8:00 a.m. each day. Our IHS Band *Snoop* may have been reproduced by hand-cranked mimeograph machine and laid out with a ruler and pen (with the end of a paper clip for correcting errors on the back side of the spirit master), but we loved it as much as we would have loved any multi-media presentation composed on Quark, Pagemaker, Photoshop, or InDesign. At the reunion in 2006, great digitally upgraded versions of the old movies and the old recordings certainly enhanced the originals, but this was one case when Marshall McLuhan may have been wrong: The medium was *not* the massage or even just the message. What we were doing together, in person, was everything, and that went far beyond the bells and whistles of technology. If he had had at his disposal all the glories of the semi-conductor technology and every wireless, digitized device now known to man, here's betting Frank Battisti would still have worked most of his magic through deep interpersonal engagement, the burning desire to create something unique and memorable, and an utterly infectious personal example.

CHAPTER 9 In the Big House: Midwest Tour—
A Second Band—Small Ensembles
Perform at Eastman School of Music,
1961–62

Marching Band

The band held its first summer chicken barbecue at Stewart Park on August 10, 1961, raising $1,200. This was the first of a series of fund-raising events to help finance the band's November 21–26, 1961 trip to Michigan and Ohio. The tour itinerary included concerts in Dayton, Ohio, and Williamsville, NY, and marching band performances in Detroit, Michigan (J. L. Hudson Thanksgiving Parade) and Cleveland, Ohio (Cleveland Browns vs. New York Giants NFL game). The trip would be the most extensive one undertaken by an IHS student organization since 1933, when the football team traveled to Florida to play a post-season game.

The last week in August found the 91 students in the 1961 IHS "Little Red" Band (76 student musicians, 1 drum major, 1 drum sergeant, 8 color guards and 5 majorettes) rehearsing at band camp in the Danby Hills. Everyone was very excited about the upcoming season and Midwest Tour. An *Ithaca Journal* reporter and photographer came to camp for the week and produced a full-page photo essay on the band's "week in the woods," **"The IHS Band . . . Its Biggest Year of All. Ithaca High's Band Prepares to Carry the Name of Ithaca Across the Nation."**

Below is a photo of the 1961 IHS "Little Red" Band (note the white-gloved "victory sign"). Mr. B is kneeling in front of the band, drum sergeant Charles Caveney is at the left, drum major Mike Miller on the right.

Below is the band's 1961 Fall Performance Schedule.

September	7	Concert for Ithaca Teachers Association	Ithaca, NY	7:30 PM
	23	Union-Endicott—IHS Football Game	Ithaca, NY	1:30 PM
	30	Band Day (Cornell—Colgate Football Game)	Cornell	11:00 AM
		Vestal—IHS Football Game	Vestal, NY	8:00 PM
October	7	Binghamton Central—IHS Football Game	Ithaca, NY	1:30 PM
	14	Elmira Free Academy—IHS Football Game	Elmira, NY	8:00 PM
	21	Johnson City—IHS Football Game	Johnson City, NY	1:30 PM
	28	Elmira Southside—IHS Football Game	Ithaca, NY	1:30 PM
November	4	Auburn—IHS Football Game	Ithaca, NY	11:00 AM
	11	Binghamton North—IHS Football Game	Binghamton, NY	1:30 PM
	23	J. L. Hudson Thanksgiving Parade (CBS-TV)	Detroit, MI	9:00 AM
	24	Concert: National Cash Register Auditorium	Dayton, OH	8:15 PM
	26	Cleveland Browns—New York Giants NFL Game (NBC and CBS-TV)	Cleveland, OH	1:00 PM
	27	Concert: Williamsville High School	Williamsville, NY	2:00 PM

Over the course of the 1961 fall season the band performed one pre-game and four different halftime shows. Each halftime show was performed twice, once at home and once at an away football game. However, consecutive home games on October 28 and November 4 necessitated the preparation of a new halftime show in just five short rehearsals (40 minutes each) for the latter date. Commenting on these "five-day wonders," Mr. B stated, "Sometimes they come off the best. The students know what they have to do and they do it."

The music performed in 1961 halftime shows included:

Climb Every Mountain
Two Different Worlds
Everything's Coming Up Roses
Zing! Went the Strings of My Heart (featuring the Percussion Section)
Great Day
Drums in My Heart
Cornet Carillon (featuring Trumpet Section)
I Could Have Danced All Night
Ain't She Sweet
What Takes My Fancy

The three photos, below, show Mr. B "in action" during a mid-September rehearsal (*Ithaca Journal*, September 25, 1961).

On the day before the band departed on its Midwest Tour (November 20, 1961), the students received the following letter from Peter Storandt, one of the 1961 band camp counselors (see excerpt, below).

Tomorrow you will be leaving on your long-awaited trip, a trip that represents the climax of three months of intensive work. [It] is a tribute to the way in which the Ithaca High School Band interprets "work." "Work" in Band is like a book is to a scholar. Give him a book and he gets as much from it as he can. You are like that—you were given work and you gained discipline, knowledge, enjoyment and a sense of the approach to perfection. Your attitudes have given you the added bonus of seeing first hand the vigor, enthusiasm and companionship that have been for years the marks of the IHS Band. No other group approaches its sense of "oneness" and teamwork. No other group can boast of its reputation of personal and public honor. I and all your other Band Camp

counselors, salute you. You are about to carry the finest institution of its kind to millions of Americans all over the nation. We are very proud of you!

Three buses loaded with 104 students, 300 pieces of luggage, 100 band uniforms, 150 individual instruments and eight chaperones (Dr. and Mrs. Reginald Farrow, Mr. and Mrs. Wilmot Carter, Mr. and Mrs. Richard Apple, and Mr. and Mrs. Charles Higgins) rolled out of the IHS parking lot on Tuesday afternoon, November 21, 1961 at 2:34 PM headed for Detroit, Dayton, Cleveland, and Williamsville. Below is a copy of the band's tour itinerary and on the following page are three pictures from the tour program booklet.

Ithaca High School Band Tour Itinerary
November 21–27, 1961

Tuesday November 21	–Leave Ithaca, New York from Claude L. Kulp Auditorium at 2:45 P.M. –Dinner stop on New York State Thruway at 5:30 P.M. –Pass through Canadian Customs at Niagara Falls –Arrive in Niagara Falls, Ontario for overnight stop at Sheraton-Brock Hotel at 8:30 P.M.
Wednesday November 22	–Breakfast at Sheraton-Brock (7:00 A.M.) –Leave Niagara Falls immediately after breakfast –Marching Band rehearsal at Central Elgin Collegiate Institute in St. Thomas, Ontario at 11:30 A.M. followed by lunch –Leave St. Thomas, Ontario at 1:15 P.M. –Clear United States Customs at Detroit, Michigan –Arrive at Park Shelton Hotel in Detroit, Michigan, at 4:00 P.M. –Concert Band rehearsal in Ballroom at 4:45 P.M. –Dinner at Ponchartrain Wine Cellars at 6:30 P.M. –Evening recreation
Thursday November 23	–Breakfast at the Park Shelton (8:00 P.M.) –Santa Claus Parade (J. L. Hudson's Thanksgiving Day Parade) in Detroit at 9:00 A.M. (TV) –Daytime sight-seeing: Henry Ford Museum, Cobo-Hall, Ice Follies, etc. –Thanksgiving Day Dinner at Park Shelton at 5:30 P.M. –Evening: Detroit Symphony Concert, Play, Movies, etc.
Friday November 24	–Breakfast at Park Shelton in Detroit (7:30 A.M.) –Leave Detroit at 8:30 A.M. –Lunch at Milano Restaurant in Lima, Ohio (12:00 Noon) –Arrive at National Cash Register in Dayton, Ohio, at 2:45 P.M. Tour plant. –Short concert band rehearsal at 4:30 P.M. in Auditorium –Dinner with National Cash Register at 5:45 P.M. –Program by Concert Band at 8:15 P.M. –Leave Dayton, Ohio at 10:00 P.M. Arrive in Columbus, Ohio at 11:20 P.M. for overnight stop at Deshler-Hilton Hotel
Saturday November 25	–Breakfast at 8:00 A.M. at Deshler-Hilton –Marching Band rehearsal on campus of Ohio State University at 9:15 A.M. after which we depart for Cleveland, Ohio –Lunch at the Loff Restaurant in Mansfield, Ohio at 12:15 P.M. –Arrive at Manger Hotel in Cleveland at 3:00 P.M. –Concert band rehearsal at Manger Hotel at 4:15 P.M. –Dinner at Manger Hotel at 6:00 P.M. –Evening recreation
Sunday November 26	–Breakfast at 8:30 A.M. at Manger Hotel –Pre-game rehearsal for Marching Band at 12:00 Noon –Marching Band national television performance at Cleveland Browns–New York Giants NFL game at 2:00 P.M. –Special dinner –Evening recreation
Monday November 27	–Breakfast at 7:30 P.M. at Manger. Leave Cleveland immediately after breakfast –Arrive in Buffalo for lunch and concert (Williamsville) at 1:00 P.M. –Leave Buffalo at 3:30 P.M. –Dinner stop on New York State Thruway at 5:30 P.M. –Arrive in Ithaca, New York at 8:00 P.M.

The band spent Tuesday night at the Sheraton-Brock Hotel in Niagara Falls, Ontario, Canada—everyone had a wonderful view of the Falls from their hotel room. On Wednesday November 22, the band traveled to St. Thomas, Ontario, rehearsed for two hours at Central Elgin Collegiate Institute and then moved on to Detroit where they checked into the Sheraton Hotel.

The Thursday morning found the band marching in Detroit's J. L. Hudson Thanksgiving Parade. Even though the parade was televised nationally, the IHS Band was not picked up by the TV cameras due to a delay in the start of the parade. However, the band was seen and heard by the 200,000 spectators who lined the parade route. The students spent the afternoon sightseeing in Detroit and then returned to the hotel for a traditional Thanksgiving Day dinner. In the evening everyone attended a concert by the Detroit Symphony Orchestra.

The following day, Friday November 23, the band traveled to Dayton, Ohio and presented a concert at the National Cash Register Company's auditorium. R. D. Fowler, Ithaca branch manager of NCR, secured the company's sponsorship for this concert. Below is the program the band performed before an audience of 1,000.

Ithaca High School Concert Band

Frank L. Battisti, Conductor

Program

The Foundation . . . . Richard Franko Goldman

Contrasts . . . . Will Gay Bottje

    Lament – Holiday

Two Chorales . . . . Johannes Brahms
                                     Arranged by Arthur H. Christmann
    O World, I Now Must Leave Thee
    Lo, How a Rose E'er Blooming

Highlights from "Gigi" . . . . Alan Lerner & Frederick Loewe

Second Suite In F For Military Band . . . . Gustav Holst
                                     Op. 28, No.2
    March
    Song Without Words "I'll love my love"
    Song of the Blacksmith
    Fantasia on the "Dargason"

William Byrd Suite . . . . Freely transcribed by Gordon Jacob

    The Earle of Oxford's March
    The Mayden's Song
    The Bells

Burlesk for Band . . . . Robert Washburn

The Black Horse Troop . . . . John Philip Sousa

Ithaca High School Band Tour

November 21–27, 1961

Immediately after the concert everyone boarded buses for the journey north to Columbus, Ohio where they checked into the Deshler-Hilton Hotel at 1:20 AM. The next morning (Saturday, November 24) the band rehearsed the "Cleveland show" in the huge parking lot next to the Ohio State University football stadium. Below is the music included in the show.

*	Climb Every Mountain (Fanfare)	Richard Rodgers
*	Everything's Coming Up Roses	Julie Styne
#	Great Day	Vincent Youmans
#	Drums In My Heart	Vincent Youmans
*	I Could Have Danced All Night	Frederick Loewe
**	Two Different Worlds	Al Frisch
***	Ain't She Sweet	M. Ager, J. Yellen Arranged by J. Cacavas
***	Charleston	C. Mack, J. Johnson Arranged by J. Conrad
##	Cornet Carillon	Ronald Binge Arranged by F. Werle

Note: (*) Indicates that permission to write these special arrangements for the Ithaca High School Band was granted by the copyright owner Chappell & Co. Inc., 609 Fifth Avenue, New York 17, New York

(#) Indicates that permission to write these special arrangements for the Ithaca High School Band was granted by the copyright owner Big 3 Music Corporation, New York, New York

(**) Indicates that permission to write this special arrangment for the Ithaca High School Band was granted by the copyright owner Princess Music Publishing, Corp. 1650 Broadway, New York 19, New York

(##) Indicates that permission to arrange a "special ending" for this number granted by Mills Music, Inc., 1619 Broadway, New York 19, New York. "Cornet Carillon" by Ronald Binge—Arr. by Floyd Werle copyright 1954 and 1961 by W. Paxton Co., Ltd. published in United States of America, South America and Canada by Mills Music, Inc.

(***) Indicates that these arrangements published by Music Publishers Holding Corporation, 619 W. 54th Street, New York, New York

Program printed by the students of the Ithaca High School Print Shop

Following the rehearsal the band left for Cleveland. Upon arrival in the city they checked into the Manger Hotel. Later that afternoon Mr. B held a one-hour rehearsal for the Concert Band. In the evening everyone attended a concert by the Cleveland Orchestra in Severance Hall.

"Game Day!!!"—Sunday, November 26. Everyone was up early, ate breakfast, put on their uniforms, loaded instruments and equipment onto the buses and departed for Cleveland Municipal Stadium at 11:00 AM. When the students entered the stadium they freaked out—the place was huge—they were stunned and speechless!! Sensing their nervousness and apprehension, Mr. B directed everyone to a secluded spot underneath the stadium where he could talk to them—"you have nothing to fear—you're well prepared. Forget the crowd—concentrate on what you have to do—you'll do a great job !!"

Gradually the students regained their equilibrium and confidence. When half-time arrived they were excited, eager and ready to perform. Everyone roared onto the field and performed brilliantly, receiving a huge ovation from, what was then, an NFL-record crowd of 80,455. The *Syracuse Post-Standard* described the crowd's response to the band's performance as a "… thunderous burst of applause …." In addition to the thousands who watched the band perform in the stadium, millions more saw them on the CBS national television network.

The following day (Monday, November 26, 1961) the *Ithaca Journal* proclaimed, **"Band's Big TV Debut A Swinging Success."** Reporter Richard O'Connell wrote,

The bandsmen, seen for the first time by a high-angle television camera, rewarded expectations here and no doubt thrilled viewers nationally as they stepped through their intricate patterns with perfect order …

Johnny Lujack (television announcer), coming at Ithacans via Channels 8 and 12, didn't tell Tompkins County residents anything new about the bandsmen and their great efforts in the marching and musical world during his commentary while the band performed. He did provide the national TV audience with an insight into the many hours of hard work by the band, highlighted by its drive to raise funds for the trip …

At Cleveland, one of the selections played was "Everything's Coming Up Roses." Today, all roses go to the Ithaca High School "Little Red" Band.

At right is O'Connell's entire story.

Band's Big TV Debut A Swinging Success

By RICHARD O'CONNELL

Cleveland Browns football fans numbering some 80,455 left Cleveland's Municipal Stadium Sunday afternoon with the bitter taste of defeat as their gridiron favorites were humbled by the New York Giants 37-21.

But sweetening the gall to some degree was the split-second precision marching and toe-tapping music provided by 104 Ithaca High School students. The kaleidoscopic movements of the Little Red Bandsmen however, were of prime interest to Ithaca viewers at half-time of the National Football League contest viewed by millions across the country.

The bandsmen, seen for the first time by a high-angle television camera, rewarded expectations here and no doubt thrilled viewers nationally as they stepped through their intricate patterns with perfect order and timing. Michael Miller, drum major, and Linda Post, majorette, led the entourage from Ithaca, while Frank Battisti directed.

Johnny Lujack, coming at Ithacans via Channels 8 and 12, didn't tell Tompkins County residents anything new about the bandsmen and their great efforts in the marching and musical world during his commentary while the band performed. He did provide the national TV audience with an insight into the many hours of hard work by the band, highlighted by its drive to raise funds for this trip.

* * *

The few moments on camera for the musicians gave friends, parents, teachers, students and "fans" just reward for patience. The unit appeared in the Detroit J. L. Hudson Thanksgiving Day Parade Thursday but TV cameras did not pick them up in the line of march.

In the half-time show the band went through geometric patterns marked by their lack of raggedness. Musical selections came out bold and brassy as the cadence continued.

Played were several selections from Broadway musicals crowned with a fast-paced Charleston number, played and danced by the band.

* * *

Arrival home for the group is 8 p.m. today at the school. Members are scheduled for a performance at Williamsville High School near Buffalo this afternoon.

This will cap a busy week. It began with three buses and an equipment vehicle carrying the 104-plus uniforms, instruments and chaperones leaving Tuesday afternoon last week. Then in quick succession came rehearsal, the Detroit parade, afternoon concert band rehearsal, tours, a trip to Dayton for a concert at the National Cash Register plant there, another rehearsal, performance at Cleveland, plus tours, and then the trip home with the last appearance for good measure.

Four months of work in practice sessions and fund-raising efforts for the trip and the trip itself are now almost history. The band raised $7,200 to make the tour, and funds were raised by band projects.

At Cleveland, one of the selections played was "Everything's Coming Up Roses." Today all roses go to the Ithaca High School "Little Red" Band.

The three Sol Goldberg photos, below, show the band performing in Cleveland as viewed on TV screens in Ithaca and throughout the nation. (*Ithaca Journal* photos) (Note: A video recording of the band's Cleveland performance is included on the 2006 IHS Band Reunion DVD.)

A headline in the Monday, November 26, 1961 edition of the *Syracuse Post-Standard*, central New York State's largest newspaper, said it all—**"Ithaca High Band Sparkles at Browns—Giants Game."**

> **The Little Red Marching Band of Ithaca High School staged a major league performance in Cleveland's huge Municipal Stadium Sunday afternoon between halves of the New York Giants-Cleveland Browns National Football League game. A capacity crowd of over 80,000 gave out with a thunderous burst of applause when the marchers and musicians completed their precision drills . . .**

Cleveland's largest newspaper, *The Cleveland Plain* Dealer, included a picture of the band (marching into the stadium before the game) in its Monday, November 26 edition. The photo was later used on the front cover of the band's LP recording of the music performed on the Midwest tour (see below).

Mr. B received many letters complimenting the band on their Cleveland performance. Below are excerpts from six of them.

Stanley B. Stone of Baschi's Leading Jewelers in Euclid, Ohio.

The people of Ithaca and your school personnel can be justly proud of the splendid performance put on display by the Ithaca High School Band at the Cleveland-New York football game Sunday. As a former Ithacan I watched with keen pride the outstanding show the youngsters presented. The tremendous crowd of over 80,000 represented the second largest crowd ever to watch a sports event in Cleveland.

Jack A. Bullock, band director at Gorham Central School, Gorham, New York.

I am writing to tell you how much I enjoyed your performance at the Cleveland Brown's halftime last Sunday. Both you and your band are to be complimented. One reason that I particularly enjoyed it was that I know that you have a well balanced music program, not just a football band. Your reputation as a concert group is outstanding also.

Joe Lanen, band director at West Technical High School, Cleveland, Ohio.

Sorry I couldn't get to the game, for we had to march our band in the annual Christmas parade. Your band must have caused a minor sensation because it's the first time they've (the *Cleveland Plain Dealer*) ever mentioned bands at the Browns games, let alone pictures! So you should feel proud of your group. I'm sure they did a terrific job!

Bill Sullivan, a former IHS Band member and in 1961, a member of the University of Notre Dame Band.

[It was] one of the best half-time shows ever . . . It's really too bad that all the people who saw the marching band . . . either in person or over television, (couldn't) hear the concert band. That would really knock them flat!!

R. D. Fowler, manager of the National Cash Register Company in Ithaca, New York, commented on both the Concert Band's performance in Dayton, Ohio and the Marching Band's performance in Cleveland.

Dayton NCR has reported to me on the visit of the Ithaca High School Band on November 24. They were very pleased with everything connected with the visit. First of all they state that the concert was excellent. They have received many comments from the people who were in attendance, all with the same complimentary theme. Mr. Robert Kline, Director of Educational Training, made the statement that they were the best behaved group of youngsters they have ever entertained. This is a high compliment because many groups of youngsters have been guests there. I watched the performance between the halves of the football game and was greatly impressed with the precision and

the music . . . Please accept the congratulations of our entire organization for the tremendous undertaking and the effective way in which it was carried out. Not only was this a wonderful trip for the youngsters but you have also greatly benefited your school and the community.

The students' behavior throughout the tour was exemplary. Dr. Reginald C. Farrow, M. D., one of the trip chaperones, wrote the following letter to the editor of *The Ithaca Journal*.

My wife and I have just returned from chaperoning the Ithaca High School Band trip, and I would like to put some of our impressions on record. Our community can take just pride in the young men and women who went forth to represent it. They handled themselves, as musicians and as people, with distinction and credit to themselves and to us. They were seen by thousands, and were regarded with favor wherever they went. The Manager of the hotel in Detroit summed it up: "They are the best bunch of kids we have ever had here." The group is described as a precision band. The leadership showed equal precision. The trip was boldly planned, and was executed without flaw or hitch. Getting 110 high school students with luggage and equipment in and out of a metropolitan hotel with quiet efficiency and dispatch was an impressive sight. With everyone invariably pitching in with good spirit, it was also a pleasant sight. No one need feel sorry for the chaperones—they had a wonderful time. It was a privilege to be on the trip.

The band's outstanding performance in Cleveland prompted the American Football Coaches' Association to invite the "Little Red" Band to perform at the 1962 All-American Game in Buffalo, NY on June 29, 1962. Because of the lateness of the invitation the band was unable to accept it.

Concert Band

Below is the 1962 Concert Band's spring semester schedule of concerts/events.

February 8, 1962	Concert-demonstration, MENC Chapter Eastman School of Music	Rochester
March 21, 1962	Band Parents' Night	Ithaca
March 23, 1962	Bach Honor Society Lecture: "Semantics in Music," Prof. Donald Wells, Ithaca College	Ithaca
April 24, 1962	Flute-Piccolo Clinic presented by William Hebert of the Cleveland Orchestra	Ithaca
May 2, 1962	IHS Band Assembly Programs, Harvey Phillips, tuba soloist, member of NY Brass Quintet, Goldman Band, Symphony of the Air	Ithaca

May 9, 1962	Annual Spring Concert	Ithaca
May 24, 1962	Performance at DeWitt Junior High School	Ithaca
May 29, 1962	Frederick Fennell Visit and Banquet	Ithaca
June 2, 1962	Youth Opportunity Camp (Nelson Rockefeller, Governor, in attendance)	Caroline Center

Richard Franko Goldman, director of the world-famous Goldman Band, conducted a rehearsal with the IHS Band in November (1961) when he was in Ithaca to guest conduct the New York State Sectional All-State Band at Ithaca High School. After returning to New York City, Goldman wrote the following letter to Mr. B (letter of November 20, 1961, excerpt below).

> **I do want to tell you again how impressed I am with what you have done and are doing, and with your whole attitude about the training of young players in high school bands. More power to you ! Of course, the playing of your own Ithaca High School Band reflects all of these things. It is a fine group, and I am very glad I could hear them, even if only for a few moments. I have already played the recording you gave me and am much impressed by it. The group is not only technically proficient, but it plays musically, and for this you are entitled to all the credit.**

IHS Band brass players continued to play Christmas carols for faculty members, friends of the band and at community institutions. Six-year-old Nancy Beeler wrote the following note to the group after they played carols at the Beeler home.

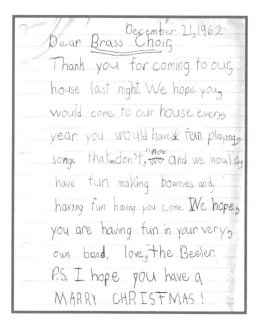

Dear Brass Choir,
December 21, 1962
Thank you for coming to our house last night. We hope you would come to our house every year. You would have fun playing songs that we don't know and we would have fun making brownies and having fun having you come. We hope you are having fun in your very own band, love, the Beelers. P.S. I hope you have a MARRY CHRISTMAS !

Because of the increased number of students playing band instruments at IHS, a new concert group, the Repertory Band (later renamed the Symphony Band), was added to the IHS Band Program in January 1962. This new ensemble ensured that all students who played woodwind, brass and percussion instruments could play in a performing concert organization.

Six of the band's small ensembles—including a woodwind quintet, flute trio, trombone-tuba quartet, clarinet-bassoon trio, and a mixed chamber group—presented a recital for the MENC Chapter at the Eastman School of Music in Rochester, NY on February 8, 1962. After the performance, William S. Larson, Chairman of the Eastman Music Education Department, sent the following letter to IHS principal John W. Graves.

> Not only was the program enjoyable to listen to but it also was highly instructive to our music education majors who plan to make school music teaching a profession . . . The band serves for a broad range of talents but by its nature and function it can hardly meet the full musical needs of the highly talented . . . Small ensembles can serve best to give the talented student desirable aesthetic experiences through fine selection of music, as was so admirably demonstrated on the program given us last Tuesday.

Lois Lounsbery, a former member of the Ithaca High School Band and in 1962 a student at the Eastman School of Music, attended the recital and wrote,

> . . . as you probably realized, everyone was very impressed and many people commented on the fine [performance of the ensembles].

The third annual IHS Band Parents' Night was held on March 21, 1962. The number of people attending this event continued to grow. Besides parents, families and friends, most school administrators were now attending the event. Band parents Carl and Helene Wickstrom wrote the following letter (March 22, 1962) to Mr. B and the band following the 1962 Band Parents' Night.

> Dear Mr. Battisti and the Band,
>
> We wish to thank you for inviting us to share in the enjoyment of your Band Parents' Night. It was good to feel the genuine interest in the musical growth of young people accomplished in such a "comradely" atmosphere.
>
> The smooth organization of the entire evening could only be accomplished by the fine cooperation of all, and for this you can be justly proud.
>
> Thanks for a nice experience.

᪲ ᪳

Harvey Phillips, one of the world's great tuba virtuosos, was the guest soloist on the band's May 2, 1962 school assembly concerts. During the next five years he performed with the band three more times and brought many of his famous friends into "the IHS

Band orbit," including composer Alec Wilder, photographer Louis Ouzer, and the members of the New York Brass Quintet.

Mr. B always received many appreciative notes after school assembly concerts. Below is one sent by Phyllis Seager (secretary to high school principal John W. Graves) after the 1962 concert.

> **THANK YOU for the thorough enjoyment I received from your beautifully selected and performed program this morning.**
>
> **Though I am no music critic—I thought it had a "professional" sound! It was so smooth, well-blended and coordinated, and so sensitive in tone and interpretation. And, of course, the soloist [Harvey Phillips] was most excellent. Really, words don't do you justice!**
>
> **CONGRATULATIONS to a very fine group of musicians and its talented conductor!**

The May 9, 1962 Spring Concert featured works by Ralph Vaughan Williams, Richard Wagner, H. Owen Reed, and Samuel Barber. Jimmy Burke was once again the featured soloist, performing Haydn's *Concerto for Trumpet* (see program, below).

```
                        Program

Fanfare pour preceder "La Peri"  .  .  .  . Paul Dukas
                                        (1865–1935)

Toccata Marziale  .  .  .  .  Ralph Vaughan Williams
                                        (1872–1958)

Elsa's Procession to the Cathedral from "Lohengrin" .  .
                                     Richard Wagner
                                        (1813–1883)
                        Transcribed by Lucien Cailliet

The Carnival of Venice (Fantasie, Theme, and Variations)
                                  Jean Baptiste Arban
                                        (1825–1889)
                    Revised and re-arranged by Erik Leidzen

Danza  Allegre .  .  .  .  .  .  .  .  James F. Burke
                                        (1923–    )
                              Arranged by Erik Leidzen

              Jimmy Burke, Trumpet Soloist

Irish Tune from County Derry and Shepherd's Hey.  .  .
                                     Percy A. Grainger
                                        (1882–1961)

La Fiesta Mexicana  .  .  .  .  .  . .H. Owen Reed
                                        (1910–    )

          Prelude and Aztec Dance
          Mass
          Carnival

Three Marches

          Commando March  .  .  .  .  . .Samuel Barber
                                        (1910–    )
          The Foundation .  .  . Richard Franko Goldman
                                        (1910–    )
          In Storm and Sunshine  .  .  .  .  . J. C. Heed
```

In a letter to Mr. B after the concert, Principal John W. Graves praised the band's performance.

The concert last night was an extra-ordinary example of what high school students can do when properly instructed and motivated. The audience was well aware of the excellence of the performance. The program was very ambitious and you deserve much credit for giving a professional interpretation (of all pieces). It was the best band concert I have heard.

Reginald Farrow, a band parent, wrote,

. . . that was a beautiful, beautiful concert.

Dr. Craig McHenry, Dean of the School of Music at Ithaca College added,

I enjoyed last night's concert by the High School Band *tremendously*. I was particularly impressed by the *unusually high caliber* of playing in the Wagner.

Below are two photos of Maestro Frederick Fennell conducting the IHS Band during his annual visit on May 29, 1962.

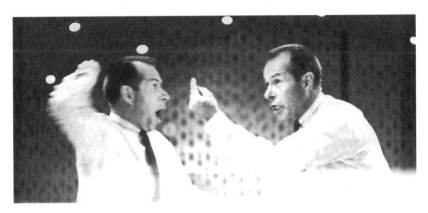

Following his visit (June 6, 1962), Fennell sent Mr. B the following note.

I am still full of good words and happy wishes of you and all the group. This was your best group thus far and as always I was really impressed with what they do and how. Keep on this kind of alert, for we desperately need this kind of discipline and standard–and keep making music.

Reflection by Bruce Musgrave, Class of 1965

Demanding in Public, Supportive in Private

Among the numerous highly elastic dynamics in the life of the IHS band member, few stand out as vividly as the apparent contrast between Mr. B's extreme public demands on the individual and his unfailing private nurture and support of the same individual. At times virtually merciless in group rehearsals with those who were unprepared, inattentive, unfocused, or otherwise unengaged, Mr. B was equally patient and encouraging during the private instrumental lessons he gave each band member throughout the school year and for six weeks each summer.

A band member might live in apoplectic dread of botching a routine in a marching band rehearsal—a faux pas guaranteed to draw Mr. B's vociferous ranting and a dressing down in front of over 100 fully attentive peers. Later in the week, however, that same band member would receive the same calm, reassuring, step-by step encouragement in the private lesson that everyone else in the band enjoyed. This patient, encouraging fellow was the same man who would explode at someone in concert band who had entered clumsily, without listening to the playing of those who had gone before, "You're about as sensitive as an angle worm!" The combination was hard to beat.

Yet any time anyone walked past Mr. B's office throughout the school day, no matter whether the sounds emanating from the private music lesson inside were ineffable or unbearable, through the long narrow windows of his door, Mr. B could be seen standing beside the student, snapping his fingers in rhythm, bobbing his head to the accents, lifting on his toes with the phrasing, singing along, willing the musician to achieve. Understated, encouraging, and endlessly patient, he made every student want to live up to his model of steady calmness in pursuit of beauty—every bit as much as his tirades in public to get it right and *right now* made each of them go all out to avoid that ire.

He would conduct a dozen of those utterly composed lessons each day; then, come full band rehearsal at the end of the day, Dr. Jekyll would become Mr. Hyde for thirty-five minutes. Despite their authentic fright of the latter, all the band members deep down understood very well that the monster's mask was only a pose, contrived—possibly even rehearsed—to convey to them the same deep desire for quality that was so evident in the calm coaching by the private teacher. By hook or by crook . . .

CHAPTER **10**   A Gift to Remember: Special
Christmas Present—Solo and Small
Ensemble Recitals—Theory and
Conducting Classes, 1962–63

Marching Band

Membership in the IHS "Little Red" Band exceeded the century mark for the first time in the fall of 1962. There were 106 students in the band (92 student musicians, 1 drum major, 1 drum sergeant, 8 color guards, and 4 majorettes).

The fourth pre-school band camp was held from August 26 through September 3, 1962. Every band member was present along with six chaperones and 17 counselors, all former band members who were in college (Cornell, Harvard, Hamilton, Mohawk, Wooster, Antioch and the Eastman School of Music). One of the established traditions of Band Camp was Rookie Day, which was held on the first full day of camp. On this day new students marched to and from all meals as a group, served tables, spoke only when spoken to and performed other assigned tasks. In the evening, gathered around a camp fire, the rookies were officially welcomed into the band as full-fledged members by the older students. Another band camp tradition was the IHS Band Olympics. These Olympics consisted of a series of competitive events among the 16 cabins. They included a series of sporting events, cabin-decoration contest, skits, and other creative endeavors. Prizes and points were awarded on the basis of each cabin's ranking in each event. The students in the two cabins with the lowest total point scores served dinner on the final day of camp.

Every camp day began with light calisthenics. Pictured, below, are band members doing "jumping jacks." (*Ithaca Journal* photo)

The band's first 1962 performance was in Elmira, NY at the IHS-Elmira Free Academy football game. The pregame show featured Latin-American and Spanish style music including *El Torero* (Fandango), *El Bailador Flamenco* (Nannigo), *Lady of Spain* (Meringue), *Cherry Pink and Apple Blossom White* (Cha-cha), *Trumpets Ole* (Guaracha) and *Temptation* (Bolero). Three new instruments were added to the percussion section (bongos, timbales, conga drum) to create a *"Latino-Americano* sound." (In the photo, below, the bongos are being played by the percussionist on the 50-yard line—the timbales and conga drum by the second and fourth players to his right.)

The Elmira halftime show featured the music of George Gershwin: *Summertime, Fascinating Rhythm, It Ain't Necessarily So, Oh, Lady Be Good, I've Got Rhythm* and *Rhapsody In Blue*.

Pictured below are the 1962 color guards marching to the practice field.

Lights were installed at Bredbenner Field in the summer of 1962. Beginning in September (1962), almost all IHS football games were played "under the lights." The photo below shows band members seated in the stands on a damp, drizzly night.

Concert Band

Below is the Concert Band's 1963 schedule of concerts and activities.

January 31, 1963	Concert by Oberlin Wind Ensemble	Ithaca
February 15, 1963	Enrichment Classes begin	Ithaca
March 5, 1963	Band Parents' Night	Ithaca
March 7, 1963	New York Brass Quintet, Recital & Clinic	Ithaca
March 14, 1963	Recital by Woodwind Quintet	Ithaca
March 18, 1963	Recital by Brass Quintet	Ithaca
March 20, 1963	Recital of Wind Chamber Music	Ithaca
April 3, 1963	Concert at DeWitt Junior High School	Ithaca
April 10, 1863	Concert at West Genesee High School	West Genesee
April 22, 1963	Concert for MENC Chapter	Ithaca College

April 24, 1963	Annual Spring Concert	Ithaca
May 3, 1963	Concerts in Seneca Falls, Williamsville, Niagara Falls, and Rochester, NY	Seneca Falls, Williamsville, Niagara Falls, Rochester
May 10, 1963	Dr. Clyde Roller visits IHS Band	Ithaca
May 15, 1963	IHS Assembly Programs, Donald Sinta, soloist	Ithaca
May 23, 1963	Percussion Clinic, Richard Schory, guest artist	Ithaca
May 29, 1963	Frederick Fennell Visits IHS Band	Ithaca

Maestro Frederick Fennell penned the following Christmas greeting to Mr. B and band members on December 14, 1962.

Dear Frank and the Members of the Ithaca High School Band:

Just a short note to wish all of you a very merry Christmas and happy New Year.

At this time of year one recalls friends and beautiful experiences. Part of this, for me, is my warm feeling for all of you and the wonderful musical moments we have shared together in my visits to Ithaca.

I am looking forward to seeing you all again later this year. I know you are all busy making music together and sharing in the "unique" experience of belonging to a group such as the Ithaca High School Band.

Affectionately,
Frederick Fennell,
Conductor

The photo below captures Mr. B and his merry band of "Christmas-caroling" brass players serenading an IHS faculty member and his family.

Robert Earle, a band parent, wrote the following letter to *The Ithaca Journal* ("Musical Christmas," December 1962), describing the IHS brass players' visit to his home.

Editor, *The Ithaca Journal*,

It was outdoors on a wintry night. They came and went like St. Nicholas and his reindeer—softly, swiftly. And their music filled the night air like happy, harmonious spirits of the season—pure, sweet, joyful. The temperature was exactly zero and they played by flashlight but their hearts were warm and bright and they played well. It's a pity the whole world could not hear them.

Band members presented Mr. B with a special gift at the December 1962 IHS Band Christmas party—a commissioned piece to be written by Warren Benson. The gift came in the form of a one-page bound score which was inscribed "*Intermezzo in d minor for Winds* by Warren Benson—for Mr. B from the 1962-63 IHS Band" (Benson later renamed the piece, *Remembrance*). The work received its premiere performance on the band's May 6, 1964 Spring Concert (see more information about this work and its premiere in Chapter 11).

All Concert Band members were now performing a solo piece and, as members of small ensembles, a chamber music work on one of the band's solo and Bach Honor Society recitals. These recitals were held on Friday afternoons at 4:00 PM in the rehearsal room. Below are samples of 1962-63 IHS Band Solo and Bach Honor Society programs.

Ithaca High School Band Solo Recitals

First Season ---First Recital

Sonata in F major....................Benedetto Marcello

    Largo
    Allegro
    Largo

    Bruce Musgrave, Trombone Soloist

Concerto in C major.......................LeClair

    Allegro
    Adagio

    Joanna Shepherd, Flute Soloist

Largo and Allegro........................Pietro Bone

    M. J. Herson, Contrabass Clarinet Soloist

Duos for French Horn, K. 487.............W. A. Mozart

    John Lounsbery, Bruce McLellan, Horn Soloists

Elegie...........................Alec Templeton

    William Fuess, Clarinet Soloist

Recitative and Slow Dance............Gordon Phillips

    Judy Swanson, Bass Clarinet Soloist

Solo for Percussion...................John Engelman

    William Storandt, Percussion Soloist

    Accompanists: Leone Buyse
              Terry McKeegan
              Stanley Tom

Friday, February 15, 1963

3:45 P. M.

BACH HONOR SOCIETY RECITALS
Third Year - First Recital
Thursday, December 20, 1962 - 4:00 P.M.

Ballad .... Henry Cowell
                                                     (1897 -   )
    Leone Buyse, Flute   Helen Myers, Clarinet
    Jean Hedlund, Oboe   Paula Mueller, Bassoon
            John Lounsbery, Horn

Clarinet Quintet K. 581 .... W. A. Mozart
                                                   (1756 - 1791)
          Helen Myers, Clarinet
          Leone Buyse, Piano

Romance No. 1, Op. 94 ....Robert Schumann
                                                   (1810 - 1856)
         William Saunders, Clarinet
          Leone Buyse, Piano

Fragments .... Robert Muczynski
    Waltz
    Solitude
    Exit
         Joanna Shepherd, Flute
         Paula Mueller, Bassoon
         Helen Myers, Clarinet

Adagio and Allegro .... Robert Schumann
         John Lounsbery, Horn
         Leone Buyse, Piano

Siciliano .... J. S. Bach
                                                 (1685 - 1750)
        Terry McKeegan, Saxophone
        Paula Mueller, Bassoon
        Helen Myers, Clarinet

Morceau de Concert .... Camille Saint Saens
    Allegro Moderato   (1835 - 1921)
    Adagio
         Bruce McLellan, Horn
         Leone Buyse, Piano

Each student, prior to performing their solo, wrote a paper about the composer and the piece. Below is an example of one of these papers written by flutist Carol Glock.

Jean - Marie Leclair

Jean - Marie Leclair, celebrated French violinist and composer, was born in Lyons on May 10, 1697. He began his public life as a dancer at Rouen Theatre. From there, he went to Turin where he became a ballet master and composed some interludes for the "Semiramide of Orlandini." This music appealed to Somis, a noted violinist, who gave Leclair further instruction and encouraged him to concentrate his efforts on the violin. Leclair stayed with Somis for only a few years; in 1729 he went to Paris where he lived for the rest of his life. During the early 1730's, he played at the Concert Spirituel, the Opéra, and at court, besides studying composition under Chéron. He also became a member of the royal orchestra, but soon lost his position due to a quarrel over the leadership of the second violins. In 1748, the Duc de Gramont appointed Leclair first violin in his private orchestra at Puteaux. Leclair spent the remainder of his life as a composer and teacher in Paris as well as making several trips to Spain and Holland. Shortly after returning from Holland in 1764, he was assassinated late at night close to the door of his home. Neither the author or motive of the crime was discovered. However, people suspected his estranged wife, Louise Roussel, who was also his publisher and engraver of music.

Leclair was considered one of the best violin composers of the eighteenth century. In his early works he followed the Italian school, but in his later works he developed a distinct style and a definite National French element. A great deal of what he wrote is antiquated, but much remains that is truly charming. On the whole, gracefulness and vivacity are more prominent in his works than depth of feeling. His employment of double stops gives much richness of sound.

Leclair composed the opera Glaucas et Scylla as well as ballets and trios. However, he is best known for his admirable violin works including fifty sonatas, concertos, trios, etc. These are noted for their technical difficulty and their expressive power.

Although <u>Concerto in C Major</u>, Opus 7, No.3 is not considered among the very best of Leclair's music, it is worth studying. When first published it was specified that " the solo may be played on the flute or on the oboe to be accompanied by strings and clavecin." Classic in structure, it is written in three movements — allegro, adagio, allegro. One writer has said:

> "The concerto is sufficiently familiar not to require a detailed analysis; it should suffice to mention the intense rhythm of the first <u>Allegro</u>, the lively motion of the <u>Finale</u> (<u>Allegro assai</u>) and especially the grandeur and incomparable lyricism of the <u>Adagio</u>. The variety and richness of both melody and harmony of Leclair's slow movements is always astonishing, and it is impossible to analyze the <u>Adagio</u> of the <u>Concerto in C Major</u> — its sublime beauty defies ~~comment~~."

Since I will be playing the first <u>Allegro</u>, though, I might add a few more words about this movement. Actually it is a " duet" between the soloist and the orchestra; each plays about the same amount and they are equally important. The orchestra begins, and states the main theme in the first few measures:

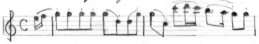

And then comes a minor theme:

As the orchestra continues, the main theme is repeated several times in slightly different variation. Just before the soloist begins another minor theme is introduced:

> The soloist comes in with a statement of the main theme, and then goes on with a lively technical passage. The use of the many embellishments throughout the concerto might be brought out here. Leclair has employed numerous mordents, trills, etc. Fortunately, though, he doesn't overdo his use of these, as did so many composers of his time. When the orchestra takes over again, it starts with the main theme. During this section all of the themes are touched. Then comes the climax of the movement. The soloist enters again with the main theme. Statements of all the themes follow as well as several striking cadenzas. The rest of the movement goes back and forth between the soloist and orchestra, tying together themes and ideas. The overall effect of this movement is certainly lively, brisk, and rhythmical.

The Bach Society recital of March 20, 1963 featured performances of selected movements from Richard Strauss's *Suite in B-flat, Op. 4*, Victor Ewald's *Symphony for Brass*, and Darius Milhaud's *La Cheminee du Roi Rene*.

⊰ ⊱

Two more distinguished composers were commissioned in 1962. One was Robert Ward, winner of the 1962 Pulitzer Prize in Music and the Music Critics' Circle of New York Citation for his opera, *The Crucible*. The other was Carlos Chavez, Mexico's most famous composer. This was the band's first commission to a non-American composer.

Mr. B continually wrote to many well known composers in an attempt to commission works from them. William Schuman, President of the Lincoln Center for the Performing Arts, stated that he was "…deeply touched by…the activities …the young players [undertake to make] possible the commissioning of original works and promised [to contact Mr. B] the next time [he was] ready to compose a band piece…." Igor Stravinsky and Samuel Barber both replied that they already had too many commissions and could not accept another one. However, both praised the band's commissioned works project. Stravinsky expressed amazement that high school students would want a piece from him. Darius Milhaud responded that "[he] could…write a piece for the band." Russian composer Aram Khachaturian misunderstood Mr. B's letters (probably because Mr. B wrote to him in English and he read only Russian). He thought Mr. B was requesting some of his scores so he could make band transcriptions of them (he sent three). Other composers Mr. B contacted were Aaron Copland, Leonard Bernstein and Duke Ellington.

The band's commissioned works project attracted the attention of many people in the musical world. One was Dr. William D. Revelli, conductor of the famous University of Michigan Band. In a letter to Mr. B (January 11, 1963), Revelli praised the band's "outstanding contribution to wind bands, music education and music."

One of the highlights of the 1963 spring semester was a concert performed by the Oberlin Conservatory Wind Ensemble, Kenneth Moore, conductor, in Kulp Auditorium on January 31 (the ensemble was en route to New York City to perform a concert in Carnegie Hall). Their program included pieces not normally performed on wind band/ensemble concerts: Paul Hindemith's *Concert Music for Piano, Brass and Two Harps, Op. 49*, Ernst Toch's *Spielmusik, Op. 39* plus two works by Aaron Copland and one by Ernst Krenek. IHS Band members were thrilled by the ensemble's performance and fascinated by the music they performed.

On February 15, 1963 Mr. B inaugurated a series of three ten-week Saturday morning classes in Music Theory I, Music Theory II, and Conducting. Students taking Theory I studied the rudiments of music and ear training; those in the Theory II, harmony and ear training. All students studied conducting. Below is a photo of Mr. B instructing the students in the conducting class. (*Ithaca Journal* photo).

—Peter Lippke

CONDUCTING STUDENTS are (from left) first row, Helen Myers, Virginia Chase; second row, Lois Jean Taber, Asher Hockett, Bob Kellogg, Toni Williams, Duane Davis; third row, David Mobbs, John Lounsbery, and Michael Miller under the direction of Frank L. Battisti.

On March 7, 1963 the New York Brass Quintet presented a recital-clinic for band members (see photo on next page). The members of the quintet were, left to right, Robert Nagel, Teddy Weiss, trumpets; Harvey Phillips, tuba; John Swallow, trombone; and John Barrows, French horn.

Performances and clinics by professional artists and ensembles informed, motivated, and inspired the students.

ॐ ॐ

The IHS Band's sixth commissioned work, *Theme and Fantasia* by Armand Russell, was premiered on the April 24, 1963 Spring Concert program (see below).

Aufwarts March	Ernst Luthold
Chester (Overture)	William Schuman
Symphony for Band	Vincent Persichetti
Adagio, Allegro	
Adagio sostenuto	
Italian Polka	Sergei Rachmaninoff
	arr. E. Leidzen
Theme and Fantasia	Armand Russell
Premiere performance	
Lincolnshire Posy	Percy Grainger
Lisbon Bay	
Harkstow Grange	
Rufford Park Poachers	
Lord Melbourne	
Pineapple Poll	Arthur Sullivan

Armand Russell was introduced to Mr. B by Frederick Fennell. (Note: Mr. B relied heavily on Fennell and Warren Benson for recommendations regarding composers he should commission.) Russell was a recent graduate of the Eastman School of Music and in 1963, a faculty member at the University of Hawaii (teaching theory) and double bass player in the Honolulu Symphony Orchestra. *Theme and Fantasia* is a series of variants based on a tranquil theme that become successively more aggressive, vigorous and expressive—it is a very dynamic work. Edward B. Marks Corporation published *Theme and Fantasia* immediately after its premiere. Two years later (1965), the composer transcribed the piece for orchestra. This is a rarity—composers seldom transcribe a band piece for orchestra.

Dr. Clyde A. Roller, newly appointed conductor of the Eastman Wind Ensemble, conducted a masterful rehearsal of Richard Wagner's *Good Friday Music* with the band on May 10, 1963. His rehearsal was one of the highlights of the year.

Mr. B met Donald Sinta in July 1962 at one of Dr. William D. Revelli's University of Michigan summer clinics for band directors and invited him to come to IHS and perform a solo with the band in May 1963. Sinta expected that his visit would be similar to those he had made to other "small-town bands." However, on arriving at IHS he realized he was in a very special environment—the students were energized, curious, and musically sophisticated; his conversations with Warren Benson and Mr. B, provocative and stimulating. Brian Norcross, in his book *One Band That Took a Chance*, quotes Sinta as saying, "My visit to Ithaca was a life-changing experience…it was worth much more [than the] stipend ($150. plus travel and lodging expenses)…."

Below is the band's May 15, 1963 school assembly concert program.

Aufwarts March		Ernst Luthold
Adagio and Samba		Maurice Whitney
Ballade		Alfred Reed
	Donald Sinta, Saxophone soloist	
Italian Polka		Sergei Rachmaninoff arr. E. Leidzen
Pineapple Poll		Arthur Sullivan

Sinta was very excited about what he experienced and discovered at IHS. So much so that when he returned to Ann Arbor he immediately cancelled a planned trip to France to study at the Paris Conservatory—he was intent on getting back to Ithaca as soon as possible. A job opening at Ithaca College opened the door for Sinta's return. When Mr. B discovered that the College was looking for a saxophone teacher he immediately contacted Dr. Craig McHenry, Dean of the School of Music, and urged him to hire Sinta. McHenry offered Sinta the job; Sinta accepted and moved to Ithaca in September (1963). During his tenure at Ithaca College, Sinta performed with the IHS Band five times—he also taught the band's saxophone players.

On May 29, 1963 Frederick Fennell returned to IHS for his annual visit, this time traveling from Minneapolis, Minnesota, where he was now associate conductor of the Minneapolis Symphony Orchestra. During his day-long rehearsal with the band, Maestro Fennell rehearsed selected movements from Mozart's *Serenade No. 10, K. 361*, Vincent Persichetti's *Symphony for Band*, Percy Grainger's *Lincolnshire Posy* and Arthur

Sullivan's *Pineapple Poll*. After rehearsal everyone adjourned to the Lehigh Valley House for the "Fennell-visit" banquet.

Reflection by Bruce Musgrave, Class of 1965

Outside the Music

There can be little doubt that the primary motives that led to the unforgettable golden age of the IHS Band were rooted in *music* education. To be sure, by building their *musical* skills, by heightening their *musical* sensitivity, by guiding and developing their *musical* tastes, by expanding their *musical* awareness, and by encouraging and enabling them "to sing" through their instruments, Mr. B sought to develop in his students a lasting appreciation of music and the perpetuation of its role in their lives. His ample successes in achieving those aims find endless documentation in this book. However, along the way, a far broader essential skill-set was building apace in his students, faultlessly modeled by the director, and of virtually inestimable value by way of transfer to numerous other enterprises quite outside the realm of music.

Teachers of mathematics commonly refer to the need to engender problem-solving skills, or tactics for breaking big jobs down into small parts. Those analytic processes—for instance, of breaking a musical composition down into its most difficult elements, and of identifying those problematic passages and working them out in isolation until they are familiar enough to be executed with facility—have their obvious analogues in the completely unmusical enterprise of executing difficult marching-band maneuvers. So too does the whole-to-parts habit apply with full benefit to a host of support activities. Whether it be planning and executing travel to a distant performance site, implementing an ambitious fund-raising effort (such as the logistical marvel that was the IHS Band chicken barbecues), or the mere lining of the football practice field at band camp, IHS Band members enjoyed opportunity after opportunity to exercise the practice habits they first learned as musicians under Mr. B.

Recent education critics decry the absence of accountability in schools, complaining that no one holds anyone else accountable, that standards of quality go unmonitored, and that no one seems to care about following through. Accountability and daily demonstration of personal responsibility *were* the musical foundations of the IHS Band, yet those same qualities were equally conspicuous in the ancillary *non-musical* activities that necessarily accompanied the musical experiences. The complexity of the program was so vast that delegation of duties was essential; those duties in turn were so substantive and real as to defy completion without significant exercise of autonomy and the granting of broad discretionary powers, not to mention substantial latitude for individual initiative. As the band grew more complex and comprehensive in its program, the extent to which students were charged with fuller responsibility and also licensed to exercise broad individual judgment grew and grew. If mid-adolescence ought to be a time for the learners to achieve increasing autonomy and, in the words of Flaubert, to "Look deeply inside [them]selves and create the most irreplaceable of things," Mr. B's band program was an utter and perpetual workshop of such opportunities.

To manage the library of concert band musical parts, students collected, distributed, maintained, inventoried, and catalogued the parts of the score for each instrument. As Mr. B completed marching band arrangements, students (and Mrs. B) copied the individual parts onto spirit ditto masters (no Xerox machine in those days), checked each others' work, reproduced the parts, cut them into sizes suitable for carrying in the marching band's transparent plastic flip folders, and saw to the distribution of them. Marching routine master plans were transposed onto individual routine sheets. When newly-commissioned works arrived in manuscript from the composers for the concert band, an army of student copyists set about creating the individual parts for each musician. At band camp time, when it was necessary to transport an entire room of band equipment from the high school to the Danby hills, the students planned and executed the operation, in both directions. Anyone who came out of the band had a sophisticated appreciation of systems, of how they work, of how to improve them, and of the necessity that everyone pitch in to make those systems prosper.

Problem-attack skills, personal responsibility, work ethic, individual autonomy, understanding of systems, internalized standards of quality . . . it was no more necessary to verbalize such matters around the IHS Band than it is necessary to say on a daily basis, "We're all breathing, and our hearts are all beating." Those who entered the IHS Band came out the other end of it able to organize, monitor, execute, and reflect on a wide range of responsibilities because they had constant practice doing so. If the variously attributed wisdom on education runs, "I see, and I *forget*; I hear, and I *remember*; I do and I *understand*," IHS band members understood *well* what work was and how to go about it. It all began with the music, and it certainly led back to the music, but the benefits derived by the students extended far beyond the realm of music.

CHAPTER **11** The Fallen Chief: New York Trip
and Grief—Persichetti Memorial
Commission—Project Creativity—
Severinsen—Contemporary Music
Festival—*Remembrance, 1963–64*

Marching Band

There were 104 students in the 1963 "Little Red" Marching Band (90 student musicians, 1 drum major, 1 drum sergeant, 8 color guards and 4 majorettes). The highlight of the band's 1963 Fall Performance schedule was a November 21-24 trip to New York City to perform at the NY Giants–St. Louis Cardinals NFL game to be televised nationally (see schedule, below).

September	21	Union-Endicott	1:30 PM at Ithaca, NY
	27	Johnson City	8:00 PM at Johnson City, NY
	28	Cornell Band Day	2:00 PM at Cornell University
October	5	Binghamton Central	11:00 AM at Ithaca, NY
	12	Elmira Southside	1:30 PM at Ithaca, NY
	18	Vestal	8:00 PM at Vestal, NY
	25	Binghamton North	8:00 PM at Binghamton, NY
	30	Halloween Parade	6:30 PM at Ithaca, NY
November	2	Auburn	10:30 AM at Ithaca, NY
	8	Elmira Free Academy	7:30 PM at Elmira, NY
	11	Veterans Day Parade	6:30 PM at Ithaca, NY
	21–24	Trip to New York City	2:00 PM at Yankee Stadium, NY, NY for Sunday, Nov. 24 performance at NY Giants–St. Louis Cardinals NFL game (National TV audience)

Each September Mr. B distributed an informational booklet to all IHS Band members and their parents. Included in this booklet were listings of student members (names, addresses and telephone numbers), membership/leadership responsibilities, schedules of rehearsals/performances and a local arts calendar. Below is the section which defined marching band student leadership responsibilities in the Fall 1963 booklet.

IHS Marching Band Student Leadership Responsibilities

Leadership Positions:

Elected Officers	Auditioned Positions	Appointed Positions
President	Drum Major	Manager
Vice-President	Drum Sergeant	Assistant Manager
Secretary	Head Majorette	Uniform Manager
Treasurer	Head Color Guard	Librarian
		Assistant Librarian(s)

Skill/Honor Positions

Section Leaders

Band Council

The band council consists of elected band officers plus the band director. The council meets on the call of either the director or the president. Its purpose is to establish policies and regulations, discuss matters affecting the band, and act as a disciplinary body regarding any inappropriate student behavior. The council's chief executive officer is the band president.

Leadership Position Duties

President
1. Act as student representative of the band.
2. Conduct band council meetings.
3. Appoint people to committees for special events, projects, etc.
4. Assist band director as needed.
5. Coordinate work of student leaders.
6. Offer suggestions, report problems.

Vice-President
1. Be prepared to assume the duties of the president, if needed.
2. Oversee the work of committees.
3. Arrange volunteer assistance.

Secretary
1. Handle all correspondence, prepare all reports.
2. Supervise mimeographing of reports/materials.
3. Record activities of the band.
4. Record minutes of band council meetings.

Treasurer	1. Handle all financial matters (income, expenditures, banking).
	2. Collect money.
	3. Handle ticket sales.

Section Leaders	1. Oversee the performance, appearance, deportment of the everyone in their section.
	2. Be a model musician/citizen/section leader.
	3. Help individual section members when needed/requested.

Drum Major	1. Lead marching band at all performances.
	2. Conduct band at football games.
	3. Assist in teaching drills.
	4. Arrange sectional rehearsals, as needed.
	5. Work with section leaders.
	6. Offer assistance to individual members when needed/requested.
	7. Be a model leader/musician.

Drum Sergeant	1. Assist the drum major.
	2. Be prepared to assume the duties of drum major, if needed.
	3. Assist in teaching drills.
	4. Inspect band instruments, equipment and uniforms prior to performances.
	5. Be a model leader/musician.

Librarian	1. Oversee distribution and cataloging of music.
	2. Assemble all concert and marching band folders.
	3. Repair/replace damaged parts.
	4. Record all music borrowed from the library.
	5. Record missing parts.
	6. Copy music/parts, as needed.

Manager	1. Ensure that all instruments and equipment are in excellent condition.
	2. Report any damage to instruments/equipment.
	3. Make minor repairs.
	4. Make arrangements for transporting instruments and equipment to performance sites.
	5. Assist in making band travel arrangements.
	6. Create needed props.
	7. Distribute information/instructions to band members.
	8. Oversee band publicity.

Uniform Manager	1. Issue and collect uniforms.
	2. Report any lost/damaged uniform parts.
	3. Oversee care and cleaning of uniforms.
	4. Inventory uniforms at the end of football season.

Hundreds of people came to Stewart Park on August 8, 1963 for the IHS Band's third annual summer Chicken Barbecue. Many more purchased "take away chicken barbecue dinners" at the band's super efficient curb-side pickup service.

The Lehigh Valley House, one of Ithaca's most popular restaurants, ran the following advertisement in the August 2, 1963 edition *of The Ithaca Journal*, urging its customers to "buy from our competitors." The money raised at chicken barbecues supported band activities and projects, primarily the commissioning of works and trips.

Below is a pre-barbecue publicity photo which appeared in the Syracuse *Post-Standard*. It shows (left to right) Mr. B, Paula Mueller, M J Herson and Bill Storandt standing next to one of the barbecue pits at Stewart Park.

Band members went to camp on August 26, 1963. The following *Ithaca Journal* photos show (left) students boarding buses for the trip to the Danby camp and (right), David Holmberg attempting to load a sousaphone onto a bus.

—Journal Photos by Sol Goldberg

A BIT OF A PROBLEM getting on the bus for band camp is encountered this morning by David Holmberg, sousaphonist in the Ithaca High Band.

The pictures on the following pages show band members involved in various band camp activities and events. From first to last: students lining the practice field, "rookie" band members preparing to march to lunch, students rehearsing a new routine, KP duty, band members listening to a recital in the main lodge, and parents, family and friends watching the band's "end-of-camp" performance.

A suspended cymbal attached to a special harness (believed to be the first of its kind), was added to the marching band's percussion section in 1963. Bill Bascom is shown playing this instrument in the photo, below. (Ithaca Journal photo by Sol Golberg)

SUSPENDED CYMBAL attached to a special harness will be in the spotlight when a special percussion section of the Ithaca High School Band presents its pre-game show at Elmira on Sept. 22—the opening game for IHS. Bill Bascom, seated, plays the cymbal—believed to be the only suspended one in the nation. Members of the section are (from left) David Mobbs on the bongos, Bill Storandt on the conga drum, cymbalists Jim Sherwood and Bascom, Mike Driscoll on Timbales, cymbalist John Lounsbery, snare drummers Jim Bliss, Jack Liang, Leo Mahool and Ken Post, and bass drummer Tom Kirby.

The 1963 IHS "Little Red" Band in front of the Music Building.

Eight new flags were added to the color guard section, one for each school in the Southern Tier Conference. The 1963 IHS Band color guards are pictured below (front to back): Dorothy Feldman, Diane Lyon, Janice and Sue Beck, Lynne Hushion, Marianna Meils, Sue Banks and Sue Ballard).

The band's 1963 pregame show included the following music: *This Could Be the Start of Something Big, I Feel a Song Coming On, Till There was You, I'm Gonna Live Till I Die,* and *With a Song in My Heart.* Its first half time show featured music from five Academy Award-winning motion pictures: *Lawrence of Arabia, Days of Wine and Roses, Exodus, West Side Story* and *Never on Sunday.*

After the band's opening season performance on September 21, 1963, Superintendent of Schools James Mason sent Mr. B the following letter.

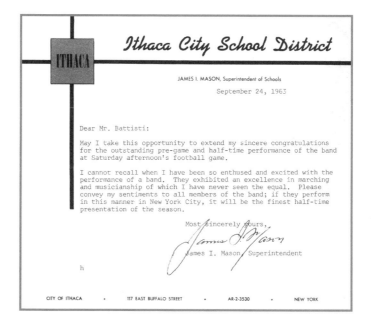

The two photographs below show the band performing precision marching routines at the IHS–Elmira Free Academy football game in Elmira, NY on November 8, 1963.

Band social events were always fun. At the 1963 Halloween party band members danced (round and square), played games, bobbed for apples, went on hayrides and enjoyed apple cider and donuts. Below is a photo of Mr. B and Charlotte (his wife) at the party.

On Thursday, November 21, 1963 the IHS "Little Red" Band left Ithaca for their Yankee Stadium performance at the NFL Divisional Championship game between the New York Giants and St. Louis Cardinals. Arriving in New York at 11:30 PM, the students unloaded luggage, instruments and equipment, checked into the hotel and then re-boarded the buses. They were driven to the southern tip of Manhattan Island and onto the Staten Island Ferry. (Note: Mr. B realized that the students would be excited and eager to "see the town" when they arrived in "the City"—settling them down would be a difficult task. He therefore decided to take them on the Staten Island Ferry where they could walk around the deck and view some of New York's famous sights.) During the cruise across New York harbor the students enjoyed spectacular views of the illuminated Statue of Liberty, Ellis Island and the almost completed Verrazano-Narrows Bridge. When the ferry arrived at the Staten Island Terminal the buses, with students on board, were driven off and immediately back onto the ferry. Once back on "terra firma," band members were driven to a restaurant (pre-arranged) where they ate hamburgers, French fries and drank Cokes. When they returned to the hotel at 3:00 AM they immediately settled down and fell asleep.

The next morning, Friday, November 22, everyone attended two symphony orchestra rehearsals—the first at Lincoln Center where they watched Leonard Bernstein rehearse the New York Philharmonic and the second at Carnegie Hall where Leopold Stokowski rehearsed the American Symphony Orchestra. After he finished rehearsing, Stokowski surprised everyone by coming into the hall and talking with band members.

Following lunch the students and chaperones set out to sightsee in the City (Times Square, Empire State Building, United Nations, etc.). Their sightseeing was abruptly halted when they heard that President John F. Kennedy had been shot—everybody rushed back to the hotel. That evening Mr. B., the students and chaperones had dinner at Mama Leone's Restaurant in midtown Manhattan. Afterwards they walked back to the hotel through a "blacked out" Times Square.

Mr. B expected the National Football League to cancel all games on Sunday, November 24. However, they did not—instead they decided that all would be played but none televised. This created a dilemma for Mr. B—he had to decide whether it was appropriate for the band to perform. He contacted Ithaca school officials and discussed the situation with them—some favored proceeding, others advised against it—but they left the decision up to him.

Because the band had a legal contract to perform, Mr. B and the students went to Yankee Stadium for their scheduled rehearsal on Saturday morning, November 23. Mr. B was still undecided about whether it was right for the band to perform. As the students prepared to rehearse, Mr. B discussed the situation once again with the chaperones and then made his decision—the band would not perform. He brought the students together and informed them. Even though they were disappointed, the students understood. Mr. B immediately went to New York Giant officials and requested that the band be released from their contract—they were very understanding and granted him his request.

The band ate lunch at a Czech restaurant (pre-arranged) and afterwards returned to the hotel, packed and boarded buses for the journey home.

During the trip back to Ithaca the students were subdued and somber. Any feelings of disappointment were overshadowed by the sadness and sense of loss everyone felt about the tragic death of President Kennedy. As one chaperone observed, "[The students] were wonderful. Not once did I hear them complain about...not [being able to perform]. They just talked about the nation's loss–not theirs."

On November 30, 1963 *The Ithaca Journal* published a photo-essay, "The Weekend That Was," which described the band's sad and disappointing experience in New York City (see the pages that follow). All photos in the essay were taken by Byron McCalmon, a chaperone on the trip and a former IHS Band member.

President John F. Kennedy's tragic death on November 22, 1963 profoundly affected everyone in the band. Mr. B and the students decided to commission a work in memory of the assassinated President. Vincent Persichetti was invited to compose the piece.

On December 16 Mr. B wrote Frederick Fennell and told him about the band's ill-fated trip to New York and their invitation to Vincent Persichetti to write a piece in honor of JFK.

We thought it would be fitting to do something to honor the "fallen chief" and to mark this sad historical event...I am optimistic that he [Persichetti] will accept the commission.

Fennell responded on January 11, 1965,

Dorothy [Mrs. Fennell] and I sat down and wept all over again when we got your letter of 16 December...What you did is exactly what I would have expected from all of you and I do hope that Vincent [will] undertake the commission.

Persichetti accepted the commission and a May 1967 date was set for the premiere of the piece.

The Weekend That Was

For Ithaca High Band Members, A Joyous Start, a Sad Ending

Photo Feature by Byron McCalmon

Off and running on a very happy Thursday.

The first meal on the road, at the Goshen Inn Thursday night, was eaten in anticipation of fun to come.

One of the tours Friday was to Lincoln Center for the Performing Arts.

The startling news that the President had been shot was received by this group when it was touring the U.N. Building (looking here into the Security Council chambers). Immediately, all groups went back to the hotel to see what would happen.

The Giants-Cardinals game was still 'on,' the band was told, so the group went to Yankee Stadium for the scheduled Saturday practice. Director Frank Battisti (left) discusses with chaperones what to do.

The decision is made. It wouldn't be right to go on. The youngsters file back out of the stadium (left) and back to the hotel to pack.

At Carnegie Hall on Friday, the main attraction was the American Symphony Orchestra in rehearsal, and conductor Leopold Stokowski, who took time out (lower right) to talk with the young musicians.

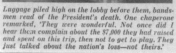

Luggage piled high on the lobby before them, bandsmen read of the President's death. One chaperone remarked, 'They were wonderful. Not once did I hear them complain about the $7,000 they had raised and spent on this trip, then not to get to play. They just talked about the nation's loss—not theirs.'

One of the last looks at New York City—flags at half-mast in Rockefeller Center.

The Ithaca Journal: Saturday, November 30, 1963

Reflection by Bruce Musgrave, Class of 1965

Marching Band-Concert Band: the Strange Synergy

In some ways the differences between the Marching Band and the Concert Band were so manifold and drastic that it seems difficult to argue that the two bands together constituted one experience—the IHS Band. But like the opposing hemispheres of our brain, the two-bands-in-one benefited from certain undeniable crossovers, in this case crossovers that enriched both experiences. The Concert Band in particular seemed very nearly to be propelled in some ways by the Marching Band.

It may be true that, at least in his earliest years of directing the band, Mr. B had less enthusiasm for the Marching Band than for the Concert Band. Yet the encouragement from Dr. Graves chronicled elsewhere in this text, to the effect that the Marching Band was something that all of Ithaca could rally 'round, seemed to register, and over the years the Marching Band became less and less an inconvenient obligation getting in the way of the real work of the Concert Band and more and more a seamless transition into that experience. In some ways, Mr. B seemed to find as many creative outlets and opportunities to build self-discipline, focus, and group dynamics in the Marching Band as he did with the Concert Band.

The two-and-a-half-month autumnal Marching Band season not only provided momentum for the seven-month Concert Band season, but it was also a fitting introduction to the work ethic and particularly the work *rate* of the Concert Band season. With as few as five thirty-five minute rehearsals—some of which might be rained out—to move from performing one show to the next, there was an acquired sense of urgency that made learning the difficult Concert Band music all the easier later on. Both bands became expert at not wasting time.

The universal expectation that everyone memorize 100% of the marching-band music challenged even the most sophisticated musicians; learning four seven-minute halftime shows and one five-minute pregame show—music and routines—by heart, within the time allotted, was a significant challenge by itself, not to mention memorizing the National Anthem, school fight songs, and other bleacher music. No one could meet all those challenges without some extra work at home alone.

One marching blunder could mar for everyone the unity and impact of a Marching Band Show; in Concert Band, where one player per voice was the rule rather than the exception, and where transparent scoring seemed to be the norm, one was already well prepared—by having marched—for the potential exposure in error and the utter necessity of reliability. One member of Marching Band showing up without a hat, the wrong color socks, or no gloves would significantly diminish the result; in Concert Band, having a good reed, a backup, and a well-swabbed horn were thus already second nature to those who had endured the austere group regimentation of Marching Band.

In Concert Band, each of the players already knew full well from the experience of Marching Band that it would require each band member functioning at optimum effectiveness if any magic were to eventuate. A marcher who didn't learn the parts, lost focus, or didn't maintain consistent distance and interval would subvert the group; small wonder then that when Concert Band rolled around, all the band members were already accustomed to pulling their own weight, already reliably meeting their obligations to themselves and everyone else, and already focused on striving together to achieve collectively something that would far transcend what any of them might have achieved alone. The Marching Band and the Concert Band *were* one band—in name and in deed. Indeed.

Concert Band

Below is the 1964 IHS Concert Band's Spring Semester schedule of events.

January 20, 1964	Composer Norman Dello Joio, guest conductor	Ithaca
February 26, 1964	School Assembly Programs, "Doc" Severinsen, soloist	Ithaca
March 6, 1964	Trip to hear Eastman Wind Ensemble perform Armand Russell's *Theme and Fantasia*, Clyde A.Roller, conductor	Rochester
March 21, 1964	Recital–Clinic by New York Brass Quintet	Ithaca
March 25, 1964	Concert at Boynton Junior High School Band Parents' Night	Ithaca
April 10, 1964	West Genesee Teacher Association Concert	West Genesee
April 13–19, 1964	IHS Band Festival of Contemporary Music	Ithaca
April 15, 1964	Concert by Eastman Wind Ensemble, Clyde A. Roller, Conductor, at Kulp Auditorium	Ithaca
April 17, 1964	Dr. Clyde A. Roller rehearses with the IHS Band	Ithaca
April 23, 24, 1964	IHS Invitational Band Festival	Ithaca
May 6, 1964	Spring Concert	Ithaca
May 29, 1964	Visit by Frederick Fennell/IHS Band Banquet	Ithaca
July 14, 1964	IHS Band/Summer Youth Band Concert at Corning Summer Theater	Corning
July 21–24, 1964	IHS Band/Summer Youth Band Concerts at World's Fair, Rockefeller Center	New York City
July 28, 1964	IHS Band/Summer Youth Band Concert	Ithaca

Mr. B posted the following announcement on the bulletin board outside of his office in January 1964:

An Original Composition, for your instrument, you compose it. Maybe you would like to write it with someone else. We will play the best ones on a recital in late spring.

This announcement triggered the start of the band's "Project Creativity." Mr. B was confident that students would find writing/creating music interesting and exciting. However, the initial response to his announcement was mixed. Brian Norcross quotes Mr. B's assessment of student reaction.

> **When it started, there was some reluctance simply because the students felt inhibited. They were exposing themselves. They began to realize the ...risk the creator takes in the creative process. I made it clear that we must have a bond of understanding. We must never make fun of anything that anybody creates. If that happens, that person might not create any more...Creating involves risk and exposure. This is [both] exciting and frightening.** (Norcross, p. 117)

Most students wrote solo works for their instruments. Some, however, were more adventurous and created pieces for small groups of instruments. One student, who had been rehearsing Stravinsky's *Ebony Concerto*, composed a trumpet trio similar in style to the Stravinsky work. Another created a tone row piece based on a mathematical system developed through the use of a computer. Writing music broadened the students' musical experiences—they were now "creators" (composers) as well as "re-creators" (performers).

Distinguished American composer Norman Dello Joio came to Ithaca College in January 1964 to discuss the Ford Foundation-MENC Composer-in-Residence Project with Warren Benson. (Note: The Ithaca City School District was awarded a Ford Foundation-MENC Composer-in-Residence in 1966-67—see Chapter 12). While in Ithaca, he visited the IHS Band and conducted a 45-minute rehearsal of his new work, *Variants on a Medieval Tune* (January 20, 1964).

Carl "Doc" Severinsen, a virtuoso trumpet player and one of New York City's busiest free-lance musicians, was guest soloist on the band's February 26, 1964 school assembly concerts. As a sideman in Skitch Henderson's "Tonight" show orchestra, he was heard and seen by millions of Americans five nights a week over the NBC national television network. His performance with the IHS band was sensational—he thrilled band members and dazzled the students and faculty. Following the concerts Severinsen conducted a clinic-rehearsal with the jazz ensemble and a masterclass for IHS and Ithaca College trumpet students. His visit generated a great deal of excitement in the community and served to reinforce the band students' feelings that they were important because famous musicians and composers visited them.

Below is a photograph of "Doc" Severinsen performing with the IHS Band.

The IHS Band and Bach Honor Society sponsored the first Festival of Contemporary Music in April 1964. The cover of the festival program was created by band oboist Jean Hedlund (at right).

Bill Storandt, a percussionist in the band, wrote the introduction for the festival program.

The creation and performance of music, more than any other art, contributes to the sublime attainment which Socrates deemed most important: the understanding of oneself. For musicians deal solely in opaque symbolism. Performers and composers, endowed with an eloquent but abstract vocabulary which no listener can be "trained" to understand, strive to convey moods, emotions, and sensations of the greatest significance exclusively by the vehicle of this often nebulous vocabulary.

The Ithaca High School Band
and the
Bach Honor Society
presents a

contemporary
music
festival

april 13-19, 1964

To express such feelings in words is difficult enough. To aim for their more powerful portrayal in music requires obviously an acutely sensitive mind, but, most important, an orderly mind which can attack this formidable task, confident in the knowledge of the unity of its ideas and the purity of its emotions.

Jean Hedlund's cover and Bill Storandt's introduction are examples of the "other than music" creative endeavors of band students.

The festival's opening event was a recital by IHS Band flutist Leone Buyse. This was followed by a recital-seminar of student compositions and a panel discussion on "Creative Thinking." Panelists included composers Warren Benson, Professor of Music at Ithaca College; Robert Palmer, Professor of Music at Cornell University; and artists Peter Kahn and Kenneth Evett, both Professors of Art and Architecture at Cornell University. On Wednesday morning, April 15 (fourth day of the festival) the IHS Concert Band presented a concert for students at DeWitt Junior High School. In the evening the Eastman Wind Ensemble, A. Clyde Roller conducting, performed in Claude L. Kulp Auditorium. Their program included a performance of *Theme and Fantasia* by Armand Russell, one of the IHS Band's recently commissioned works. The festival ended with a pair of concerts, one by the Ithaca College Faculty Woodwind Quintet and Percussion Ensemble, the other by IHS woodwind, brass and percussion ensembles.

Four days after the Contemporary Music Festival, the band hosted the Ithaca High School Invitational Band Festival (April 23, 24, 1964). Participating bands included the Lockport Senior High School Band, Lackawanna Senior High School Band, Barker Central Senior High Band, Williamsville Junior High Band, Maine-Endwell Senior High School Band, Plattsburg Senior High School Stage Band, and the host IHS Band. Four-hundred students and directors attended performances and clinics by distinguished artists and ensembles, including saxophonist Donald Sinta, the New York Brass Quintet, Ithaca College Woodwind Quintet, Ithaca College Jazz Ensemble, and Ithaca College Concert Band.

Articles about the band's commissioned works project appeared in numerous national publications. Below is an excerpt from a March 1964 Associated Press story that appeared in many newspapers throughout the country.

ITHACA, N.Y. (AP)—The opportunity for a high school band in a small city to play under the baton of a noted conductor is rare. To premiere an original work is rarer; to exert a vital influence on the music world is even less likely. Yet this is happening in Ithaca.

If a mathematician ever took time to compute the odds of success in such a venture, the figure probably would be astronomical. Each year, Ithaca High School music pupils raise funds to commission a composer to write an original piece for symphonic band, for them to premiere.

The composers attracted to the project include Robert Ward, a 1962 Pulitzer Prize winner in music, and Carlos Chavez, a major Mexican musical figure. To raise funds, pupils sell magazine subscriptions, prepare chicken barbecue dinners and play concerts.

An article in the December 1964 issue of the *Selmer Bandwagon*, **"How a farsighted director made his band a patron of music–GOLDBERG, RASOUMOWSKY & ITHACA HIGH,"** describes the band's commissioning project. Below is an excerpt from this article, quoting Mr. B:

> **The [commissioned works] project is continuing to serve the purposes for which it was established. It has fostered a deeper appreciation, on the part of students, for the importance of the creator's role in music (and all the arts). Besides the benefits and experiences gained from the rehearsing and performance of these works, we have, I feel, also been able to contribute to the good literature for the concert band.**

A section in Brian Norcross's book is devoted to "Student Reactions to the Commissioning Project." In it he quotes former band members commenting on the project. Flutist Leone Buyse stated, "There was a sense of importance in that we were adding to the Literature." Percussionist Jack Liang said that the students sensed "…that these outside composers and musicians believed that we were committed to what we were doing and to them. We [took] them seriously." M J Herson, who played contra-bass clarinet, recalled, "Benson was wonderful. He was a quiet man. We loved his music. He could explain what he wanted us to do…I could say 'hello' and he knew me." Trombonist Bruce Musgrave felt, "It was the thrill of the era, having composers like Benson writing for band in their style…not writing down [to us]…We were jumping out of our skins….".

Below is the IHS Concert Band's May 6, 1964 Spring Concert program:

Program

FANFARE POUR PRECEDER "LA PERI" ....Paul Dukas (1865-1935)

Paul Dukas was a French composer of solid attainments whose talent showed to greatest advantage in the larger instrumental forms. He is probably best known for his masterful orchestral scherzo "L'Apprenti Sorcier." This fanfare was written to precede his ballet "La Peri" composed in 1912.

TRAUERSINFONIE ....Richard Wagner (1813-1883)

The most important figure in 19th century opera is Richard Wagner who achieved a fusion of the arts in his musical dramas. The "Trauersinfonie" is an instrumental work of historical interest. Eighteen years after the death of Carl Maria von Weber (1844), a patriotic movement in Germany resulted in the transference of his remains to his native land. Wagner took a leading part in the impressive ceremony at Dresden by reading the solemn oration and composing this march based upon the two themes from Weber's opera "Euryanthe."

NIGHT SOLILOQUY ....Kent Kennan (1913-   )

"Night Soliloquy" for flute and orchestra was first performed in 1938 by the N.B.C. Symphony Orchestra with Arturo Toscanini conducting. The present arrangement by the composer is for a small wind ensemble and is characterized by its delicate scoring. Mr. Kennan studied at the University of Michigan, Eastman School of Music, and at the Royal Academy of St. Cecilia in Rome, Italy.

Leone Buyse, *Flute*

REMEMBRANCE ....Warren Benson (1924-   )

World Premiere Performance

The piece was written by Mr. Benson on a commission from the members of the Ithaca High School Band as a Christmas present to their conductor, Mr. B. Mr. Benson is on the faculty of the Ithaca College School of Music where he teaches composition and percussion. He has been a resident at the MacDowell Colony for Artists in New Hampshire and the winner of two Fulbright Fellowships and numerous ASCAP awards. This is the third commissioned work Mr. Benson has composed for the Ithaca High School Band.

INTERMISSION

LE JOURNAL DU PRINTEMPS ....J. K. Ferdinand Fischer (1665-1746)

Overture
Menuet
Chaconne

Johann Kasper Ferdinand Fischer was one of the most proficient keyboard performers of his time. His "Ariadne Musica Neo-Organoedum," a collection of twenty keyboard preludes and fugues, was an extremely important influence on J. S. Bach. "Le Journal du Printemps" is a series of eight French orchestral suites written for five voices without any specific reference to instrumentation. This number is from the third suite and was arranged for wind ensemble by Keith Wilson of the Yale School of Music.

CONCERTO ....Paul Creston, Op. 26B (1906-   )

Meditative
Rhythmic

Donald Sinta, *Alto Saxophone*

Mr. Donald Sinta is an internationally-known saxophone virtuoso and teacher of Saxophone at the Ithaca College School of Music. In 1961, he was the featured soloist with the University of Michigan Band when the group toured Russia, the Middle East, and Western Europe. Newspapers everywhere reported on his brilliant solo performances. This is Mr. Sinta's second performance with the Ithaca High School Band.

LA FIESTA MEXICANA ....H. Owen Reed (1910-   )
Prelude and Aztec Dance

The fiesta is an integral part of the Mexican social structure. "La Fiesta Mexicana" by H. Owen Reed attempts to musically portray one of these Mexican holidays. The first movement, of this three part work, is entitled "Prelude and Aztec Dance." Church bells and fireworks announce the opening of the fiesta. At mid-day, a parade is announced by the trumpets and a band marches into the plaza. The attention is focused upon the Aztec dancers, brilliantly plumed and masked, who dance in ever-increasing frenzy to the end of the movement.

THE ITHACA HIGH SCHOOL CONCERT BAND

The Concert Band, organized in 1917, is a select group of 57 students. It rehearses and performs the very best in wind and band literature and has, through its many performances, established itself as one of the finest school bands in the country.

The basic goal of the band is to stimulate interest in the arts, in general, and music in particular. It is hoped that the student, who is constantly striving for fine musical performances, will develop a keen sense of values and a broader concept of life.

All pieces performed on this concert were very challenging. The featured work, Warren Benson's *Remembrance* (originally titled: *Intermezzo for Woodwinds, Brass, Percussion and Piano*), was commissioned by the 1962-63 IHS Band as a Christmas gift to Mr. B. The students were embarrassed to ask Benson to write the piece because they could offer him only $75.00. However, he was so touched by their sincerity that he immediately accepted the commission. Benson recalled that while he was writing the piece, students arrived at his house at regular intervals to pick up "just composed pages of the score" so they could copy out parts.

Remembrance is an eleven-minute long monothematic work consisting of a chorale, variations and fugue—there are many passages for solo players. Benson wrote the following note about the piece.

> **This gift in kind was their best "thank you," a kind of "we understand what you're trying to do for us" statement that would, at the same time, afford each of them [the students] the opportunity to participate directly, individually and collectively with him, in the opening of the gift—taking off its wrapping of silence, shaping and polishing this bit of time and sound as they went, together—a memorable experience for any teacher, this significant return on a long range investment…the various moods of the piece perhaps reflect some of the experiences we [the students, Benson and Battisti] have shared together in the past, in this present work, and, in the unique bond of understanding through mutual creative effort and commitment that we bring to the future.**

Band members never considered Warren Benson to be a guest—he was a valued friend and composer. This made the premiere performance of *Remembrance* an extraordinary emotional experience for everyone.

Donald Sinta, soloist in the Creston *Concerto for Saxophone and Band*, was also a special friend of the band. He spent a great deal of time at IHS conversing with students, attending their recitals and performances and rehearsing/performing with the band. The Creston *Concerto* was the first of three concertos Sinta performed with the band. The other two, Warren Benson's Star *Edge* in 1966 and Alec Wilder's *Concerto for Saxophone and Band* in 1967, were both world-premiere performances.

⁂

Warren Benson was the guest speaker at the annual band banquet on May 29, 1964. He read a poem he had written for the occasion. It was titled, "What Music Is."

Love	Stars	Now
Sing	Joy	Work
Listen	Soul	All
Being	Giving	Forever
Iron	Tears	I
Velvet	Waiting	You
Risk	Depth	We
		Together

Summer Band

Ed Sebring, Director of Recreation for the City of Ithaca, started the Ithaca Youth Summer Band in 1948. Dr. John W. Graves, IHS Band Director at the time, was the group's first conductor. The band consisted of current IHS Band members and former students home from college for the summer. Concerts were performed at school playgrounds throughout the city. Mr. B became the band's conductor in 1956.

In early 1964 the Ithaca Youth Bureau Summer Band received an invitation to perform at the New York World's Fair in July. It was decided that for this special occasion the IHS Concert Band would become the Ithaca Youth Bureau Band. Following two weeks of rehearsals in early July the band performed a pre-New York trip concert at the Corning, NY Summer Theater on July 14.

The band had accommodations in a section of New York City that had experienced some racial unrest and turmoil (Columbia University). This was a concern for some parents and prompted Mr. B to contact local authorities and inquire about this safety issue. They assured him that the students would be safe.

The band's first World's Fair performance was on July 21 at the RCA Pavilion—a 30-minute concert which was video-taped and played many times during the Fair's two-year run. Later in the day the band performed at the New York State and United States Pavilions. Below is a photograph of the band performing at Enterprise Common in the New York State Pavilion.

On July 23 the band presented an outdoor concert at Rockefeller Center Plaza in midtown Manhattan before a large and enthusiastic noontime crowd (see photo, below).

William F. Schneider, Assistant Director of Public Relations at Rockefeller Center, praised the band's performance (letter to Mr. B, July 24, 1964).

> As I told you last evening, and want to repeat, the concert by the Ithaca Youth Band was one of the best we've had here at Rockefeller Center. It was a delight to listen to the excellent program played so expertly by your young people.

Eileen Walsh of Sunnyside, New York was in the crowd that heard the band's performance at Rockefeller Center. She wrote the following note to Mr. B (July 24, 1964).

Usually high school bands are just average and enjoyable mostly to the families of the fellows and girls playing in it. But I was honestly sorry to see the concert come to an end, and judging by the reactions of others there, this was their feeling too. I wish you lots of success…

Reflection by Bruce Musgrave, Class of 1965

Creativity

What may have begun as a student organization based on recreating the standard music repertoire for the wind band/ensemble quickly metamorphosed into something far more complex and comprehensive. Before Frank Battisti's tenure with the band came to an end, the outlets for *student* creativity it nurtured were in some ways as remarkable as the band's famous program of commissioning works by some of the most creative *professional* composers of the day. While all these creative acts grew out of the central activity of music making, their range— across numerous genres and modes—and variety were remarkable. If the quality was uneven, ranging from crude doggerel to sublime portraiture, the energy and enthusiasm were unflagging.

To help the students appreciate the commissioned works more fully, Mr. B added to the established tradition of individual student recitals the expectation that each band member would also compose an original piece for the instrument he or she played in the band. Consequently, a whole new species of student recitals sprang up to showcase those new student works. The array of performance opportunities in any calendar year thus came to include marching band shows and parades, concert band concerts, summer band performances, sectional and all-state band festivals, jazz band appearances, brass choir caroling at Christmas, small ensemble recitals such as those by the brass and woodwind quintets, individual performances of standard works from the literature, and recitals of fellow students' compositions. An impressive number of these performances included premieres of compositions that never would have existed were it not for the IHS Band. But the creativity fostered by the band was hardly limited to musical creativity.

At the low end of the non-musical scale, the band spawned any number of irreverent acts of literary creation—including but not limited to editions of the *IHS Band Snoop* (a jocular band newspaper that at times rivaled the *IHS Tattler*, the official school newspaper, for mirth and inventive features: "All the news that fits, we print"), the epic band poems (mixed-quality group efforts delivered annually at the band banquets), student-generated scripts for marching-band shows or program notes for concert band programs and recordings, and even some more solid lyric verse, philosophical essays reflecting on music and creativity, and other occasional pieces. The advent of super-8 movies provided a whole new creative outlet for the band members, and several deft portrait photographers created memorable black and white still images of their fellow band members as well.

Not infrequently, band alumni had a hand in creating marching/dance routines, musical arrangements, and percussion parts for the marching band. There will be no mention of the countless skits, royal rookie brigade presentations, morning wake-up radio programs at band camp, and numerous other ad hoc creations of that ilk, but suffice it to say that every creative impulse—from the highest to the lowest—found a fertile proving ground in the IHS Band. Flaubert told us, "Look deeply inside yourselves and create the most irreplaceable of things." The band members delighted in doing so. Perpetual creativity had become a treasured way of life.

CHAPTER **12**   A Great One: On His Own Dime—
Benny Goodman Visits IHS—
ABC Performance—Composer-
in-Residence—Premieres of Three
Commissioned Works, 1964–65

Marching Band

Of the 111 students in the 1964 IHS "Little Red" Band, fifty-eight were new. To ensure that all new members would be "up to speed" when band camp started, a series of five orientation/instructional sessions was held during July and August. As a result, these "rookies" were quickly integrated into the full group, and the band made excellent progress during the week at camp. Mr. B told *Ithaca Journal* reporter Jerry Langdon,

> **We're going to have a terrific band…This group [has]… developed very rapidly…They have a terrific dedication to a goal…the desire to come as close to perfection as possible…**

The band's 1964 pregame show featured arrangements of classical music: William Walton's *Crown Imperial March*, Aaron Copland's Shaker theme from *Appalachian Spring*, Modest Moussorgsky's *Great Gate of Kiev*, Samuel Barber's *Commando March*, and the finale of Stravinsky's *Firebird Suite*. Halftime shows included music from two popular Broadway musicals, *West Side Story* and *Hello Dolly*.

Below is a photo of the 1964 Ithaca High School Marching Band. Drum Major Bruce Musgrave is at the right end of the front row.

Following the band's first performance on September 20, 1964, Mr. B wrote the following note to the students:

To the most exciting and enthusiastic group of students in the world !!

Your Saturday performance was excellent !!!! It represented a terrific achievement for 111 "special people" who have been working, living and thinking together for 20 days. I want you…to know that you have made these first 3 weeks of the 1964-65 school year one of the most enjoyable and enthusiastic periods in my teaching career.

A month later, after the Union-Endicott game performance (October 19, 1964), he sent them another note.

To the greatest group of young people…anywhere,

Last Saturday was one of the best days, ever !!!!!!! Your performance was TREMENDOUS…

IHS Principal, Dr. John W. Graves also praised the band's U-E game performance (and Mr. B's leadership).

The band did an outstanding show at the U. E. game. The music, the precision was perfection…Your leadership continues to produce excellence through music.

The photographs that follow show the band performing at IHS football games during the 1964 season.

In early November the band received an invitation to perform at the American Football League Championship game in Buffalo, NY on December 26, 1964. At the end of the IHS football season (mid-November), the marching band went into a state of suspended animation, holding only occasional rehearsals—outdoors when weather permitted, indoors otherwise. In the week prior to the Buffalo performance, the band rehearsed in Cornell University's football-field-sized armory, Barton Hall. A diagram of a football field was mapped out in masking tape on the armory floor for the rehearsal. This was probably the only time the full IHS Marching Band ever marched on a hardwood floor.

Band members enjoyed Christmas Day with their families. The next morning (December 26), they were up early for a 7:00 AM rehearsal in Barton Hall prior to departing for Buffalo (see *Ithaca Journal* photographs on the following page).

A steady drizzle greeted band members when they arrived at Buffalo's Memorial Stadium. However, the less-than-perfect weather did not dampen the students' enthusiasm or determination to present a great half-time performance. When half-time arrived, the students took to the field, Drum Major Bruce Musgrave gave three blasts on his whistle and the band proceeded to perform magnificently for the 50,000 people in Memorial Stadium and millions more who saw and heard them on the ABC national TV network. A testimony to the band's extraordinary performance can be found in George Clay's December 29 *Ithaca Journal* article, **"The Little Red Band's Busy Day in Buffalo."**

The best measure of critical judgment [regarding the band's performance] was given by television officials who gave the band 12 full minutes of…airtime, without commercial[s], station break[s], or play recaps.

SHUFFLING OFF TO BUFFALO this morning was the Ithaca High School Band, but not without a final practice session at 7 o'clock in Barton Hall (top), some final directions from director Frank Battisti (center left), a dash for the bus (center right) and farewells to friends and families (bottom). The band was scheduled to play during halftime of the American Football League championship between Buffalo and San Diego, and nationally televised on ABC.

—Journal Photo by Sol Goldberg

The ABC TV cameras remained on the band for the entire half-time performance!! There were no interruptions of any kind. The ABC producers praised the band's precise marching and especially, its **"great musical sound !!!"**

The following two photos show the band performing in Buffalo Memorial Stadium.

The picture on the next page captures band members bowing at the end of their Buffalo performance. (*Ithaca Journal* photo)

Reporter George Clay, in his article "The Little Red Band's Busy Day in Buffalo", described some of the challenges/difficulties encountered by band members prior to and during their half-time performance.

Drum Sergeant David Holmberg was injured in an accident on the way to the early-morning practice at Barton Hall, but insisted on going with the group and taking care of his responsibilities.

The families of Allen Fisher and Belinda Vail…were visiting in the Washington, D. C. area and the bandsmen arranged to fly from Washington to Buffalo for the performance. They were told that their plane left at 11:50 AM. When they arrived early they found the plane already on the runway ready to take off and literally ran out and flagged it down. Troubles did not end there. When they arrived in Buffalo the person who was to meet them was not at the airport, so they took a cab and arrived with three minutes to go to halftime.

Mary Hall waited at the Buffalo stadium for nearly two hours in chilling weather, so that she would be available for any practice that might be held in Buffalo.

During the performance Penelope (Penny) Behn lost her shoe in the mud and continued through the remainder of the routine, walking in her stockings. Her only hope was that some other bandsman didn't trip over it and ruin the band's appearance on television. A referee later picked up her shoe and returned it to her.

On January 11, 1965 the Ithaca Board of Education passed a resolution congratulating the band and Mr. B on their Buffalo performance. The commendation read, "The Ithaca Board of Education hereby extends congratulations to Band Director Frank L. Battisti and all members of Ithaca High's 'Little Red' Marching Band on the outstanding performance during half-time of the American Football League championship game in Buffalo on December 26, 1964."

Dr. Leonard Buyse, Assistant Superintendent of the Ithaca Public Schools, also praised the band's performance.

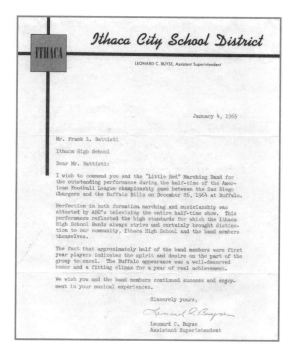

Mr. B and the band received many congratulatory letters and telegrams from people throughout the country (see excerpts from four, below).

David L. Armstrong, Boston, Massachusetts:
I just want you to know what an excellent job I think your band did during the halftime of the American Football League championship game in Buffalo. Everything was superb !!—the selection of music, the tempo, the movements of the members and the togetherness of the group ! I've never written a letter of praise such as this in my life, but I feel I should let you know how impressed I am with your group.

Mr. Ralph Pastore, Claremont, New Hampshire:
May I express my enjoyment where your fine band is concerned. I saw the whole unit on TV at intermission time and must compliment [you]…Usually

I do not care for this type of music but yours was so great. I just had to express
how much I enjoyed the music, marching, etc.

Dr. Paul Bryan, Director of Bands, Duke University, Durham, North Carolina:
I enjoyed your TV performance the other day *very much* !! First rate as always.
Congratulations to you and your kids !

Mr. and Mrs. Robert Anderson, Mission Hills, California:
The extraordinary fine work of the Ithaca High School Band was seen by our
family. We could not let this pass by without a word of compliment on the performance. It was one of the most outstanding displays of any halftime entertainment we have ever enjoyed. To you and your band we say, well done !!

Concert Band

In 1965 the Ithaca City School District was one of 11 school systems in the United States
awarded a MENC Ford Foundation-sponsored composer-in-residence. The purpose
of this project was to promote vitality in the musical life of schools and communities,
expand the body of music for young performers, raise the standards of music for students in public schools, and allow promising young composers to pursue their craft.
Having a composer-in-residence in the Ithaca Public Schools added to the already vital
musical life at IHS.

David Borden was chosen to be Ithaca's composer-in-residence in 1966–67. A native
of Boston, he was studying at the *Hochschule für Musik* in Berlin, Germany when he
received his appointment. Borden was educated at the Eastman School of Music where
he studied composition with Bernard Rogers and Howard Hanson and Harvard University where he studied with Leon Kirchner and Randall Thompson.

❧ ☙

Mr. B considered school assembly concerts the most important the band performed.
Over the years many well-known artists such as Carl "Doc" Severinsen, Donald Sinta,
Harvey Phillips and Jimmy Burke, had performed on these concerts. Even though he
realized it was a long shot, Mr. B decided to try to get popular band leader and "clarinetist extraordinaire" Benny Goodman to perform on one of these concerts. Goodman,
the "King of Swing," was an American jazz icon. Through hundreds of performances in
the 1930s–40s, he and his band established the "swing era" of popular music. Known as
the "Patriarch of the Clarinet," he inspired a whole generation of jazz clarinetists with
his definitive solo-playing style. Goodman brought jazz to Carnegie Hall through his
historic concert of January 16, 1938 and was the first white band leader to include black
musicians in his band.

Since Benny played a Selmer clarinet, Mr. B decided to call Harry Randall at the
Selmer Instrument Company and ask him if he thought there was any possibility of
getting Benny to come to Ithaca and perform with the band. His response was an

emphatic, "No—impossible." Randall said that the Selmer Company had offered Benny thousands of dollars to present clinics for them but he had always turned them down. However, he did make a suggestion—"Why don't you write Benny and tell him about your commissioned-works project? He might find it interesting and decide to come to Ithaca and check it out." (Note: Goodman had commissioned Bela Bartok and Aaron Copland to write pieces for him—Bartok, a chamber work, *Contrasts*, and Copland, a *Concerto for Clarinet and Orchestra*.) Mr. B followed Randall's suggestion and wrote Goodman telling him about the commissioned-works project. A month went by with no response. Then one day as he was teaching in his office, Mr. B was interrupted by a telephone call. The voice on the telephone asked, "Is Frank Battisti there?"

Mr. B: "Yes, speaking."

Caller: "This is Benny Goodman—how about next week?"

Mr. B: "Next week ?…Well…Yes… *Yes!!* … that would be fine."

After finishing his conversation with Goodman, Mr. B rushed over to Principal John Graves's office and told him about Benny's offer to come to IHS the following week. Mr. B inquired, "Would it be possible to arrange an assembly program for next Friday, March 12?" A startled and surprised Graves replied, "Definitely!!"

On Friday, March 12, Mr. B picked Goodman up at the Syracuse, NY airport. During the drive back to Ithaca, Mr. B discussed the day's schedule with him. Goodman showed no interest in playing—"high school students don't like 'my kind of music' (swing)—they only like rock'n'roll." It became clear that the primary motive for Goodman's trip to Ithaca was to observe/check out "the high school band that commissioned composers to write music for them" and not to perform. The photo, below, shows Mr. B trying to assure Goodman that IHS students were eager to hear him play "his kind of music."

Happily, Mr. B succeeded in convincing Goodman to perform. However, there was still a problem: because Goodman hadn't intended to perform, he didn't bring his clarinet with him—one had to be found for him to use (Benny insisted that it be a Selmer). Luckily, one band student, Brian Earle, played a Selmer (all other clarinetists played Buffets). Brian was called out of his class and brought Goodman his instrument (he was thrilled to have "the King of Swing" play his clarinet).

In the early afternoon Goodman rehearsed with the IHS Jazz Ensemble in the gym (Mr. B thought the gym would be a more relaxed, less formal environment than Kulp Auditorium). Goodman didn't play a note during the rehearsal—he just listened to the band and offered suggestions. When it was over he told the students, "I'll see you on the battlefield."

At 2:40 PM the students filed into the gym, filled the bleachers and sat on the floor in front of the band. The jazz ensemble opened the program with two numbers made famous by the Goodman Band, *Sing, Sing, Sing* and *One O'Clock Jump*. When Mr. B introduced Goodman he was greeted with loud cheers and prolonged applause—he appeared genuinely surprised by the enthusiastic reception. Goodman's smooth and stylish playing provoked many outbursts of applause and cheers throughout the concert—the students loved "his kind of music" and the way he played it !! It was a great once-in-a-lifetime experience for everyone.

After the concert Goodman returned to Mr. B's office and signed autographs on LP recordings, saxophone and clarinet reeds, note paper, tardy excuse forms, etc. One student even offered a stranger $2 to take a picture of him standing next to Goodman.

The three photographs that follow show Benny Goodman during his visit to Ithaca High School.

Goodman rehearsing the IHS Jazz Ensemble prior to the assembly program.

Goodman "swinging" with the IHS Jazz Ensemble during the concert.

A smiling Benny Goodman in Mr. B's office after the concert.

In the evening Mr. B drove Benny back to the Syracuse airport. They had dinner together after which Benny boarded a flight to Boston. Goodman's visit to Ithaca didn't cost the band anything. Benny came on his own dime to see "the band that took a chance and commissioned music." In June (1965) two band members traveled to New York City and presented Goodman with a thank-you gift—a painting by Cornell University artist Peter Kahn (Benny collected paintings).

A few days following Goodman's visit, Principal John Graves sent Mr. B the following note.

> **The assembly featuring Benny Goodman was thrilling to all who attended. It was a short but cherished glimpse of a Great in American music.**

Mr. B. also received a letter from Jack Feddersen, President of the H. & A. Selmer Instrument Company (dated June 1, 1965). In it he commented,

> **I saw Benny about a month ago, and he told me about his trip to Ithaca and how thrilled he was with the work you are doing there.**

Below is a photo of the 1964-65 Ithaca High School Concert Band

The band's April 28,1965 Spring Concert program included premiere performances of new works by Leslie Bassett, Warren Benson and Barney Childs. All three composers attended the premiere performance of their pieces (see program on the next page).

OVERTURE AND ALLEGRO from "La Sultane" ....F. Couperin – D. Milhaud

Following the bold and vigorous art of the virginalists, a new and sharply contrasting school of keyboard composers, the "clavecinists", arose in France about the middle of the seventeenth century. Its founder was Chambonnières, who took over many features of lute music in his graceful and refined pieces. The clavecinist style reached its climax in Handel. A favorite musician of Louis XIV during the first part of the eighteenth century François Couperin, called "le Grand", whose works were greatly admired by Bach and Couperin cultivated the art of the miniature; his pieces have a polished, witty and elegant charm that reflects the "galanterie" of the court to which he was attached.

The "Overture and Allegro", which the band will perform to open tonight's concert, has been scored for band by the distinguished contemporary composer from France, Darius Milhaud.

IRISH TUNE from County Derry ....Percy Grainger

Percy Grainger's impressionable associations with Edward Grieg awoke in him a desire to know all he could about the English folk song and its singer. Like his contemporary Bela Bartok, he pursued the folk song with a passion for its accurate notation. After becoming a United States citizen, a period of military service in the band program of the U. S. Army in 1917 afforded him unlimited opportunities to experiment in scoring for the wind instruments. Following this experience, Mr. Grainger scored many folk songs for the band medium.

SIX EVENTS FOR FIFTY-EIGHT PLAYERS ....Barney Childs
Premiere Performance

Mr. Childs graduated from the University of Nevada in 1949 and then earned both Bachelor and Master of Arts degrees from Oxford University as a Rhodes Scholar in 1951 and 1955, respectively. In 1957 he earned his Ph.D. from Stanford University. As a composer, Elliott Carter. His awards include the Stanford Humanities Prize in composition; Koussevitsky Memorial Award in composition; Woolley Memorial Commission from Bennington College.

Currently Mr. Childs composes and teaches English at the University of Arizona.

SOIREES MUSICALES ....B. Britten – T. Brown
Canzonetta
Bolero
Tirolese

Benjamin Britten is the gifted English Composer, pianist, and conductor. His attraction to the theatre as a medium for expression drew him to Rossini as a model for his first compositional excursion in this area. Using some of Rossini's small pieces for material he composed a film musical score in the late 30's. This later became the "Soirées Musicales."

INTERMISSION

DESIGNS, IMAGES, AND TEXTURES ....Leslie Bassett
Premiere Performance

Oil Painting
Water Color
Pen and Ink Drawing
Mobile
Bronze Sculpture

Mr. Bassett is an associate professor in composition at the University of Michigan School of Music. He served with the Army Bands during World War II. His Prix de Rome were awarded in 1961 and 1962. In 1960 he won the award from the Society for the Publication of American Music.

STAR EDGE ....Warren Benson
Premiere Performance
Mr. Donald Sinta, *Alto Saxophone Soloist*

1958 Mr. Benson has written four compositions which have received premiere performances by the I.H.S. Band. "Star Edge" is Mr. Benson's most recent composition. It is a Colony for Artists in New Hampshire and the winner of two Fulbright Fellowships and dence at the Ithaca College School of Music. He has been a resident at the MacDowell work for solo alto saxophone and band. At present Mr. Benson is the composer-in-residence many ASCAP awards.

Mr. Sinta is an internationally-known saxophone virtuoso and teacher of Saxophone at the Ithaca College School of Music. This marks Mr. Sinta's third solo appearance with the Ithaca High School Band.

THE ITHACA HIGH SCHOOL CONCERT BAND

The Concert Band, organized in 1917, is a select group of 64 students. It rehearses and performs the very best in wind and band literature and has, through its many performances, established itself as one of the finest school bands in the country.

The basic goal of the band is to stimulate interest in the arts, in general, and music in particular. It is hoped that the student, who is constantly striving for fine musical performances, will develop a keen sense of values and a broader concept of life.

Leslie Bassett was chairperson of the composition department at the University of Michigan and the recipient of numerous commissions including a recent one from the Philadelphia Orchestra for their bicentennial celebration. The piece he composed for them, *Variations for Orchestra*, won the 1966 Pulitzer Prize in Music.

Designs, Images and Textures was Bassett's first piece for band. It is a brilliant five-movement work, each of which relates to a different medium of modern art (*Oil Painting, Water Color, Pen and Ink Drawing, Mobile, and Bronze Sculpture*). Like Moussorgsky's *Pictures at an Exhibition*, the piece invites players and listeners to "associate music with visual art."

Mr. B received the score and parts to *Designs, Images and Textures* on November 10, 1964. Enclosed with the music was the following letter from Bassett.

Dear Mr. Battisti,

I took you at your word that the Ithaca band is a good one, and I've heard many reports from musicians who know of your work and tell me that your group is excellent. These pieces are difficult and will require careful preparation. There are technical challenges, naturally, but I would imagine that the biggest challenge might be that of getting each performer to play his/her own part independently rather than as part of a group. Each person will be exposed at some time during the work and will have his chance to be heard. I hope that this prospect is an attractive one rather than one that might frighten. In any case, I like to think that the students will respond favorably to this sort of writing and that it will result in a quality of sound that is not often heard in band music. I am truly excited by this piece and hope that it can be welcomed as a rather radical but long-awaited addition in the band repertory that presents that marvelous ensemble in a fresh way, free of doubling and over-scoring.

After rehearsing the piece for two weeks, Mr. B wrote Bassett the following note (January 26, 1965):

> We think your piece is GREAT and very exciting…!!!!! The students find it challenging both technically and musically. However, they are fascinated by the new and interesting sounds and have become more excited and happy with the piece the more they work on it. I am confident we will be able to give the piece an excellent premiere performance.

Star Edge was Warren Benson's fourth work for the IHS Band. It is a concerto for saxophone and band and is dedicated "to the IHS Band, Frank Battisti, conductor, Donald Sinta and a Friend." Brian Norcross states that *Star Edge* is

> …a musical experience that must be heard and felt. The work exposed the students to a more dissonant style of composition from Warren Benson… students were…offered the opportunity to…interact with the soloist in the "free," somewhat improvised sections, and the cadenza.

Following the premiere performance of *Star Edge*, Donald Sinta wrote band members the note at the right on the back of a napkin.

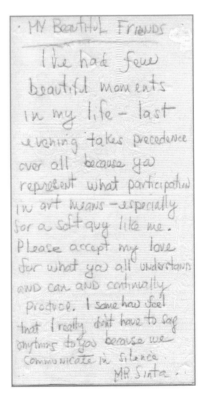

When Mr. B met Barney Childs in 1964 he invited him to write a piece for the band (he extended this same invitation to every composer he met). *Six Events for 58 Players* is Childs's response to Mr. B's request. There is no score for the piece—just a single page of instructions on how the piece should be created. Each player's part contains information on what to play and when (ex. "hold any note 10-15 seconds"; "say ch-ch-ch-ch- loudly on the same pitch"; "play any fast trill or tremolo 6–10 seconds—pp"; "play any five eighth-notes at random—mf," etc.). *Six Events for 58 Players* is structured in fifteen "systems"— any consecutive six of which may be selected for a performance of the piece. This variable option ensures that every performance is unique and different. Mr. B did not conduct the band at rehearsals or at the premiere performance of Childs's piece. Instead, a remote-controlled sweep-hand, constructed by band clarinetist David Wickstrom (and named "Igor" by the students), was used to measure out the length of each system and lead the players. *Six Events for 58 Players* is probably the first aleatoric (chance) piece ever written for high school band.

When Childs sent Mr. B the score and parts to *Six Events for 58 Players* he enclosed a letter offering advice on how to introduce the piece to the students.

> …I suspect your hardest job will be in convincing your players that the formal means and esthetic of the piece are legitimate. Perhaps if you explain to them that music is, after all, simply sound organized in time and that this piece gives each one a chance to help the composer present a musical experience in process; that it's a kind of kaleidoscope of sonority; that chance music works constantly to keep the expectation at a minimum…and to keep listening pleasantly and continuously surprised—in these terms I think they will soon accept the piece happily and enjoy playing it a great deal…*I have been told by at least two composers, on explaining the piece, "You're out of your mind; you'll never get fifty-eight kids to be interested and serious enough even to read it, much less play it in performance."* I don't THINK they are right, but it IS possible. We'll see. If any outfit can do it I'm sure yours can.

Following the premiere of *Six Events for 58 Players*, Childs sent the students the following letter (May 15, 1965):

> I am glad you…enjoyed the piece. I have always felt that music should be pleasure, often fun…and in the very act of playing it one can derive a much greater pleasure than someone who is simply listening. I tried, therefore, in the piece to arrange things so that everyone would have their own personal creative responsibilities to making the whole work go, allowing him to use his own sense of invention and inspiration and yet being aware that he was part of a group of friends all doing the same thing. This piece is simply music about music—it doesn't have a program or a story or even a kind of emotional progress to it—and as such I hope it allowed all of you to learn something for yourself about the nature and variety of *music for its own sake.*

In November (1965) the *Selmer Bandwagon* published an article on the students' reaction to *Six Events for 58 Players*. Overall their responses were very positive. Many commented that playing Childs's piece increased their understanding of all types of music and elevated their appreciation of the individual player's importance in the performance of a piece. Below are excerpts from four student reactions:

> The whole musical experience–the rehearsals and performance–was to me very exciting. I had the freedom to do whatever I felt like and yet I learned to use discipline and discrimination. It was a strange idea but it made my understanding of music grow. Knowledge can only grow by trying unprecedented ideas. The chance piece was a profound experience.

I learned to listen to the total "event" and to judge the limits of what I should do. I listened and this sharpened my listening ability for other pieces. I learned to distinguish what should be brought out and what should be used as a subtle complement to the main theme. This knowledge has become invaluable to me.

The most exciting aspects were the realization of meaning in a practically meaningless phrase on the (part). Bringing out the ostinato to a climax, a combination of these phrases made by instruments or by the human body, was the fulfillment of the piece. Also, when I had a solo, the spirit of cooperation—the good accompaniment could augment and enhance its possibilities.

In that, the piece was priceless, indeed it was a lesson in democratic thinking. I value the piece because I could let my imagination and temperament work while I performed what was written before me, and then perform harmoniously with others.

Rehearsing and performing *Six Events for 58 Players* proved to be an exciting experience in spontaneous discretion and creative judgment for the students.

The sixth annual Band Parents' Night took place on March 24, 1965. A record number of 375 parents, brothers, sisters, grandparents and friends attended the event. As in past years, the highlight of the evening was the performance of the IHS Band Parents' Band. Below is a photo of the 1965 "blast from the past" with Mr. B conducting.

In mid-April (1965) Thomas Beversdorf—trombonist, composer, conductor and member of the faculty at the Indiana University School of Music—conducted the IHS Band in a rehearsal of his *Symphony for Band*. He also presented a trombone recital and clinic for the students. In a letter to band members following his visit Dr. Beaversdorf wrote,

Dear Band Members,

In the past I have had the opportunity to work under some of the great conductors, Leinsdorf, Reiner, Rodzinski, Bernstein, Munch, Paray, etc. and I have had many thrilling moments of music making. Also, I have had occasion to conduct some fine professional and college ensembles such as the Houston Symphony, the Eastman Summer Symphony, the Indiana University Symphony, the Indianapolis Philharmonic to mention a few. What I want to convey to you is that in working with you as an ensemble, I had one of those singular experiences which any musician, be he composer or conductor, treasures as unique. You are the most responsive, interesting, and exciting ensemble with which I have ever worked. Your perception and open-mindedness is far superior to any professional or college group with which I have ever worked, and, in general, I must say, that I had more fun during our hard musical workout than I can remember with *any other* group. I was caught completely by surprise–to my utter delight. Congratulations for being such a wonderful ensemble.

In conclusion Beversdorf stated that the IHS Band program was

…perhaps the most creative high school band program in this hemisphere.

The IHS Band continued to sponsor concerts by outstanding college and university bands and wind ensembles. In 1965 the Luther College Concert Band from Decorah, Iowa, Weston Noble, conductor, presented a concert in Claude L. Kulp Auditorium.

Frederick Fennell's annual visit on May 28 concluded the 1964-65 band year. As he had done every May since 1960, Fennell created another "magical day of music making" for the students.

Reflection by Bruce Musgrave, Class of 1965

Leadership, Role Models, and Mentors

Educational theorists expound at length on the necessity of schools' providing opportunities for students to develop leadership skills—at times actually devising workshops or even regular classes on leadership. The phrase "Talk is cheap" springs readily to mind when it comes to the efficacy of many such programs. The band was a different story. The organization of close to 150 adolescents had only one adult director and perhaps the occasional part-time assistant, to help with percussionists, for example. To ensure the band's day-to-day growth and development, student leadership was not only desirable but also essential. Otherwise, how could several simultaneous sectional rehearsals occur at once? How could the director be free to work with one segment of the band, while others functioned productively elsewhere at the same time?

As was the case with so much of the band's yearly rhythm, student leaders began to develop early in the marching-band cycle. Busy giving weekly individual instrumental lessons, selecting music, studying scores, writing arrangements and routines for the marching-band, Mr. B of necessity delegated to upper-class students the tasks of teaching new band members the rudiments of marching, of instructing the color guard in the basics of carrying their flags, and of beginning to learn the new music by sections (the flutes in one room with their student section leader, the trumpets in another, etc.). It was critical for the departing drum majors to teach their successors the specialized skills of that post; those who had served as music librarians needed to pass on their insights to their successors. The leadership of the Bach Honor Society had to pass along the particulars of fostering the society's events and programs.

When the time for band camp actually came, each cabin needed a counselor, and there were myriad on-field supervisory duties to be performed—all ably discharged by recent band alumni, most of whom were college students at the time. In some ways it brought to mind the medieval guild system that band members had learned about in their history classes—the apprentices (the rookies), the journeymen (the underclassmen), the master craftsmen (the upperclassmen), and the guild leadership (the alumni counselors). With so many opportunities to lead, the band members developed leadership skills naturally. The program was forever perpetuating itself, and each new cycle of leaders would contribute more competencies and new ways of prospering to that culture.

In the spring of the concert-band cycle, usually following the spring concert, the band would select its officers/student leaders for the coming year so that the summer duties could unfold smoothly and with nominal authority. Even without those elections, the leadership was there already, and the elected officers enjoyed abundant support in *de facto* leadership from rank-and-file upperclassmen. Some former officers of the band—along with many others who never held IHS Band office—have risen to high prominence in their adult lives, not only in business, the professions, and education, but also in virtually all levels of government—including national cabinet-level posts—but more than a few of them are most proud of their service as leaders of the IHS band. At the time, being elected to office in the band meant far more to most of them than being elected to the school's student government, an athletic captaincy, or a position of leadership in a religious or civic youth group.

Those former student leaders of the band include international-level leaders in music pedagogy, major-university-program leaders in the arts, leaders in law, education, the military, engineering, medicine, social services, philanthropy, religion, commerce, the sciences, the trades, and broadly throughout the arts. That their experiences helping lead the band prepared them directly for their effectiveness in subsequent positions of responsibility and authority is uniformly agreed on by all of them.

CHAPTER **13** A Program in Full Stride: Midwest
Clinic Concert with Fennell, Revelli,
Beeler, Sinta, Buyse and New York
Brass Quintet—Second Contemporary
Music Festival—Premieres of Three
More Commissioned Pieces, 1965–66

Marching Band

Over 2000 people attended the IHS Band Chicken Barbecue at Stewart Park
on July 15, 1965. Afterwards many moved over to the park's lakeside pavilion
and listened to the Summer-Ithaca jazz-by-the-lake concert.

Below is a photo of some of the people who attended the chicken barbecue. (*Ithaca
Journal* photo)

❧ ☙

Every July and August Mr. B held a series of meetings for the band camp staff (camp
counselors, IHS Band officers and drum major[s]). Listed below are the agendas for
those held in summer 1965.

   Meeting No. 1—Friday, July 16, 1965
      Review of last year's camp
      Suggestions for improvement and changes
      Cabin counselor assignments
      Distribution of camp preparation assignments

Meeting No. 2—Friday, July 23, 1965
  Discussion of special events
  Goals of band camp and the band experience

Meeting No. 3—Monday, August 23, 1965
  Supervision details
  Rehearsal plans
  Discussion of camp organization and finalizing of camp program

Meeting No. 4—Wednesday, August 25, 1965
  Pre-camp briefing
  Rookie Day plans
  Opening-day schedule
  Rehearsal plans finalized
  Student conduct
  Final check of all details

A Band Camp Informational Booklet was distributed to band members and their parents each fall. Below are excerpts from the top letter included in the 1965 booklet.

This is our seventh camp and I anticipate it will be our finest! August 29th will find 118 band members (34 new ones) and 21 counselors (all former IHS Band members) gathering in the Danby Hills to participate in a week of intensive rehearsing in preparation for our fall schedule of performances. Besides performing at all home and away IHS football games…the band will make a nationally-televised appearance (in color) on the NBC television network on October 5, 1965 at the Buffalo Bills–Oakland Raiders AFL game in Buffalo, New York…My contact with new members during the summer gives me great confidence [in their] ability to "come up" to the standards we seek…it should be a great and exciting year…It is my sincerest hope that the challenge…to become the BEST musician, student and person possible will result in [an] appreciation of…the value of discipline, dedication and hard work in [the pursuit of musical] excellence.

The 1965 "Little Red" Band was the largest ever—118 students, including 92 student musicians, 16 color guards, 4 majorettes and 4 managers. For the first time in its history, the band had two drum majors, juniors Al Fisher and Greg Mosher.

Band camp began on Sunday, August 29, 1965—each student paid $30.00 to attend. The photo at the top of the next page shows band members "walking through" a new precision marching routine on the first day of camp.

Even though students spent many hours rehearsing and practicing, there was also time for dancing, playing games, talking and relaxing (see photos, below and on the next page).

Alto saxophonist, friend-of-the-band Donald Sinta, and the New York Brass Quintet performed recital programs at the 1965 Band Camp. Both Sinta and the Quintet would perform with the band later in the year at their Chicago Midwest Clinic concert.

Everyone worked very hard at camp and much was accomplished. When camp ended on Sunday, September 6, the band's "esprit de corps" was sky-high—everyone was excited and ready to start the new year.

The band's first performance was on September 18, 1965 at the IHS-Union Endicott game. Once again, its pregame show included music not normally performed on a football field—arrangements of music from Prokofiev's *Love of Three Oranges*, Warren Benson's *Transylvania Fanfare*, the march from Peter I. Tschaikowsky's *Symphony No. 4, Op. 74*, *Normandie* from Darius Milhaud's *Suite Francaise*, and the march from Gustav Holst's *Suite No. 1*. This music was arranged by Alpha Hockett, a former band member and in 1965 a student at the Eastman School of Music in Rochester, NY. The band's halftime show featured precision marching routines to music by Richard Rodgers: *Victory at Sea Fanfare*, *Lover*, *Slaughter on Tenth Avenue*, *The Sweetest Sounds*, and *Climb Every Mountain*.

The following photo shows the band performing at a fall 1965 night game.

The band traveled to Buffalo, NY in October to perform at the Buffalo-Oakland AFL game (televised over the NBC-TV national network). The following four photos were taken during the band's performance.

IHS Band alumnus Michael Salamino ('65), who was attending college in Binghamton, NY, viewed the band's performance on TV and wrote the following note to Mr. B.

Congratulations on a tremendous performance…in Buffalo, NY. The routines simply looked great!! I hate to say it, but they looked better and sounded better than last year's band. The performance made me feel very proud of being a member of *the Greatest Band in the World*.

Bill Youhas, IHS Band percussion coach, watched the band's performance in Champaign, Illinois and sent band members the following two-sentence telegram in Buffalo.

The show was a gas!! It looked great and the charts really cooked too much!!!

Frank Del Russo, band director at Williamsville, NY High School (suburb of Buffalo), sent Mr. B an article from the *Buffalo Evening News* praising the band's performance. He also enclosed a personal note that read, "Great Show Frank, this is the longest 'write up' about a band's performance at a Buffalo Bills game ever to appear in the *Evening News*—**BRAVO!!!!!!!!!**"

A large colored picture of the 1965 IHS "Little Red" Band appeared on the front page of the October 9 edition of *The Ithaca Journal* (reproduced on the next page in black and white).

ITHACA HIGH SCHOOL'S BIGGEST LITTLE RED BAND will perform today for the crowd at the Ithaca High School-Elmira Southside football game, which begins at 11 a.m. on Bredbenner Field. At halftime, the band will present a program of marches based on classical symphonic literature: March from the 'Love of Three Oranges Ballet' by Prokofieff; 'Transylvania Fanfare March' by Ithaca's Warren Benson; a march based on the second movement of Tchaikovsky's Sixth Symphony; 'Normandie' from the Suite Francaise by Darius Milhaud; and the 'First Suite for Band' by Gustav Holst. After the game, the band will play 'Taste of Honey' and 'Peter Gunn.'

Every fall the band performed in two parades in Ithaca—the Tompkins County Halloween and Veterans' Day parades. The photo, below, shows the band marching in the 1965 Veterans' Day Parade (*Ithaca Journal* photo).

The first thing IHS Band members did when they arrived at school each morning was read the notices and announcements posted on the band bulletin board outside Mr. B's office. These announcements included information about rehearsals, band activities/events, newspaper/magazine articles about the band, etc. In the photo that follows, students crowd around the bulletin board to read the announcements. (Note the partially exposed sign above Mr. B's office doors. It reads, "All who pass under this sign are striving to become perfect musicians and individuals.")

Concert Band

The IHS Concert Band was one of four high school bands in the United States invited to perform at the Midwest National Band Clinic in Chicago, Illinois in December 1965. The invitation letter stated that the band was selected because of its **"continuously high musical performances" and "[its] excellent contribution to the repertoire of serious literature for concert band through its unique series of commissioned works."** Being selected to perform at the Midwest Clinic was a very prestigious honor. Thousands of band directors/conductors and music educators from the United States, Canada, and throughout the world attend this clinic every year.

Midwest Clinic regulations in 1965 restricted the music performed at Clinic concerts to pieces not longer than 6 ½ minutes and published in the last year. Conductors were instructed to select music from new pieces sent to them by music publishers. Mr. B found those he received to be of inferior musical quality. He therefore proceeded to select a program that was representative of those the band performed at home.

His program was rejected by the Midwest committee. They stated that it did not conform to Midwest Clinic regulations—too many pieces were longer than 6 ½ minutes and the Wilder and Benson pieces were in manuscript. Overall, the committee deemed the program to be "too non-traditional" and requested that it be revised. Mr. B refused to do so. He informed the committee that he would not subvert the integrity of the IHS Band by programming music of inferior quality. Faced with the possibility of the IHS Band not performing at the Clinic, the committee finally accepted the program (see below).

PROGRAM
Mid-West National Band Clinic
December 16, 1965

Fanfare pour preceder "La Peri" . . . . Paul Dukas

La Fiesta Mexicana . . . . H. Owen Reed
    Mass

Festive Overture . . . . Dmitri Shostakovich
                      Arranged by Donald Hunsberger
    Mr. Walter Beeler, Guest Conductor
    Ithaca College School of Music

Concertino . . . . Cecile Chaminade
  Arranged by Clayton Wilson, Flute Solo edited by Frederick Wilkins
    Miss Leone Buyse, Guest Flute Soloist

Remarks by Dr. John W. Graves, Principal, Ithaca High School

Remembrance . . . . Warren Benson

Aeolian Song . . . . Warren Benson
    Mr. Donald Sinta, Guest Alto Saxophone Soloist

Trittico . . . . Vaclav Nelhybel
    First Movement
    Third Movement
        Dr. William D. Revelli, Guest Conductor
        University of Michigan School of Music

Dypitch for Brass Quintet and Band . . . . Gunther Schuller
    New York Brass Quintet, Guest Soloists
  Robert Nagel, Trumpet-Paul Ingraham, French Horn-Robert Heinrich, Trumpet-John Swallow, Trombone-Harvey Phillips, Tuba

Le Journal du Printemps . . . . Johann K. F. Fischer
    Overture   Arranged by Keith Wilson
    Chacoone

Entertainment III . . . . Alec Wilder
    Dr. Frederick Fennell, Guest Conductor
    University of Miami School of Music

Danza Final . . . . Alberto Ginastera

Rehearsals for the Midwest concert began in mid-October. Guest soloists Leone Buyse, a former member of the band (in 1965, a student at the Eastman School of Music), and Donald Sinta both rehearsed with the band in October and November. Walter Beeler, one of the guest conductors, rehearsed Shostakovich's *Festive Overture* twice with the band during the first week of December.

Mr. B had met Alec Wilder in February 1965 and invited him to write a piece for the band's Midwest Clinic concert. Wilder was a self-taught composer who created a unique kind of music that didn't fit into any preordained musical categories. It was a blend of jazz, the American popular song and classical music techniques. Many well-known jazz musicians, popular singers and classical artists/ensembles performed his music including Benny Goodman, Jimmy Dorsey, Frank Sinatra, Peggy Lee, Judy Garland, New York Brass Quintet, New York Woodwind Quintet and Rochester Philharmonic.

Mr. B received the score and parts for Wilder's new piece, *Entertainment III*, on November 29. It was an extremely difficult piece and the students worked very hard to prepare it for the composer's arrival on December 8. The photo, below, shows Wilder clarifying a point in the score to Mr. B at one of the rehearsals. (*Ithaca Journal* photo).

Frederick Fennell and the New York Brass Quintet arrived in Ithaca on Tuesday, December 14. That evening Fennell rehearsed *Entertainment III* for an hour and a half (he would conduct the premiere of the piece at the band's Midwest Clinic concert). Afterwards he told *Ithaca Journal* reporter Jane Marcham, **"There's no group like this one in the country."** Mr. B spent the remainder of the rehearsal rehearsing Schuller's *Diptych* with the New York Brass Quintet.

The next day (Wednesday, December 15) the students, chaperones and Mr. B traveled to Syracuse and boarded a United Airlines charter plane to Chicago (this was the first time many of the students had ever flown). The band arrived at Chicago's O'Hare Field at 7:00 PM and was transferred to the Sherman House on Gray Line buses. At 8:30 PM the guest conductors and soloists joined Mr. B and band members for dinner in the hotel's coffee shop. Afterwards everyone went to the Tabarin Room and rehearsed from 10:00 PM to 12:30 AM. The photo on the next page shows (left to right), Dr. William D. Revelli, Harvey Phillips, Michael Walters (behind Phillips), Warren Benson and Frederick Fennell listening to Mr. B rehearse the band.

The IHS Band's Midwest Clinic concert brochure included a picture of the Concert Band, list of pieces, program notes and biographical information on the composers, guest conductors and soloists (see below and the top of the next page).

PROGRAM
Mid-West National Band Clinic
December 16, 1965

Fanfare pour preceder "La Peri" . . . . Paul Dukas

La Fiesta Mexicana . . . . H. Owen Reed
    Mass

Festive Overture . . . . Dmitri Shostakovich
        Arranged by Donald Hunsberger
        Mr. Walter Beeler, Guest Conductor
        Ithaca College School of Music

Concertino . . . . Cecile Chaminade
    Arranged by Clayton Wilson, Flute Solo edited by Frederick Wilkins
        Miss Leone Buyse, Guest Flute Soloist

    Remarks by Dr. John W. Graves, Principal, Ithaca High School

Remembrance . . . . Warren Benson

Aeolian Song . . . . Warren Benson
        Mr. Donald Sinta, Guest Alto Saxophone Soloist

Trittico . . . . Vaclav Nelhybel
    First Movement
    Third Movement
        Dr. William D. Revelli, Guest Conductor
        University of Michigan School of Music

Dypitch for Brass Quintet and Band . . . . Gunther Schuller
        New York Brass Quintet, Guest Soloists
    Robert Nagel, Trumpet-Paul Ingraham, French Horn-Robert Hein-
    rich, Trumpet-John Swallow, Trombone-Harvey Phillips, Tuba

Le Journal du Printemps . . . . Johann K. F. Fischer
    Overture   Arranged by Keith Wilson
    Chacoone

Entertainment III . . . . Alec Wilder
        Dr. Frederick Fennell, Guest Conductor
        University of Miami School of Music

Danza Final . . . . Alberto Ginastera

The photo, below, shows the overflow crowd in the Grand Ballroom of the Sherman House awaiting the start of the IHS Band's concert.

Prior to the start of the concert, band members, guest conductors and soloists posed for the official Clinic photograph (see below). Standing in front of the band are (left to right), Dr. Frederick Fennell, Robert Heinrich, Paul Ingraham, Robert Nagel, John Swallow, Harvey Phillips, Leone Buyse, Mr. B, Walter Beeler, Donald Sinta and Dr. William D. Revelli.

Below, the band performing at the Midwest Clinic concert

The pieces on the band's Midwest concert were very different in style and content than those performed by the other clinic bands. Four of the works were written by composers whose music was seldom (if ever) performed by bands (Benson, Schuller, Wilder, Ginastera); two were for small woodwind/brass ensembles (Dukas, Fischer) and four were longer than 6 ½ minutes (Wilder, Schuller, Benson, Nelhybel). Even though these pieces were not the usual "band fare," the audience's response to them was very enthusiastic. At the end of the concert the band received a lengthy standing ovation. Donald McCathren, Band Director at Duquesne University, was so excited and thrilled by the performance that he immediately rushed back stage and invited the band to perform at the 1967 Mid-East Instrumental Music Conference in Pittsburgh, PA. A few band directors, however, did find the program "disturbing"—"this isn't band music."

On December 18, 1965 *The Ithaca Journal* proclaimed:

Ithaca Band Earns Ovation—The Ithaca High School Concert Band received a standing ovation in Chicago Thursday night.

Mr. B received many letters congratulating the band on its Midwest performance. George C. Wilson, Vice-President of the Interlochen National Music Camp, wrote,

May I take this opportunity to again congratulate you and the fine Ithaca High School Concert Band on your performance in Chicago at the Midwest Band Clinic. This was a most unusual program and the performance of the players was exciting and convincing. We're all indebted to you and the band for your continued fine efforts in connection with contemporary band literature. Your contributions are significant and add greatly to the repertoire for the band.

Harry Begian, Director of Bands at Wayne State University, stated,

I am amazed at the competency with which your students tackled the contemporary idiom and how well you had trained them to present the difficult program you performed.

Al Wright, Director of Bands at Purdue University, added,

Your Ithaca Band was simply tremendous at the Midwest Clinic in Chicago… It simply knocked us all out musically. The sensitivity and musicianship with which your group performed was the talk of the convention. I know that the youngsters in the band are just as proud of their performance as you are.

Alec Wilder's letter to the band began, **"Dear (followed by the names of every student in the band)."** At the bottom he wrote, **"THANK YOU !!!"** in red pen and huge capital letters.

On January 1, 1966 the *Ithaca Journal* published a full-page photo-essay about the band's Midwest Clinic concert entitled, **"The Feeling Was Satisfaction."** (see excerpt on the next page):

... the center of the excitement was the music. "My main feeling was the satisfaction of achieving something," one bandsman reminisced. "We had been working on the concert for so long, and in the last two weeks the pace was furious, and then, in a short space of time, it was all there." Especially exciting, he said, was the opportunity to work with the composers of their music, guest conductors and guest artists. "It complicated things technically, but the experience of being around these brilliant people was tremendous."

Then there was the music itself, all of it contemporary. "It wasn't really too wild for us, we're used to it, although I realize it's unusual for high school bands. But Mr. B [Conductor Frank Battisti] has this great knack for interpreting this stuff. It comes off."

One Midwest Clinic administrator was critical because there was nothing on the Ithaca program by Sousa. He changed his mind. The audience was enthusiastic, and the Ithacans apparently converted many listeners to new music.

Dr. Thomas E. Mosher, a band parent and one of the chaperones on the trip, praised the students' behavior and deportment in a letter to the editor of *The Ithaca Journal* (excerpt, below).

...Not only did the High School Concert Band produce the most exciting music written to a packed concert hall which gave it a standing ovation, but they did it with the utmost poise and dignity...Their self and group discipline and courtesy was always evident.

French horn player Dave Smith sent Mr. B the following note:

Needless to say, the trip to Chicago was really the greatest experience I have ever had...Until now, I thought I'd quit Horn after high school and just enjoy *listening* to music in college. I've changed my mind; playing music is a hell of a lot better way. I've applied to Northwestern and Indiana University, so I'll have a good chance to be in a *good* band again, since they both have fine music schools. Thanks for everything, especially for showing me that much good can come from dedication and hard work.

Mr. B believed that whenever the band traveled to perform somewhere, it was very important that the students explore, visit and do things that expanded their knowledge and experiences. In Chicago the students heard a concert by the Chicago Symphony, went on a three-hour bus tour of the city, had dinner at both the Stock Yard Inn and the Kungsholm Scandanavian Smorgasbord Restaurant where they also saw a Miniature Opera production (puppets) of Humperdinck's *Hansel and Gretel* and attended a musical, *Funny Girl*, at the Schubert Theatre.

In January (1966) Netty Simons, director of programs for the American Composers Alliance and radio station WNYC in New York City, wrote to Mr. B requesting permission to use the IHS Band's April 28, 1965 premiere performances of Barney Childs's *Six Events for 58 Players* and Leslie Bassett's *Designs, Images and Textures* for broadcasts during 1966.

⁂

There were now forty-five students in the Symphony Band. It was conducted by Michael Walters, a part-time assistant in the band program. In 1966-67 Walters became Assistant Band Director at IHS.

The Concert Band's first concert of the spring semester took place at Ithaca College on March 24, 1966. Three band members were featured as soloists—Nancy Gibson played Vivaldi's *Concerto for Piccolo*; Bruce Corson, W. A. Mozart's *Concerto No. 1 for French Horn*; and Philip DeLibero, Alfred Reed's *Ballade* for alto saxophone and band. A month later the band performed its annual junior high school concert at Boynton Junior High. Margaret Weaver, school student secretary, sent Mr. B the following note after the concert.

> **Dear Mr. Battisti,**
>
> **Thank you and the band for coming to Boynton on April 13 and giving us the fine assembly that you did. Your band gave an excellent performance that was enjoyed by the whole school. It gives the band members at Boynton something to look forward to in the next few years. Our many thanks.**

Concerts by outstanding American wind bands and wind ensembles continued in 1966. On April 22 the United States Air Force Band, conducted by Col. Arnold Gabriel, presented a concert in Kulp Auditorium. Gabriel had strong ties to central New York State. He was born in Cortland, graduated from Ithaca College and served as Director of the Sampson Air Force Base Band near Seneca Falls, NY prior to his appointment as Commander/Conductor of the U. S. Air Force Band in Washington, D. C.

The band's second Contemporary Arts Festival took place on May 2–18, 1966. In addition to musical events, the festival included a modern dance program, a movie produced by IHS students, a folk song recital and an exhibition of paintings and photographs by IHS students. Below is the festival's schedule.

May 2	Ithaca College Jazz Lab concert
May 3	Recital of Ithaca High School student original compositions
May 4	Recital, Ithaca College Brass Quintet
May 5	Contemporary one-act play, Ithaca High School students
May 6	Recital, Don Jaeger, oboe
May 9	Open Rehearsal: Ithaca High School Band rehearsing premiere works for May 11, 1966 concert

May 10	Open Rehearsal: Ithaca High School Band, Lukas Foss, guest conductor (event cancelled)
May 11	Ithaca High School Spring concert, premiere of three new works
May 12	Modern Dance Program, Ithaca High School students
May 13	Recital, Shaul Ben-Meir, flute, and Edward Marks, piano
May 16	Movie produced by three Ithaca High School students
May 17	Recital of Contemporary Music, Ithaca High School students
May 18	Folk Song Recital, C. Swank
	Exhibit of paintings and photographs by Ithaca High School students in the foyer of Claude L. Kulp Auditorium.

The May 11, 1966 Spring Concert included three commissioned works, Walter Hartley's *Sinfonia No. 4*, Alec Wilder's *Concerto for Alto Saxophone* (Donald Sinta, soloist), and Warren Benson's *Recuerdo* (Donald Jaeger, Oboe/English horn, soloist). This was the second time three commissioned works were premiered on a concert program (see program, below).

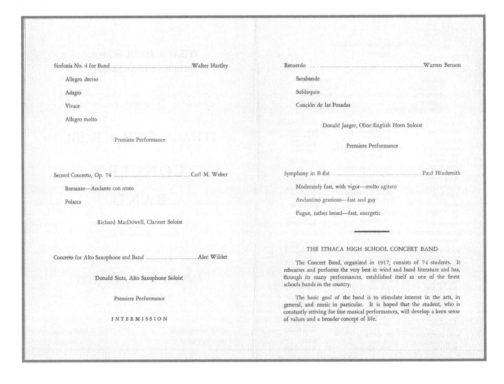

Walter Hartley was a composer recommended to Mr. B by Frederick Fennell (in 1957 he wrote his *Concerto for 23 Winds* for Fennell and the Eastman Wind Ensemble).

He composed *Sinfonia No. 4* in 1965 when he was in London on sabbatical leave from his teaching position at Davis and Elkins College. *Sinfonia No. 4* is a four-movement tonal work with many passages for solo players.

Hartley planned to be in Ithaca on May 10 so he could attend a rehearsal of *Sinfonia No. 4*. However, he got on a wrong flight and ended up in Hartford, CT. He finally made it to Ithaca the following day, just a few hours before the start of the concert. Hartley heard *Sinfonia No. 4* for the first time at the concert and was extremely pleased with the performance. On May 13 he wrote the following letter to the students.

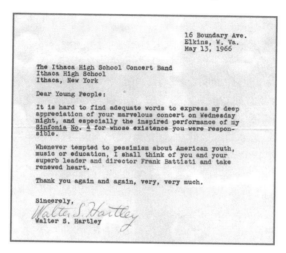

Donald Sinta's artistry and the band's excellent performance of *Entertainment III* on their Midwest Clinic concert inspired Alec Wilder to compose his *Concerto for Alto Saxophone and Band* for Sinta and the IHS Band. It is a very difficult piece for both the soloist and band—many hours were spent rehearsing it. Happily, the work paid off—the performance went well and everyone, including Wilder, was elated and jubilant. After the concert he wrote the following letter to Mr. B and the students.

Dear Mr. Battisti and the Members of the Band,

…**eight-year-olds are buying five rock-and-roll albums at one crack…television keeps insisting that we buy things we know we don't want, don't need and which go to pieces immediately so that we'll have to buy new ones; newspapers keep pumping us full of half-truths…No one's happy, everyone's confused, nobody trusts anybody, morality's gone down the drain–and Muzak goes on playing its pallid, pointless sounds everywhere but the graveyard.**

And that's about it.

Or so I thought before I went to Ithaca.

There I found a miracle.

I found a group of young people believing in something besides Westerns, Playboy, new cars, picture windows, The Rolling Stones, wrong chords on badly tuned guitars, status seeking, the stock market and Muzak. I found people who believed in something as sturdy as an oak and as delicate as a humming bird—music. I found people who were willing to work every day for the purpose of proving that something they believed in really could be made to live and breathe. I found people who knew that this miracle could never exist unless they forgot their own egos long enough to work with and listen to the sounds and ideas of others; people who were concerned with realizing the impossible; people who were eager to take chances, risk failure; who could never be accused of not trying; people who never remained static, but who grew just as surely as does a tree or a flower and, like a tree or flower, wouldn't stop growing until they burst into bloom.

And I also met a very remarkable head gardener, a man who knows soil and fertilizer, seeds and plants, sunlight and rain; a man who lives for miracles, who helps create them; whom I am proud to know, to whom I plan to bring plants for proper planting and fruition.

Occasionally Louis Ouzer joined Alec Wilder on his visits to IHS. Ouzer was a well-known photo artist whose photographs appeared regularly in numerous national magazines and publications. Sometimes he brought along his camera and took photos of band members at rehearsals. At right is one of oboe player Cheryl Bliss.

Warren Benson spent the 1965-66 school year as a visiting artist at the Interlochen Arts Academy in Michigan. While there he met Donald Jaeger, conductor of the wind ensemble and teacher of oboe. *Recuerdo*, the band's eleventh commissioned work and Benson's fifth piece for the band, was composed for Jaeger and the IHS Band. It was the second of Mr. B's hoped-for concerto-type pieces for solo woodwind/brass instruments and wind ensemble. Each movement of *Recuerdo* is scored for a different instrumentation—the first for solo oboe, brass and marimba, the second for English horn and percussion and the third for oboe, woodwinds, trumpet, marimba and string bass.

Like Hartley and Wilder, Benson was also very pleased with the premiere performance of his piece. On May 16, 1966 he wrote to Mr. B:

By now most everyone here has heard great things about Ithaca—*not* from me, but from Jaeger. I talk so much about it anyway that I thought they'd believe it easier from the lips of one of their own. Everyone comes up to me to say how much they've heard about "the great work in Ithaca" from "the horse's mouth–namely, Jaeger." For once I've kept my mouth shut and scored a big hit for IHS …The concert was most satisfying for me. It was the best sustained performance of a whole program that I can remember–and, in many ways, the most exciting…As much of the tape I was able to hear seemed to bear this out. I was impressed by the maturity of the band's sound and the solidity in all sections…

Enclosed with the letter was a poem for band members.

Dear IHS Band—a motley crew of diamonds, emeralds, gold, silver, roses, gentians, bluebirds, larks, clouds, zephyrs, fires, speed, coolness, slow ease, grace, pluck, affection, thrills, calm, momentum, insight, dreams, honey, Spring, cedar, fern, muscle, silk, dusk, fur, tears, crystal, magnetism, shadows, reflections, woods, rain, stars, sun, earth, moon, curls, spume, deer, ginger, heather, roots, sweat, trains, jet trails, bubbles, mint, dawn, love and music.

Thanks,
Warren Benson

A few days later (May 17, 1966), Mr. B received a letter from Donald Jaeger.

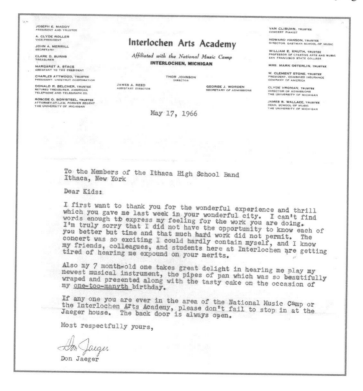

Many pictures were taken after the April 28, 1965 Spring Concert including the following two. The first is a group photo of the jubilant band members, guest soloists and commissioned composers. The second, of the happy composers and soloists back stage after the concert (left to right: Walter Hartley, Don Sinta, Warren Benson, Don Jaeger, Alec Wilder, Mr. B).

There were seven Bach Honor Society recitals during the 1966 spring semester—one in January, two each in February and March, and one in both April and May. Mr. B also organized informal "Listening Sessions" which were designed to help students better understand and appreciate music *as listeners*.

Frederick Fennell's annual visit on May 27, 1966 concluded the band's very busy and exciting year.

Reflection by Bruce Musgrave, Class of 1965

Band Director as Coach

The best that can be said of coaches applies *a fortiori* to Mr. B. Athletes have recalled the legendary coaches of whom they are fondest as "never getting on us for unavoidable errors, but always calling us on avoidable mistakes." Likewise, they have often recalled that what they learned from the coach was less about the particular sport than about more universal qualities of human endeavor. Or they have noted the habits of coaches who praised hustlers, defenders, assist-men, and other exemplars of team play in front of the team, and praised scorers and individually talented players in private—fully aware that both kinds of contributions are essential to the team's success, but that those contributions originate from very different places. Numerous other athletic shibboleths spring to mind, and ring curiously true to the philosophy of the IHS band: "Many have the will to win, but not many have the will to prepare to win." "Success is one percent inspiration and 99% perspiration." "There is no 'I' in team." "A chain is no stronger than its weakest link." "Practice doesn't make perfect—only *perfect* practice makes perfect." "Winning isn't the only thing; trying hard to win is everything."

In general, both coaches and band directors lead their charges through arduous preparations for game day/concerts (performing). With all the pains-taking preparations behind them, "the die is cast," "the Rubicon has been crossed," and various other platitudes all attest to the need to realize, "You got to dance with who brang ya," because there is no more time for getting ready—only the opportunity to motivate and refocus the "troops" by bringing them together in a new way. All that can remain is to summon, through oratory and body language, the very best that resides within them.

On a late-autumn Friday night, under the lights on Bredbenner Field, the IHS football stadium, two IHS band alumni got a telling first-hand glimpse of those similarities between a high-quality football program and a high-quality band program. At half-time of a game with Vestal, the two alums mounted to the top rail of the stands just vacated by the IHS Band, which had taken the field to perform. Also resting their backs on that top rail were several members of the Maine-Endwell football coaching staff, who were in attendance to scout an upcoming opponent. The band alums—Cornell students at the time—had spent their summer months mentoring the band members; they were eager to see how their charges had progressed a month or so later.

As the Little Red Band prepared to take the field, one of the Maine-Endwell coaches turned to the two alums and said, "I see you two are interested in this band. You're in for a real treat. This band is something special." Disingenuously, one of the alums (who at the time knew more or cared more about precious few things in life than the IHS band) replied, "Oh? What is it you like so much about this band?" The Maine-Endwell coach said something to the effect of, "These kids have such intensity, energy, and focus, that as football coaches we are in awe of the training, education program, and leadership that have brought all that out of them." Just then, the band entered the field through the goal posts at the south end of the stadium, chanting in unison, and executing a double-time quickstep, reminiscent of the rhythm and flare of the Southern University Jaguar Marching Band, and the precision and poise of the Coldstream Guard. The football coach said, "See what I mean?" When the first notes of the fanfare resounded in the cool night air, the football coach added, "Now that's what I'm talking about. This band director would be a great coach!"

Mr. B himself often quoted Vince Lombardi, who strove to be "so demanding, intense, and impossible to please in practice that the pressure of the game itself was a snap by comparison." He also borrowed liberally from then-Notre Dame football coach Ara Parseghian in ending his marching band rehearsals. Like Parseghian, Mr. B would bring the band together briefly at the end of rehearsal in a large but close huddle—for announcements, reminders, previews of upcoming obligations, and a positive reassertion that all the huffing and puffing of rehearsal was a vehicle to help the band accomplish together something of unequalled high quality. And like Parseghian, invariably at the end of those post-rehearsal remarks, throughout the mid '60s, he would punctuate the meeting with, "Right?"—to which the enrapt assembled band members would as one resound, "RIGHT!" And it was.

CHAPTER 14

The Beat Goes On: Yankee Stadium
Performance—Boston MENC
Concert—Mr. B's Final Concert, 1966–67

Marching Band

When the IHS "Little Red" Band gathered at band camp in late August (1966), 65 of its 150 members were new. Their presence fueled the band's enthusiasm and energy. By the end of band camp everyone was excited, energized and committed to making the 1966-67 IHS Band "the best, ever." (It was already the largest.)

Band members were wearing new uniforms (the previous uniforms were 28 years old) for their opening-day performance on September 25 in Binghamton, NY. Everyone knew the importance of this performance—it was the only opportunity to "run the show" prior to performing it in Yankee Stadium the following weekend. The students were nervous as they awaited halftime. When it came their performance started tentatively—the marching lacked energy and the playing was unfocused and not tight. Fortunately, about a minute into the show, everything came together and "jelled"—the rest of the performance was excellent.

The band arrived in New York City on Thursday evening, September 29, 1966. The next morning they rehearsed at Rye (NY) High School (a 45-minute drive northeast of NYC) for two hours. Returning to the City the students spent the remainder of the day sightseeing in New York City.

It was raining on Saturday morning (October 1) when the band left the hotel for their rehearsal in Yankee Stadium. Unable to get onto the field, Mr. B took the students to a covered section of the stadium where he had them run through the show mentally. The question on everyone's mind was—would it be raining tomorrow, the day of the performance?

Happily, Sunday (October 2) dawned sunny and clear. The students were up early, ate breakfast, packed and were on buses to Yankee Stadium by 9:15 AM.

Mr. B was hopeful that an early arrival at the stadium would prompt officials to allow the band to get onto the field and run through their show once. He was surprised and delighted when they told him he could use it for a whole hour. Following a very energized and productive rehearsal the students moved to seats along the sideline, ate box lunches and waited for half-time. When it arrived, they charged onto the field (see photo, below) and performed their 13-minute halftime show brilliantly—the routines were sharp and the playing dynamic and resonant.

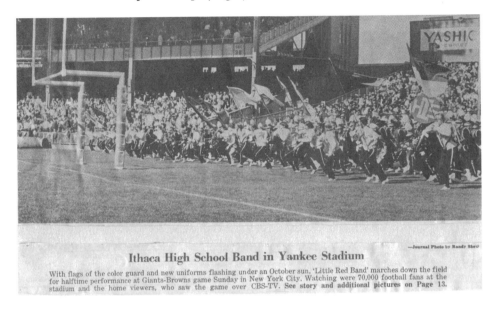

Ithaca High School Band in Yankee Stadium

With flags of the color guard and new uniforms flashing under an October sun, 'Little Red Band' marches down the field for halftime performance at Giants-Browns game Sunday in New York City. Watching were 70,000 football fans at the stadium and the home viewers, who saw the game over CBS-TV. **See story and additional pictures on Page 13.**

(Ithaca Journal, October 3, 1966, front-page photo)

On October 8, 1966 *The Ithaca Journal* ran a full page photo-essay about the band's New York experience. ("After a Dismal Saturday in New York…A BIG, BRIGHT, BEAUTIFUL DAY FOR IHS BAND.") The three photos that follow are from the story:

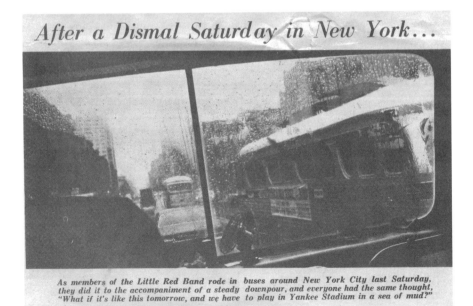

As members of the Little Red Band rode in buses around New York City last Saturday, they did it to the accompaniment of a steady downpour, and everyone had the same thought, "What if it's like this tomorrow, and we have to play in Yankee Stadium in a sea of mud?"

It was a dismal day Saturday, with rain falling steadily. Under cover in Yankee stadium, band members listen as Battisti goes over the plans for Sunday with them, and watch as rain beats against the plastic that covers the stadium playing field.

...A Big, Bright Beautiful Day For IHS Band

But they needn't have worried, because Sunday was clear and bright and 70,000 fans looked on at the stadium as the band, led here by its color guard, took the field for the halftime show at the Giants-Browns pro football game.

A band parent took the following photograph of the band performing a dance routine in Yankee Stadium as seen on TV screens in Ithaca and throughout the nation (televised by CBS).

The following are three of the many letters received by Mr. B congratulating the band on their Yankee Stadium performance.

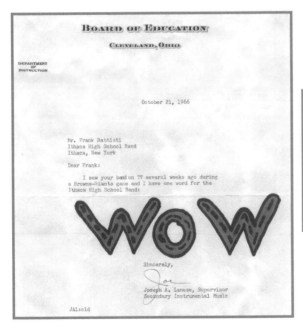

```
              WRIGHT STATE CAMPUS
                    MIAMI UNIVERSITY
                 THE OHIO STATE UNIVERSITY


                                      COLONEL GLENN HIGHWAY
                                       DAYTON, OHIO 45431
                                       Phone 513-426-6650



                                      October 3, 1966



      Mr. Frank Battista
      Ithaca High School
      Ithaca, New York

      Dear Mr. Battista:

      You may not remember me by name--I was Neal Glenn's cohort at the
      Music Institute in Iowa City this past summer.  I am writing to
      tell you how thrilled I was with your band's performance at the
      Brown-Giant football game yesterday.  It was positively the most
      thrilling football show I've seen given by a high school band--it
      was well-planned, cleanly and precisely executed, and sounded great,
      even on television.  I also appreciated the quality of the music,
      and the student announcer.

      Here's wishing you continued success.

      Sincerely,


      Robert Glidden
      Assistant Professor of Music
      Band Director

      RG:ls
```

"Howie" Myer was the Music Department Building custodian (and an honorary IHS Band member). He contributed much to the success of the band and took great pride in his work, especially in the precise way he arranged chairs, music stands and equipment for band rehearsals and concerts.

Leone Buyse, a former band member/camp counselor and, in 1966, a student at the Eastman School of Music wrote,

> BRAVO! Sunday afternoon's performance left me proud, thrilled astonished, misty—you name it. That was my first exposure to the "new" band…It's huge! Nevertheless, the lines seemed actually straighter than ever before…Since Sunday I've thought often of the tremendous, well-earned sense of accomplishment you and the kids are now able to glow in. (October 5, 1966)

Anthony C. DeGiacomo, President of the Ithaca Chamber of Commerce, extended the Chamber's congratulations to the band.

> On behalf of the Ithaca Chamber of Commerce and the entire community, I would like to commend you and your organization for the outstanding performance at Yankee Stadium last Sunday. The marching maneuvers were sharp and precise and the musical executions outstanding. (October 4, 1966)

A video recording of a portion of the band's 1966 Yankee Stadium performance can be viewed on the 2006 IHS Band Reunion DVD.

ॐ ॐ

Below are two photos of the band performing at IHS football games during fall 1966.

ॐ ॐ

A fire in Claude L. Kulp Auditorium on Thursday afternoon, October 27, 2006 caused extensive smoke and water damage throughout the Music Department building. It was caused by a short in the stage electrical system, which ignited the overhang of the stage curtain. None of the individual student-owned instruments were damaged but some of the large school-owned instruments were. In the photo, below, Mr. B is seen talking to IHS Band students outside the burning Music Department building. (*Ithaca Journal*, October 28, 1966).

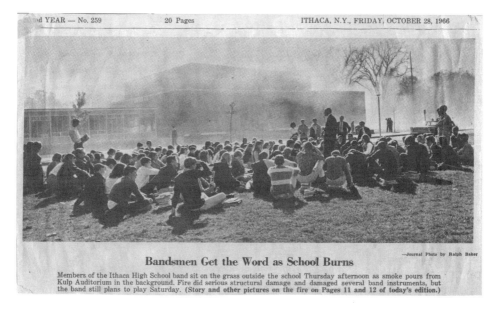

d YEAR — No. 259   20 Pages   ITHACA, N.Y., FRIDAY, OCTOBER 28, 1966

—Journal Photo by Ralph Baker

Bandsmen Get the Word as School Burns

Members of the Ithaca High School band sit on the grass outside the school Thursday afternoon as smoke pours from Kulp Auditorium in the background. Fire did serious structural damage and damaged several band instruments, but the band still plans to play Saturday. (Story and other pictures on the fire on Pages 11 and 12 of today's edition.)

The band's new uniforms were rescued from damage when John Whitney, high school orchestra conductor, rushed to the storage room and wheeled the racks of uniforms out of the building. A local dry cleaning company employee, driving nearby, heard about the fire on the radio, rushed to the school, picked up the uniforms and took them away in his van. It was impossible to have them cleaned in time for the band's weekend performance, so students wore improvised uniforms consisting of a white shirt, black trousers, and white shoes (can be seen on the 2006 IHS Band Reunion DVD).

The photos on the next page show (left to right), Mr. B carrying a sousaphone out of the Music building, cleanup workers placing bass drums and sousaphones on the lawn outside the Music building and the damaged rehearsal room (*Ithaca Journal*, October 29, 1966).

Band instruments and Band Room suffered heat, smoke and water damage in Kulp Auditorium fire Thursday.

Severe Ithaca High Fire Confined To Auditorium; Cause Still Sought

The fire damage made Kulp Auditorium unusable. However, a speedy cleanup of the other areas of the building made them usable in a few days.

Concert Band

On December 19, 1966, Mr. B wrote the following note to IHS Band students.

> I appreciate your friendship; your willingness and desire to share…your time and energy in creating things we find valuable, beautiful and exciting; your willingness to risk …your openness to musical experiences which are new and different…your confidence in my ability as a teacher and a musician.
>
> I love you all and music. Thank you…for being so beautiful.

The 1967 IHS Concert Band schedule:

February 10–13, 1967	Trip to Boston for MENC Performance	Boston
March 15, 1967	DeWitt Junior High Concert	Ithaca
March 22, 1967	Band Parents' Night	Ithaca
April 12, 1967	IHS Symphony Band Concert	Ithaca
April 19, 1967	IHS Assembly programs, Armando Ghitalla, trumpet	Ithaca
April 20, 1967	IHS Percussion Ensemble	Ithaca
May 2, 1967	University of Michigan Symphony Band	Ithaca
May 5–19, 1967	IHS Band Contemporary Music Festival	Ithaca
May 5, 1967	Trip to Eastman Wind Ensemble Concert	Rochester

May 17, 1967	Spring Concert—IHS Band's 50th Anniversary Concert	Ithaca
May 19, 1967	Fennell visit to IHS Band and Band Banquet	Ithaca
May 26, 1967	Combined IHS Symphony and Concert Band Concert for National Honor Society's Honduras Project	Ithaca

(Note: In addition to the events listed above, band members performed on twelve Bach Honor Society and band solo recitals during the 1967 spring semester.)

The IHS Concert Band traveled to Boston, MA on February 9, 1967 to perform at the Eastern Division Meeting of the Music Educators National Conference (MENC). While there, they also performed two other concerts on Friday, February 10—one at Brookline High School (bus drivers had to fight their way through a snow storm to get there), the other at Boston University's School of Music.

The next morning (Saturday, February 11), Mr. B rehearsed the band for two hours at the hotel. The students spent the afternoon sightseeing in Boston. That evening everyone, except a few die-hard hockey fans who went to a Boston Bruins NHL game at Boston Garden, attended a concert by the Boston Symphony Orchestra in Symphony Hall.

The band's MENC concert took place on Sunday afternoon, February 12, at 3:00 PM in the main ballroom of the Boston Sheraton Hotel. The program consisted of five IHS Band-commissioned works including the world-premiere performances of John Huggler's *Celebration, Op. 68* and Warren Benson's *Helix*, Harvey Phillips, tuba soloist (other pieces on the program were Vincent Persichetti's *Serenade for Band*, Armand Russell's *Theme and Fantasia*, Warren Benson's *Star-Edge*, Donald Sinta, alto saxophone soloist, and Herbert Bielawa's *Prisms* for pre-recorded electronic sounds and band). See program, at right.

About a thousand music educators crowded into the hotel's ballroom to hear the concert (those

Program

PRISMS ....Herbert Bielawa

STAR-EDGE ....Warren Benson
Mr. Donald Sinta, *Alto Saxophone Soloist*
This work was commissioned by the Ithaca High School Band and premiered in May 1964.

SERENADE FOR BAND ....Vincent Persichetti
Pastoral
Humoreske
Nocturne
Intermezzo
Capriccio
This work was commissioned by the Ithaca High School Band and premiered in April 1961.

CELEBRATION, OP. 68 ....John Huggler
This work was commissioned by Kappa Gamma Psi, National Music Fraternity and dedicated to the Ithaca High School Band. This is the premiere performance of this work.

THEME AND FANTASIA ....Armand Russell
This work was commissioned by the Ithaca High School Band and premiered in May 1963.

Helix ....Warren Benson
Dancing
Singing
Mr. Harvey Phillips, *Tuba Soloist*
This work was written for and dedicated to Mr. Phillips. This is the premier performance of this piece.

not able to get in listened to it on large speakers in an adjacent room). The photo, below, shows Mr. B and band members accepting the audience's applause after performing one of the pieces on the program.

At the end of the performance the band received a *very long* standing ovation.

Music critic Alan Raph reviewed the concert for the *National Student Musician* (March 1967 issue). See below.

> One of the highlights of the recent MENC (Eastern Division) Conference in Boston was the performance of the Ithaca High School Band directed by Frank L. Battisti. The band of some 65 young and dedicated players performed a program of six contemporary works for concert band. Only one of these works was not specially commissioned by the school band and associated organizations. Two of the works were premiere performances.
>
> While members of the audience had their own reactions to the music, and comments varied as personal preference, all selections were received with interest and obvious respect for the level of performance by this excellent ensemble. It was evident that a great deal of rehearsal time has gone into the shaping of the Ithaca H. S. Band as well as a sincere dedication on the part of the members and conductor.
>
> Mr. Battisti and his associates work hard in developing fine players, and in shaping their collective efforts in a fine musical organization such as the Ithaca High School Band. I doubt if there is any high school band in

existence today that would sound substantially better than this one. There are other organizations that might sound as well in similar types of programs, and there are other bands that would sound as impressive with their own special musical focus, but the Ithaca band has utilized as many capabilities of high school students as I have ever heard anywhere. Other band directors upon hearing such a band might well become inspired to reach higher; on the other hand perhaps hearing this performance can have a depressing effect on those directors who can never hope to have the physical facilities of the band to work with (equipment, rehearsal-practice rooms, sponsorship, etc.) and perhaps a director will feel the need to rationalize his own position. The point is that with each performance of the Ithaca band and those like it, everyone concerned with the broader aspects of musical growth and youngsters' potential will have the first hand knowledge that such a degree of competence is possible and therefore perhaps gear their sights to this potential rather than the "fun and games" approach that often goes on long past the "fun and games" age and interest. The members of the Ithaca H. S. Band, Mr. Battisti and all others concerned with the formation and development of this wonderful ensemble are to be highly complimented on their fine showing.

Mr. B received many letters praising the band's MENC concert performance. Below are excerpts from seven of them.

Mr. Robert A. Meseroll, Music Director, Moorestown Township Pubic School, Moorestown, NJ wrote,

> …It goes, without saying, that you and your students have achieved a very high standard of performing ability. This reflects the high standards and the Music Education program in your school…My one wish, upon hearing your students was, "if only my students could be here to hear and see this program."

Mr. Lawrence Eisman, Assistant Professor of Music at Queens College in Flushing, NY, expressed his

> …deepest appreciation, and slight case of envy, for the magnificent performance of your band at the recent MENC convention in Boston.

[Later in his letter Eisman inquired about the possibility of using the IHS Band's performance of Herbert Bielawa's *Prisms* in a junior high school general music book he was preparing for publication.]

Constance Price, Hartford, CT Public High School, stated that she

> …thoroughly enjoyed the performance of the Ithaca High School Concert Band during the MENC Eastern Conference. The band's performance of *Prisms* left me speechless. Believe it or not, your performing group opened my ears to the beauty found in [contemporary music].

William L. Gagnon, Jr., President of Kappa Gamma Psi, National Music Fraternity, commented that

> For years I have heard many wonderful things about the Ithaca High School Band. I can say in all honesty that I have never heard any band—high school or college—perform as beautifully as your performance in Boston.

Cole Biasini, Head, Music Department, Ramapo Central School District No 2, Spring Valley, NY wrote,

> I can't tell you how much I enjoyed your Concert Band in performance at the recent MENC Eastern Division Conference. The performance was brilliant !!

Clif Symons, Band Director, Greenfield, MA Public Schools, congratulated the band on their

> ...amazing performance at the Eastern Conference. The work that you are doing must rank with the very best being done anywhere...please tell the students that at least one man in the profession thinks they are the best he has ever heard.

George R. Borich, Chariman, Music Department, Lake Forest High School, Lake Forest, IL, stated that he

> ...was impressed by many things at the meeting, but mostly by the superb concert presented by...the Ithaca High School Concert Band. Congratulations !!...thanks for the great concert and the inspiring thoughts it provoked.

Prisms by Herbert Bielawa is probably the first piece ever written for high school band in which pre-recorded electronic sounds are used with traditional concert band sonorities. Bielawa composed the piece in 1964-65 when he was an MENC-Ford Foundation composer-in-residence in the Spring Branch Independent School System in Houston, TX. Two large speakers, one on each side of the band, projected the pre-recorded stereo sounds into the hall during the performance. The audience's response to Bielawa's piece was *extremely* enthusiastic—it became the talk of the conference.

John Huggler, composer of *Celebration, Op. 68*, was the Boston Symphony Orchestra's composer-in-residence in 1967. Huggler lived in Ithaca in 1964-65 composing music and reviewing concerts for *The Ithaca Journal*. *Celebration, Op. 68*, is a *very* difficult and complex work (the band spent many hours rehearsing it). Huggler attended the work's premiere and afterwards wrote the following message to Mr. B and the band members.

> It was a pleasure writing the piece for the band, and I must say that you did, I think, a marvelous job of playing, considering especially that it was difficult and you had a relatively short time to prepare it. I had thought at times during the writing of the piece that it must be made simpler, and I found myself unable to get interested in doing something about it: largely, I must admit because I was interested in the way it was shaping up.
>
> [Congratulations] on the remarkable things you are doing and the wonderful spirit in which they are done.

Warren Benson's *Helix* for tuba and band was the IHS Band's third commissioned work for a solo wind instrument and concert band. It is dedicated to tuba virtuoso Harvey Phillips and the IHS Band. One of the unusual features of the work is Benson's use of tuned clay flower pots in its instrumentation. Mr. B searched many garden stores in and around Ithaca before finding ones that sounded at the pitches specified in the score. Benson was unable to attend the premiere performance of *Helix* in Boston due to illness—everyone was very disappointed.

The IHS Jazz Ensemble, which began as a "dance band" in the late 1950s, was now an important component in the IHS Band program. Below is a photo of the 1967 Jazz Ensemble, which was directed by IHS orchestra conductor John Whitney.

❧ ❧

The band's third Contemporary Music Festival was held from May 4–19, 1967 (see schedule, below).

May 4	Recital of original compositions by Ithaca High School students
May 5	Trip to Rochester, NY for an Eastman Wind Ensemble Concert, program to include Walter Hartley's *Sinfonia No. 4* (Ithaca High School Band-commissioned work)
My 9	Recital of Brass Music
May 11	Recital of Contemporary Music
May 15	Open rehearsal: Ithaca High School Concert Band with guests Fennell, Ward, Persichetti, Borden, Benson, Phillips
May 16	Open rehearsal with guests listed above
May 17	Ithaca High School Band Spring Concert
May 19	Bach Honor Society Induction and Recital

Three more commissioned works were premiered on the band's 50th-Anniversary Spring Concert on May 17, 1967—Vincent Persichetti's *Turn Not Thy Face*; Robert Ward's *Fiesta Processional*; and David Bordon's *All-American; Teenage; Lovesongs*. An article in the May 10, 1967 edition of *The Ithaca Journal* by reporter Jane Marcham, "**Work Commissioned in Kennedy's Memory Featured in IHS Concert**," contained information about these composers and their works. (see at right)

The other pieces on the program were Warren Benson's *The Leaves Are Falling* and *Helix*, Herbert Bielawa's *Prisms* and Percy Grainger's *Lincolnshire Posy* guest conducted by Frederick Fennell. Persichetti, Ward and Borden were all present for the premiere performances of their pieces. The photo, below, shows (left to right) Vincent Persichetti, Warren Benson, David Borden, Robert Ward, Mr. B and Frederick Fennell standing outside the IHS Music Building during a break in one of the band's rehearsals.

Scheduled Next Wednesday

Work Commissioned in Kennedy's Memory Featured in IHS Concert

By JANE MARCHAM
Journal Staff Writer

A work commissioned by the Ithaca High School Band in memory of John F. Kennedy will be performed for the first time at the Concert Band's spring concert, set for 8 p.m. Wednesday, May 17, in Ford Auditorium at Ithaca College.

Composer Vincent Persichetti, a leading figure in contemporary music, will be present to hear the premiere of his chorale prelude, "Turn Not Thy Face."

So will composers Robert Ward, a Pulitzer winner, and David Borden and Warren Benson, whose works also will receive first performances.

The band was in New York City awaiting a football game half-time performance in Yankee Stadium when President Kennedy was assassinated.

The performance was canceled, and upon their return to Ithaca the band members decided to commission the Persichetti memorial. A copy of the score has been sent to Mrs. Kennedy.

Persichetti is a prolific composer as well as a virtuoso performer, scholar, teacher a n d author. More than 80 of his compositions have been published. They include works in every genre and are frequently performed. He is chairman of composition at the Juilliard School of Music and publications director at Elkan-Vogel Music Co. in Philadelphia.

The Ward premiere is "Fiesta Processional". Robert Ward won the Pulitzer Prize in music in 1962 and the New York Music Critics Circle Citation in 1962 for his opera, "The Crucible". He has taught at Juilliard, is executive vice president and managing editor of Galaxy Music Corp. and Highgate Press, and is a past president of the American Composers Alliance.

David Borden's "All-American; Teenage; Lovesongs" will receive its first complete performance. He is composer-in-residence at Ithaca High School under a grant from the Ford Foundation administered by the Music Educators National Con-

VINCENT PERSICHETTI   **ROBERT WARD**

ference. Borden has received degrees from Eastman School of Music and Harvard University, where he studied composition under Leon Kirchner, and was in Berlin on a Fulbright grant last year.

Two compositions by Warren Benson, composer-in-residence at Ithaca College, will be performed. They are "The Leaves Are Falling", composed in 1963, and "Helix" which will have its first Ithaca performance.

"Helix" was dedicated to Harvey Phillips of the New York Brass Quintet, and he will be tuba soloist with the band in Wednesday's performance. Phillips has performed at Ithaca and throughout the world as soloist, in chamber music and with orchestras, and will become vice president of the New England Conservatory of Music next year.

Frank L. Battisti is the band's director. A guest conductor on the program will be Frederick Fennell of the University of Miami, who has had a long association with the Ithaca band.

Fennell, who will conduct Percy Grainger's suite "Lincolnshire Posy", is founder a n d former conductor of the Eastman Wind Ensemble, and now is a professor and conductor at Miami. He has made many recordings and has guest-conducted in nearly every state.

Tickets for the concert will be available at the door, and season passes for music department concerts may be used for admission.

The Gala May 17, 1967 Spring Concert was performed at Ithaca College's Ford Hall (see program, below).

PROGRAM

Prisms . . . . Herbert Bielawa

Herbert Bielawa is presently Assistant Professor of Music at San Francisco State College, teaching theory and composition. He holds degrees in Music from the University of Illinois and the University of Southern California. His composition teachers include Darius Milhaud, Elliott Carter, Nadia Boulanger, Lukas Foss, Roger Session and Ingolf Dahl. He was composer-in-residence, under a Ford Foundation Grant, in the Spring Branch Independent School System, Houston, Texas in 1964-65.

"Prisms" is a work which combines electronic sounds with the colors of the wind band medium.

Turn Not Thy Face (Chorale Prelude) . . . . Vincent Persichetti
PREMIERE PERFORMANCE

This work commissioned by the 1963-64 Ithaca High School Band in memory of President John F. Kennedy.

Vincent Persichetti has established himself as one of the leading figures in contemporary American music. He is a virtuoso performer, scholar, artist teacher and the author of one of the great books on the art of music. This prolific composer has written a major literature including works in almost every genre. His music is regularly performed both here and abroad. Over 80 of his compositions have been published, and his works have been recorded by the leading record companies. Mr. Persichetti headed the composition department of the Philadelphia Conservatory from 1942-62. In 1947 he joined the faculty of the Juilliard School of Music and is presently head of its composition department. Since 1952 he has been director of publications at Elkan-Vogel Music Company.

"Turn Not Thy Face" was written by Mr. Persichetti on a commission from the 1963-64 Ithaca High School Band. On Friday, November 22, 1963 the members of the I.H.S. Band were in New York City awaiting their scheduled Sunday performance in Yankee Stadium. The tragedy of President Kennedy's assassination in Dallas brought the trip to an abrupt halt and the band returned home on Saturday night. Soon after their return the members decided to commission a work to honor the memory of John F. Kennedy. Tonight we present the premiere performance of this work.

This work is based on the eleventh hymn, "O Lord, Turn not Thy Face From Them", from Mr. Persichetti's Hymns and Responses for the Church Year.

All-American; Teenage; Lovesongs . . . . David Borden
Before
All-American
;
Teenage
;
Lovesongs
After
PREMIERE PERFORMANCE

Mr. David Borden is the MENC-Ford Foundation Composer-in-Residence in the Ithaca City School District. He holds degrees from the Eastman School of Music and Harvard University, where he studied with Leon Kirchner. During the 1965-66 academic year, he was in Berlin, Germany on a Fulbright study grant.

Concerning the work to be premiered tonight, the composer states: "There is not much one can say about a piece of music, aside from its technical or structural idiosyncrasies. The music and only the music contains the valuable information, not verbal description. Emerson said, "No man can quite emancipate himself from his age and country, or produce a model in which the education, the religion, the politics, usages and arts of his times shall have no share. Though he were never so original, never so wilful and fantastic, he cannot wipe out of his work every trace of the thoughts amidst which it grew." This piece reflects a desire on my part to explicitly display the "...age and country..." which helped shape its content. Contained within it are sounds, voices and melodies all of us are familiar with; it's the combination that baffles us."

Fiesta Processional . . . . Robert Ward
PREMIERE PERFORMANCE

Robert Ward attended the Eastman School of Music, where he majored in composition under Bernard Rogers and Howard Hanson. He went on to the Juilliard Graduate School, studying composition with Frederick Jacobi and conducting with Albert Stoessell and Edgar Schenkman. In 1942, he worked with Aaron Copland at the Berkshire Music Center. Mr. Ward has taught at the Juilliard School of Music, where he was also Assistant to the President from 1954-56, and at Columbia University. From 1952-55 he served as Music Director of the Third Street Music School Settlement. At present, he is Executive Vice President and Managing Editor of Galaxy Music Corporation and Highgate Press, as well as a past Chairman of the Board of Directors and a Past President of the American Composers Alliance. In 1964-65 he was chosen to serve on the Joint Committee of the Contemporary Music Project for Creativity in Music Education, administered by the Music Educators National Conference. In 1962, Mr. Ward received both the Pulitzer Prize in Music and the New York Critics Circle Citation for his opera, "The Crucible".

INTERMISSION

Helix . . . . Warren Benson

Dancing
Singing
                              Mr. Harvey Phillips, Tuba Soloist

       Warren Benson is composer-in-residence and Professor of Music at the Ithaca College School of Music in Ithaca, New York. He has many published works to his credit. During the 1965-66 academic year, he conducted a MENC-Ford Foundation Contemporary Music Project, "Learning Through Creativity", at the Interlochen Arts Academy. Mr. Benson is a graduate of the University of Michigan and a former timpanist with the Detroit Symphony Orchestra, Ford Sunday Evening Hour Orchestra and the Brevard Music Festival Orchestra. He has received six ASCAP Awards for Serious Music and was a resident composer at the MacDowell Colony in 1955 and 1963.

       "Helix" was composed by Mr. Benson last fall. It was given its premiere performance by Mr. Phillips and the Ithaca High School Concert Band at the Music Educators' National Conference in Boston, Massachusetts last February.

       Harvey Phillips is the world's greatest tuba virtuoso. He has performed throughout the world as a soloist, chamber music player, and orchestra performer. As a member of the New York Brass Quintet, he has helped gain new acceptance for brass chamber music throughout the world. During the 1966-67 academic year, Mr. Phillips is serving as an administrative assistant in the Concert Department and member of the Association of College and University Managers (ACUCM) at Rutgers State University of New Jersey.

Lincolnshire Posy . . . . Percy Grainger

Dublin Bay
Harkstow Grange
Rufford Park Poachers
The Brisk Young Sailor (returned to wed his True Love)
Lord Melbourne
The Lost Lady Found

                       Dr. Frederick Fennell, Guest Conductor

       Percy Grainger (1882-1961), celebrated pianist and composer, was born in Melbourne, Australia. In 1914 Grainger settled in the United States and from 1940 he lived mostly in White Plains, New York. His philosophy of life and art calls for the widest communion of peoples and opinions. Grainger made a profound study of folk music and a determined effort to recreate in art music, the free flow of instinctive songs of the people.

       "Lincolnshire Posy" is Mr. Grainger's most impressive work for wind instruments. Grainger writes "that 'Lincolnshire Posy,' as a whole work, was conceived and scored by me direct for wind band early in 1937. This bunch of "musical wildflowers" (hence the title "Lincolnshire Posy") is based on folksongs collected in Lincolnshire, England, and the work is dedicated to the old folk singers who sang so sweetly to me. Indeed, each number is intended to be a kind of musical portrait of the singer's personality no less than of his habits of song..."

       Dr. Frederick Fennell is conductor of the University of Miami Symphony Orchestra and Wind Ensemble at Coral Gables and Professor of Conducting in the University's School of Music. Dr. Fennell's background includes a long and distinguished career as a conductor at the Eastman School of Music of the University of Rochester, where he founded the famous Eastman Wind Ensemble and Associate Music Director of the Minneapolis Symphony Orchestra for two seasons. He is one of the country's most sought after guest conductors and annually appears with many professional symphony orchestras and high school and university festival bands and orchestras. Dr. Fennell's outstanding recordings for Mercury Records have been a model for educators everywhere for over a decade.

The Leaves Are Falling . . . . Warren Benson
       This work was inspired by the poem HERBST (Autumn) from <u>Buch der Lieder</u> by Rainer Maria Rilke. Rather than attempting the impossible, namely to describe with words what could only be expressed with music, the poem itself is reprinted here in lieu of any other form of introduction.

                        AUTUMN

The leaves are falling, falling as from way off,
as though far gardens withered in the skies;
they are falling with denying gestures.

And in the nights the heavy earth is falling
from all the stars down into loneliness.

We are all falling. This hand falls.
And look at others: it is in them all.

And yet, there is one who holds this falling
endlessly, gently in his hands.

Vincent Persichetti's *Turn Not Thy Face* is a quiet, reflective work. It was commissioned by the band in 1963 as a memorial to President John F. Kennedy (the IHS Band was in New York City in November 1963 when Kennedy was assassinated). Senator Robert Kennedy, the President's brother, was invited to attend the premiere performance of the piece but congressional duties in Washington, DC prevented him from doing so.

Besides composing music, David Borden was also an excellent illustrator. Below is a poster-invitation he created for the premiere performance of *All-American; Teenage; Lovesongs* (poster-invitation originally in color).

All-Ameican; Teenage; Lovesongs is a very complex collage-type piece which calls for pre-recorded electronic sounds and transistor radios. The texture of the piece is often very dense and dissonant (the final chord of the piece contains every tone in a three and one-third octave range [43 consecutive pitches]). David Borden provided the following note about the piece:

> There is not much one can say about a piece of music aside from its technical and structural idiosyncrasies. The music and only the music contains the valuable information, not verbal description. Emerson said, "No man can quite emancipate himself from his age and country, or produce a model in which the education, the religion, the politics, usages and arts of his times shall have no share. Though he were never so original, never so willful and fantastic, he cannot wipe out of his work, every trace of the thoughts amidst which it grew." This piece reflects a desire on my part to explicitly display the "…age and country…the education, the religion, the politics…" which helped shape its content. Contained within it are sounds, voices and melodies all of us are familiar with; it's the combination that baffles us.

Robert Ward's *Fiesta Processional* is a short overture-like work and the composer's first piece for high school band. In 1966 Ward won the Pulitzer Prize in Music for his opera, *The Crucible*, which is based on Arthur Miller's play of the same name. Students in two English Literature classes were reading *The Crucible* when Ward visited IHS. They invited him to talk to them about the challenges he faced in setting Miller's play to music.

Even though Frederick Fennell had visited the IHS Band numerous times, his performance of *Lincolnshire Posy* on the Spring Concert was his first (and only) appearance with the band on a public concert in Ithaca (his other visits were day-long rehearsals with the band). It also marked the band's first complete performance of *Lincolnshire Posy*. Previously only selected movements from the piece had been performed on concert programs.

The last work on the program, *The Leaves are Falling*, was commissioned for the IHS Band by Kappa Gamma Psi (national music fraternity) in 1964. It was fitting that the final work Mr. B conducted with the IHS Band was one composed by his long-time mentor and friend, Warren Benson.

(Note: The other two pieces on the 1967 Spring Concert, *Prisms* by Herbert Bielawa and *Helix* by Warren Benson were discussed earlier in this chapter.)

Shown below are, on the left, Frederick Fennell conducting *Lincolnshire Posy*; on the right, (left to right) Harvey Phillips, Robert Ward, Frederick Fennell, Warren Benson, David Borden, Vincent Persichetti and Mr. B conversing on Ford Hall stage after the Spring Concert. (*Ithaca Journal* photos, May 18, 1967)

Thursday, May 18, 1967   ITHACA JOURNAL   3

On-Stage for Ithaca High Band's 50th Birthday: Concert and Congratulations

Guest conductor Frederick Fennell leads the Ithaca High School Concert Band at its 50th anniversary spring concert in Ford Auditorium Wednesday night. Capacity audience of 800 greeted an all-contemporary program, including electronic music and four premieres, and band and composers applauded each other. Assembling for picture-taking formalities afterwards are, from left, tuba soloist Harvey Phillips, Pulitzer award-winning composer Robert Ward, Fennell, Ithaca College composer-in-residence Warren Benson, Ithaca school composer-in-residence David Borden, composer Vincent Persichetti and Frank Battisti, the band director. Compositions by Ward, Benson, Borden and Persichetti received first performances.

Frederick Fennell commented on the uniqueness of the 1967 Spring Concert in a note to Mr. B on May 24, 1967.

> **To say that the events [of the concert] were memorable is to speak in small truths about mountainous facts. Truly, Frank, that concert would simply not have been possible anywhere else but Ithaca.**

He also wrote a letter to band members.

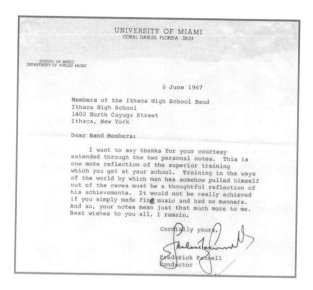

The band commissioned four more composers to write works for them in 1967—Karel Husa, Gunther Schuller, Alvin Etler, and Ernst Krenek. These commissions were withdrawn when Mr. B left Ithaca High School in November 1967.

Three previous IHS Band-commissioned works were published in 1967: Leslie Bassett's *Designs, Images and Textures* by C. F. Peters; Robert Ward's *Fiesta Processional* by Galaxy Music; and Vincent Persichetti's *Turn Not Thy Face* by Elkan-Vogel.

The Symphony Band continued to grow in size and especially in the quality of its performances. The 58-member ensemble was conducted by Michael Walters, Assistant IHS Band Director (see photo, below).

The final event of the year was an outdoor concert performed by the combined Concert and Symphony Bands on May 26, 1967 to raise money for the National Honor Society's Honduras relief project.

Reflection by Bruce Musgrave, Class of 1965

Competition and Cooperation

A convenient way of looking at educational enterprises divides them into competitive and cooperative activities. Convenient though those handles may be, the realities of any learning experience, or for that matter of any group undertaking whatsoever, seem to defy pat categorization as merely competitive or cooperative. Accordingly, the ethos of the IHS Band under Frank Battisti blended complex elements of both traits.

From day one, the band members *appeared* to be in competition with one another; membership in the Concert Band was, after all, by audition. But it quickly became clear to everyone involved that the initial evaluation of players was an expedient to seating them in their sections and getting quickly down to work rather than a competitive gambit to pit them against one another, or ensure survival of the fittest. On the contrary, everyone knew full well that for the band to prosper, the least fit had to excel. What everyone understood so well that no one bothered to express it was that the real competition was with the self . . . to reach the individual's fullest potential, and thereby enable the ensemble to excel.

There was little question that the better player would earn the lead chair, and no one resented even slightly that reality, which seemed only just. What was far more important to everyone than who sat first chair was the ongoing competition with the self—am I doing all I can be doing to optimize my playing and personal growth? The question was never, "Am I better than so-and-so?" but always, "Am I justifying my presence in this organization whose existence is so precious to me and my fellow band members?" Not external competition, but the test of how fully one could achieve within the limits of individual talent was what motivated everyone.

In fact, in all ways, the band was highly averse to external competition. Neither the Marching Band nor the Concert Band nor any individual students ever went to contests or adjudications—the foundation of numerous instrumental programs elsewhere. Mr. B clearly preferred that his bands compete against their own perceived standards of excellence, against the demands and challenges posed by the music itself, and against his own aesthetic ideals. There was also a degree of relativism to his standards: a player of modest ability could be expected to achieve a solidly workmanlike performance, but clearly gifted players had to surpass that standard to satisfy their director.

If the attitude of the program toward competition was unorthodox, the orientation toward cooperation was unequivocal. Mr. B expected cooperation, he devised tasks that were impossible to achieve without it (both in Marching Band and Concert Band, and especially in the non-musical enterprises that supported both bands), he lauded clearly cooperative effort, and he demanded cooperation when it was absent. Nowhere were those demands more apparent than in the rehearsal of the full ensemble. He saved his most lavish praise for those whose voices continued harmoniously what others had begun, and he reserved his most scathing admonishments for those who played out without listening sensitively to those around them.

The message was plain: *Cooperate* fully with those around you as you *compete* against the standard of the best that you can be. Then, if we are all equal to that competition with the self, and if we all work together for the common good, we have the chance of achieving together sublime moments that others may not have managed to contemplate.

PART IV   Departure and Reunion

CHAPTER **15**   Departure:
Mr. B Leaves IHS, 1967

ccording to the liner notes on the back of the 1967 IHS Marching Band LP recording, band camp was "an unbelievably productive and exciting week." The 1967 "Little Red" Band was the largest ever, 158 members including 130 student musicians, 2 drum majors, 20 color guards, and 6 majorettes.

The following three photos were taken at band camp. They show (below) Mr. B speaking to band members at an evening meeting in the Main Lodge, (p. 180, top) Assistant IHS Band director Michael Walters rehearsing the band "under the big top" and, (p. 180, bottom) Mr. B studying a score.

The increased number of students in the "Little Red" Band necessitated the purchase of additional uniforms. A week prior to the band's opening-day performance the company supplying the uniforms notified Mr. B that they would not be able to deliver them on time. A group of students, aided by some band parents, sprang into action and assembled eight "substitute uniforms" by dyeing old hats, jackets and trousers red, black and gold, making them look like the new band uniforms.

The music performed in band's 1967 halftime shows:

THE MAN SHOW

    Man from La Mancha

    Dulcinea

    Little Bird, Little Bird

    Impossible Dream

BIG CHARTS SHOW

    Watermelon Man

    Georgy Girl

    Born Free

    I Love You

    Music to Watch Girls By

SOUNDS OF MUSIC

    The Sound of Music Fanfare

    My Funny Valentine

    Lover

    The Sound of Music

THE BEETLES SHOW

    Michelle Fanfare

    Yesterday

    Michelle

    Run for Your Life

    When I'm 64

    Sgt. Pepper's Lovely Hearts Club Band

Once again the band traveled to Buffalo, NY on October 15, 1967 to perform at the Buffalo-Oakland AFL football game. For some unknown reason its half-time performance was not televised in the Ithaca area. However, it was televised to other parts of the country, and thousands of people saw the band perform. NBC TV apologized for "their goof" and told Mr. B that the band's performance was the best they had seen. According to *The Ithaca Journal* the performance was **"beautiful, the kids did an especially good job."**

Below and on the following page are photos of the band's Buffalo performance.

Mr. B's Departure from Ithaca High School

Rumors began to circulate in late September that after 14 years at Ithaca High School, Mr. B was leaving to accept a faculty position at Baldwin-Wallace College in Berea, Ohio. On October 2 Mr. B informed the students that he was indeed leaving IHS in November. Perhaps it was the knowledge of Mr. B's departure that spurred band members on to greater heights—the band's last five performances were extraordinary. At the final game of the season the students, marching in the mud at Bredbenner Field, performed an emotion-filled halftime show for their departing leader.

Mr. B left Ithaca High School on November 3, 1967 to become Conductor of the Symphonic Wind Ensemble and member of the Music Education Faculty at Baldwin-Wallace College Conservatory in Berea, Ohio.

Below are two *Ithaca Journal* articles about his departure.

Frank Battisti Is Departing

By JANE MARCHAM
Journal Staff Writer

Frank L. Battisti is leaving the Ithaca schools on Nov. 3, he announced today.

Conductor of Ithaca High School bands since 1955, the director of instrumental music has accepted a post as director of bands for Baldwin-Wallace, a college near Cleveland that has a Conservatory of Music.

No replacement has been announced.

Battisti, 36, is credited with building one of the most outstanding high school bands in the nation on the foundation of already strong music programs in the Ithaca schools.

In recent years the High School Concert Band has performed to acclaim at Midwest and national music conferences in Chicago and Boston. The "Little Red" Marching Band has appeared during half-time at nationally televised games of the National Football League.

The band's program to commission new music by contemporary composers was one of the first of its kind, and is believed to be unique in that it has continued for many years. The students, with the cooperation of parents, have raised their own money for band trips and the commissioning program.

Battisti has been considering the college offer since this summer. Baldwin-Wallace held the post open so that he could

The Ithaca Journal

PAGE 13

Monday, October 2, 1967

stay here long enough to start the high school band off on its fall program, he said. The formal announcement was made to band members and school officials today.

A native of Ithaca, Battisti was graduated from Ithaca High School in 1949 and from Ithaca College in 1953, where he was a trumpet major in the School of Music.

He joined the Ithaca schools in 1953 as a part-time instructor in instrumental music while working on his master's degree. At that time John Graves, now the high school principal, was band director, as he had been when Battisti was in high school.

When Battisti was named band director in 1955, the band

had 60 members. This fall, at its peak of membership it has 160.

The commissioning program, through which 22 new works for concert band have been written, started in 1958. Week-long band camps, primarily to train the marching band for its fall appearances, have been annually since 1959.

The band director was named head of instrumental music for the Ithaca schools in 1962.

Known to students as a perfectionist, Battisti said his philosophy is to challenge each individual student to do his best work because the performance of the band as a group depends on the performance of each individual.

While music educators list no ranking of high school bands, he believes the Ithaca band is outstanding and unique and has served as an example to many other bands.

He said he is looking forward to training other band directors and teachers of music at Baldwin-Wallace, which has 300 students at its conservatory. He will also teach wind instruments and plans to work on his doctor's degree.

Baldwin-Wallace has 2,200 students, including 300 at the conservatory where members of the Cleveland Orchestra are among the instructors. Music groups there have commissioned new music and have held Bach festivals, indicating the breadth of musical insterest.

In Yankee Stadium: "Mr. B." appraises the Marching Band from the sidelines at the Giants-Browns National Football League game in October 1966

Students Are Subdued

Wish Battisti Well in New Position

By JANE MARCHAM
Journal Staff Writer

"I doubt if there is any high school band in existence today that would sound substantially better than this one," a music critic for The National Student Musician said after the Ithaca High School Concert Band's performance before music educators in Boston last winter.

Assistant Superintendent Leonard Buyse quoted the review today in paying tribute to band director Frank Battisti,

while students, school administrators, and parents regretted the impending loss of the director and wished him well in his new college post.

Buyse noted that many Ithaca students have become professional musicians due to the "stimulation and challenge of the Ithaca school's music program, with Mr. Battisti a key influence."

Battisti stressed his debt to students in announcing his "difficult decision" to them at a band rehearsal Monday afternoon.

"This is the best band in the country because it has the best kids in the country," he said. "I've discovered things in teaching, and most of the discoveries have come from members of the band. And the kids, have taught me things about myself and about life, I'm very sincere about that."

Discussing the high school's losses this year, which he said had influenced him to leave, he

said the new post as band director at Baldwin-Wallace will give him "an opportunity to grow. I can function as an imaginative teacher more perfectly there than I can here."

The students were subdued and some were tearful.

In response to their questions, Battisti said he will "try to secure as many things as possible," including the band camp and orientation programs, before he leaves. Then they collected their instruments and trooped outside for a marching rehearsal.

The band president, Elliot Carlin said Monday night, "Although the students had heard rumors that he was leaving up until Monday afternoon there was some hope that he might stay.

"The kids were really moved, that we're losing somebody like 'Mr. B'. He means a lot to us, and we're sorry to see him go, but we can only sympathize with his decision and wish him luck."

Elliot, a senior who moved to Ithaca a year ago and is a clarinetist with the band, added, "We hope his leaving won't create a void that can't be filled. It would be terrible to see the whole thing crumble because of the loss of one man. The band is a wonderful learning experience, and many former students have said how anxious they are that other students have the opportunity for the same experience."

John Graves, high school principal and his predecessor as band director, said, "I've known Frank ever since he was in grade school. I've admired the growth he's made, the vitality of his teaching and his devotion to the students.

"I hate to see him leave, but I'm not surprised he received a better offer. I'm only

sorry the environment here wasn't enough to encourage him to stay. He has gained for the community a respect, here and elsewhere, that I don't think it otherwise would have had."

The president of the Band Parents Assn. for the past year, Frank Howell, said, "The band parents think he's just about the greatest. Like all the children we're really disappointed in his leaving. It's a blow to the music department. But we wish him well, foremost, even though we'd love to keep him. We realized he'd probably move on someday."

Praising Battisti's achievements with the band, Howell remarked that high school students at football games "show as much enthusiasm for the band as they do for the football team."

Superintendent Roger Bardwell was out of town at a state superintendents' conference when Battisti announced Monday he plans to leave Nov. 3. In his absence, Buyse stated:

"Throughout his years of service Mr. Battisti has developed in the marching and concert band a tradition of excellence which has inspired the young musicians under him to achieve at an unusually high level of technical skill.

"Under his leadership these groups have demonstrated a strong dedication to their musical projects each year and have brought distinction to our school and community. We wish him the best of success in his new and challenging assignment at Baldwin-Wallace."

Buyse, whose daughter Leone was a band member and is currently a senior at the Eastman School of Music, and whose son Alan is a present member of the band, added:

"The stature of Ithaca High School band organizations is attested by a tribute to Mr. Battisti and the 1966-67 Concert Band which was made by Alan Ralph, music critic for the National Student Musician, March 1967, after the Concert Band performance at the Music Educators National Conference in Boston last February.

"The critic said, 'Mr. Battisti and his associates work hard in developing fine players, and in shaping their collective efforts into a fine musical organization such as the Ithaca High School Band. I doubt if there is any high school band in existence that would sound substantially better than this one.'

The Ithaca band has utilized as many capabilities of high school students as I have heard anywhere.'"

By coincidence, the band director Battisti will succeed, Kenneth Snapp, will be coming to Ithaca. He will become band director at Ithaca College after Battisti replaces him at Baldwin-Wallace in November.

Two hundred and eighty former and present band students, parents, friends and colleagues gathered at Cornell University's Statler Hotel on Saturday night, November 4, 1967 to honor Mr. B. Below are copies of the dinner program and a November 6 *Ithaca Journal* article describing the event.

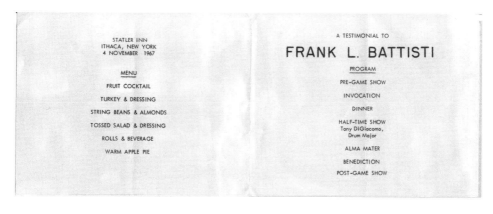

Ohio-Bound Battisti Is Honored by Friends

By JANE MARCHAM
Journal Staff Writer

Stacks of good wishes and a watch "that hums in F-sharp" accompanied Frank L. Battisti to his new post as band director at Baldwin-Wallace College, Berea, Ohio, over the weekend.

Two hundred and eighty persons attended the Statler Ballroom dinner Saturday night, honoring the director of the Ithaca High School bands for the past 12 years. They were present and former students, Band Parents, friends and colleagues in teaching and music.

The ballroom was decked with red and gold, the high school colors, and banners of the band.

As a tribute to "Mr. B.," students in this year's band have commissioned a new work by Alec Wilder which they hope will be ready in time for the spring concert. The band president, Elliot Carlin, said they felt their gift is especially appropriate because Battisti started the commissioning project which has expanded the repertoire of high school bands.

Dozens of telegrams and letters read at the dinner event honored Battisti as both teacher and musician. His wife, Charlotte, wearing a white orchid, shared the spotlight.

Wilder wrote of the director's "inspiring" personality and musicianship. The composer said that what Battisti does with his music is "magic — the band knows it, and I know it, but all he knows is that next time it had better be better."

Praising Battisti's talents as a teacher, the high school principal, John Graves, said that the band director "didn't just pass through, he became a part of students' lives, and because he is a great teacher they became a part of his life too."

Battisti said he believes the teacher's job is the help students "think for themselves," and his own "vehicle" has been the "true, exciting experience of participation in music."

He reminisced about events from the performance of a "scared" band in Cleveland Stadium six years ago to "the intensity of yesterday afternoon's rehearsal." He said, "What we have done could not have been done by one person."

A black-and white sketch of the director watching, arms folded, while the marching band performs was the cover for dinner programs. The artist, Charles Allaben of the Band Parents Assn., gave the original to Mrs. Battisti. The watch, presented to Battisti by Don Gibson, was the gift of the association.

Warren Benson, professor of composition at Rochester's Eastman School of Music and composer of music for the band while he was at Ithaca College, returned to speak at the event. Music, he said, is "love, sing, listen, being, iron, velvet, risk, stars, joy, soul, giving, tears, waiting, now, work, all, forever, I, you, we, together."

Mayor Hunna Johns observed that Battisti has brought "great honor" to the Ithaca community.

Tributes also came from other composers for the band, Vincent Persichetti, Walter Hartley and Norman dello Joio; performers Harvey Phillips of the New York Brass Quintet and Benny Goodman; conductors William Revelli of the University of Michigan, Frederick Fennell of the University of Florida and John Lounsberry of the Milwaukee Symphony; former superintendents of Ithaca schools, James I. Mason and William Gragg; former students including Bill Storandt, who was a drummer with the band and is now at the Juilliard School of Music; and John Whitney of West Genesee High School, director of the high school orchestra last year.

Other guests introduced were Battisti's parents, Mr. and Mrs. Frank Battisti of 413 Spencer Rd., his sister, Mrs. Mary Streeter of Cortland, Superintendent Roger Bardwell, Dr. Charles deProsse who is Ithaca Board of Education president, Joseph Tatascore and Joseph Moresco of the athletics department, composers Karel Husa and David Borden, and former superintendent Claude Kulp and former principal Frank Bliss.

Band director Frank L. Battisti mimicks portrait of himself presented as a farewell gift Saturday night to h's wife, Charlotte (left). The black-and-white sketch is by Charles Allaben.
—Journal Photo by George Clay

The banquet program cover was a reproduction of a painting of Mr. B standing in front of the IHS Band by band parent Charles Allaben.

Reflection by Bruce Musgrave, Class of 1965

Why It Happened

Elsewhere in this history Frank Battisti has detailed the factors that came together to create the memorable experiences described in this book. To be sure, a forward-looking school system, intent on growth and eager to support the arts, was a most helpful condition. Likewise, the quick recognition by families of the benefits that came to their children from involvement in the IHS Band made for astounding degrees of trust and support when it came to sustaining the time commitment, transportation demands, and significant costs involved in attaining high levels of instrumental musicianship. A sympathetic and supportive school administration, highly appreciative of the values inherent in music education, was more than willing over time to allocate the space, time, and fiscal resources to foster a music program of high quality. The presence in Ithaca of college-level music educators, both at Ithaca College and Cornell University, was yet another catalytic ingredient—both in supporting the training of the student musicians, and in providing counsel and a sounding board for Frank Battisti's developing aesthetic and pedagogical philosophies. It was a magical time, brought about by a magical combination of factors, but all of those who lived the experience know for certain that those contributing factors would have come to next to nothing had it not been for Frank Battisti himself. In fact, all of us know beyond doubting that absent some or even many of the supports detailed above, Frank Battisti still would have crafted both an eminent band program and an educational experience of everlasting value for the students fortunate to be present and participate.

Over the four and five decades since our days in the band, most of us have reflected endlessly on what it was about Mr. B that made him so magnetic, so dynamic, and such a pied piper, for we gladly followed wherever he led us. No doubt, those with innate musical talent discovered a godsend in Mr. B, whose rare skills at developing student musicians filled an immense void in their lives. But in fairness, it is clear that each of Frank Battisti's bands consisted of a few genuinely talented musicians surrounded by many more absolutely average Joe's and Jane's, neither musically talented nor otherwise motivated on their own to become musically competent. Frank Battisti made believers of all of them, and they often performed in ways that made it temporarily hard to distinguish them from the real musicians in their midst. What enabled this humble son of Ithaca to inspire so many in such profound ways? The question still burns in our minds fifty years later.

High energy and an incomparable work ethic were a good start. No one we knew worked either longer hours or with more sustained focus than our band director. He found ways of making every minute of the day productive, cramming in individual music lessons, processing voluminous professional correspondence (all personally executed by hand or on his Smith Corona electric typewriter), studying scores, and tending to the myriad details essential to such a high-functioning endeavor. Even when he was standing still for obligatory lunch duty in the IHS cafeteria, it was clear his mind was grinding away on the various details of the program, and he would frequently reach into his shirt pocket to jot down reminders to himself in his meticulously legible handwriting. (To this day he is the only professional most of us know whose handwriting resembles most nearly that of a fifth-grade penmanship teacher.) He usually returned to work after supper, working out the details past ten or eleven at night. One or both weekend days, passing by the high school we would find his station wagon parked in the music building parking lot for long hours at a stretch.

Supreme organizational skills and a knack of systematizing things were traits nearly as prominent in Frank Battisti as were the superhuman energy, work ethic and staying power. Seeing how hard he was working, we naturally wanted to share some of the load, and he was quick to organize student volunteers into efficient teams to sort music, mimeograph handouts, assemble pamphlets, copy marching routine sheets, orchestrate chicken barbecues, or do whatever else was necessary. Over time, he could completely delegate such tasks as lining the practice field at band camp or filing parts in the music library or supervising a sectional rehearsal to students whose alacrity and autonomy were fully inspired by his own, if never quite its equal.

In an era when mistrust of adults was rampant among adolescents, what inspired such perfect trust in and utter devotion to Frank Battisti? In part, it was because he provided something for everyone. None of us knew anyone else who was so high-functioning is so many realms, for Frank Battisti may be the world's most perfectly integrated appreciator of things low-brow, things middle-brow, and things high brow. It's impossible to forget him guffawing in the Strand Theatre over a summer matinee showing of *The Producers* with Zero Mostel. That night, he would certainly be tuned in to *The Tonight Show* to appreciate Johnny Carson's latest antics. Yet he was just as likely to be reading a new book by Mark VanDoren, Archibald MacLeish, Robert Henri, Harold Taylor, or Ben Shawn. He could revel equally in eating a Bo-Burger at the State Diner, or drinking good champagne in a fine restaurant in Rochester. He was equally at home with a hot dog in the bleachers of Cleveland Municipal Stadium watching the Indians and Twins in a double header, as he was alone in his office poring over a philosophical or psychological treatise by Eric Hoffer or Erich Fromm. He would extol with equal ardor the latest recording by George Szell and the Cleveland Symphony Orchestra, Stan Getz and Eddie Sauter, or the Beetles. He rhapsodized on the virtues of everyone from A.S. Neill (the founder of Summerhill) to the Pope.

Because of his immense enthusiasms, and his utterly wholesome modeling of deep appreciation of the attainments of others, it was impossible not to develop enthusiasms of our own and not to want to deepen our appreciation of what others had accomplished. He would laugh deeply, sigh deeply, reflect deeply, lament deeply . . . and live deeply. Vitality was his secret. We learned from him what was truly vital—essential—as well as what had great vitality—life and liveliness. Surrounded by adolescents brim-full of vitality of the most natural sort, he was the most vital one of all, right in their midst. He was getting every last drop of life out of living—right down to limiting himself to five hours of sleep a night . . . so as to give himself nineteen hours bursting with life. Listening to the *Brandenburg Concertos* and reflecting on Hinduism, it was hard not to suspect that Frank Battisti was some reincarnation of J.S. Bach, with his bubbling baroque energy and insatiable thirst for life. There was an unforgettable IHS Band era because there was an even more memorable Frank Battisti.

CHAPTER 16

Returns: Ithaca High School Band
Reunion—"The Best Reunion Ever!!!,"
June 23–24, 2006

A Battisti Birthday Reunion

By Elizabeth Peterson

During the weekend of June 23-24, 2006, more than 300 alumni and friends celebrated Frank Battisti's 75th birthday in Ithaca, New York. Many were graduates of Ithaca High School, where Frank directed the band from 1954-1967 when he left to teach at the New England Conservatory. "This is all about Mr. B. We are overcome with memories of barbecues, magazine sales, practice rooms, and music rehearsals. We remember the music

we performed in Ithaca, Danby, New York City, and Chicago. We all share the good fortune to have been in Ithaca at that time," Gregory Mosher said.

A series of guest artists performed solos and chamber works, and Donald Sinta gave the world premiere of *Elegie*, a work commissioned in memory of Warren Benson. The recital concluded with the premiere of *Frank Dialogue* by Dana Wilson, which featured a number of soloists and closed

with a rousing finale, with all soloists playing together.

On Saturday morning the alumni recreated the marching camp at the site they had used decades before. They marched down the field to recorded excerpts of their marching performances, then lined up and presented Mr. and Mrs. Battisti with band letters for their dedication, commitment, and perfect attendance. Nancy Scholes of the class of 1960 remembers Battisti's "charisma. He was a born leader who brought out the best in everybody." Mike Driscoll of the class of 1964 recalled Battisti as "inspiring and full of intensity – just as he is today." After the marching drills everyone enjoyed a picnic lunch in the same spot the band camp was held forty years ago.

At the formal dinner Saturday evening composer Dana Wilson described his new piece honoring Battisti, who had commissioned several works during his tenure at Ithaca High School. Among these are *Night Song*, *Nocturne and Rumba*, and *Star Edge* by Warren Benson; *Serenade*, *Op. 85* by Vincent Perichetti; *Theme and Fantasia* by Armand Russell; *Design's Images and Textures* by Leslie Bassett; and *Six Events for 58 Players* by Barney Childs.

photo by Robert Weiss

Photo at top by Jack Liang.

The story depicted on the opposite page appeared in the September 2006 issue of *The Instrumentalist*. It is an edited version of Elizabeth Peterson's original story (see below).

"Affectionately Known as Mr. B"

During the weekend of June 23-24, more than 235 people gathered in Ithaca, New York to pay tribute to Frank Battisti and the Ithaca High School Band program in which they participated and he directed between 1955-1967. The Ithaca High School Band Reunion weekend led by several alumni committee leaders consisted of a recital, picnic, marching band camp, several rehearsals, a reception and a formal dinner.

The opening event was a recital at the Ithaca College School of Music in which many alumni and friends performed. Tony Award-winning producer and director, Gregory Mosher gave the opening address: "This is all about Mr. B. We are all overcome with memories… from barbecues, to magazine sales, practice rooms and music rehearsals—we remember the performances in Ithaca, Danby, New York City and Chicago—the music created by us. We all share the ASTONISHING good fortune to have been in Ithaca at that time—this one tiny place in this one narrow moment of time! We found ourselves here with Frank Battisti—a great teacher, a great artist and a great person."

Featured performers in the Friday evening recital included Damian Bursill-Hall (co-principal flute, Pittsburgh Symphony); Leone Buyse (Professor of flute, Rice University, former member Boston Symphony/Pops Orchestra); Joyce Catalfano (Associate Professor of flute Emerita, West Virginia University); Brian Earle (clarinet/sax player, Central New York); Myra Kovary (teacher and professional harp performer); Richard MacDowell (Associate Professor of clarinet, University of Texas at Austin); Donald Sinta (Professor of Saxophone, University of Michigan); Alpha Hockett Walker (pianist, oboist, collaborative chamber musician and teacher); Michael Webster (Professor of Clarinet, Rice University); and David Weiss (principal oboist, Los Angeles Philharmonic and musical saw virtuoso). Each guest artist performed a solo or chamber work including the world premiere, "Elegie" which was commissioned and performed by Donald Sinta in memory of Warren Benson. The recital concluded with another premiere called *Frank Dialogue* written by Dana Wilson, which included all of the aforementioned artists. Wilson constructed the piece so that each soloist would enter the texture of the piece in the order in which they entered Frank's life—concluding with a rousing finale in which all soloists were a part.

On Saturday morning, [all the] registered alumni drove 15 miles south of Ithaca to recreate, at the original site, their marching band camp and marching drills. Marching up and down the field to recorded excerpts of their own marching performances, the members lined up and presented Mr. and Mrs. B with their band letters—for "dedication, commitment and perfect attendance!" One marching member, Nancy Scholes, class of '60, said she remembers Battisti's "incredible charisma—he was a natural born leader who could bring out the best in everybody—we learned to work hard, the whole band experience taught us valuable life long skills." Scholes said that the whole weekend felt like they were all really living *Mr. Holland's Opus*. Another alumnus, Mike Driscoll class of '64, remembered the group discipline. About Battisti, Driscoll said, "He was inspiring and full of intensity—same as today— he still has it—he kept us so involved and engaged." After the marching drills ended, all participants including the Battistis enjoyed a picnic lunch in the same place where the band camp was held [over fifty] years ago.

The following photo shows Mr. B with brother and sister John ('62) and Lois ('60) Lounsbery at IHS Band Camp in Danby during Reunion weekend.

Below are two "reflections" written by former band members following the 2006 reunion. The first is by Lynn Hushion ('64).

June 25, 2006

Like Odysseus we returned to Ithaca. His journey was ours; his trials were ours to overcome. It seems we did prevail and arrived back home no worse from the wars we've fought, and still infused with that indomitable band spirit. Our disguises are age and wisdom, only meant to fool ourselves.

A dictionary would certainly define our experience as a reunion. We've all been to some such gathering, but this was not one. It's easy to sentimentalize, but I liken it more to a rebirth and an affirmation of our collective and individual uniqueness back then and now. It showed us our ability to be the best when the best was demanded of us, from the best.

We all have our own recollections, but we all agree that Mr. B gave us good wind to set sail, one strong enough to bring us back home. Watching the last bit of the video Saturday night summed it up.

We were all sitting at tables, yet we were not. We were hovering above the earth watching our young lives below marching in and out of miracles, not circles. When the last band member placed that last foot on the mark to form a perfect line of excellence, there was little more anyone else could say other than Mr. B, to make us realize what good fortune befell us. We prepared for our voyage out in a climate of excellence, and we got to return to it all again, one more time before we finally go.

Hugs for all the roads left to travel,

Lynn Hushion

The second is by Bob Weiss, a clarinetist in the 1965-67 bands. Bob writes about a "substantial intangible thing" he gained from his IHS Band experience.

I don't recall the name of the work…[a] "chance piece" conducted by Igor the clock. Frankly, I didn't like it, on principle. I didn't see how the bizarre notation and semi-random procedure could produce music. I guess I've never been much of a modernist. For a few years after high school I continued to have a feel for the modern idiom, but I'm really a Mozart person. Dipping into Bartok and Stravinsky a little is as far as I go these days. And of course I have a lingering fondness for Richard Strauss.

I don't perform music as such now, but certain aspects of synagogue prayers seem to me a collective musical performance. I don't mean cantorial flourishes, which mostly have me looking at my watch. But for significant parts of the service the congregation reads along, mostly in low voices, collectively producing a kind of textured hum, and individually keeping rough time with the cantor, who speaks/sings aloud the beginnings and ends of paragraphs to indicate the place to the others, who can choose to treat these hints a bit casually and proceed on their own schedules. Occasionally, a member of the congregation will raise his voice for a phrase or a sentence loudly enough to stand out. When I do this, it's mostly as a concentration aid, but for others it often seems to have a more spiritual significance. I find the collective audio result pleasant to listen to and to participate in.

So imagine my surprise when I realized that the closest musical analogy I could think of to these prayers was the chance piece. Perhaps one of the substantial intangible things about the band experience was to open my mind to experiences it didn't take to naturally.

Note: The "chance" piece referred to, above, is Barney Childs's *Six Events for 58 Players*, which was premiered by the band in 1965.

Below is a sampling of messages written by 1955-67 Band members, which were posted on the IHS Band Reunion website.

Greetings from the foothills of North Carolina. I have been holding out to the last minute with hopes of being able to attend the "reunion of reunions". What a very special event to honor a very special person—Mr. B! Unfortunately, I will not be able to attend. I enjoyed reading the testimonials on the message board that brought back many memories. I went back 50 years (WOW!) when Mr.B was giving me my first trumpet lessons in the cafeteria of the old I.H.S. building. I reflected back to my first year in the I.H.S. band—marching down to the practice field, the intensity of Band Camp, the infamous concert band sectional rehearsals (I still get anxiety thinking about them), the fellowship at band parties and trips (we did have fun, didn't we!), and the satisfaction of knowing we did our very best at each performance. Thanks, Mr. B for the legacy you left with me of self-mastery, self-discipline, accountability, and integrity that have profoundly affected my personal and professional life. A special thanks to all my fellow band members for the privilege of knowing you and allowing me to be part of a very special and unique group of people. Although I can't be with you in person, I want you to know that I am alive and well, my life has been truly blessed beyond what I deserve, and I am with you in spirit. Take care and have a GREAT time for me!

Tony Dale
June 17, 2006

The upcoming reunion has certainly made me do a lot of thinking about band and high school experiences. Without a doubt, band made me a better person. I certainly was intimidated by Mr. B., but learned many things, such as the skill of learning how to pay attention to details; the desire "to be the BEST"; being forced to balance, prioritize, and complete multiple tasks; to be a team player; to love and appreciate good music; and most of all, I benefited from my friendships. I am looking forward to seeing everyone soon.

Nancy Alexander Davison
June 5, 2006

Well, here we are on the brink of the mother of all reunions! What a testament to the band experience that happened SO long ago that so many people would find it important to gather one more time to relive the memories. Obviously those years changed our lives in different yet common ways. That's why we're coming back. To thank the man who influenced us beyond explanation. I am now a Speech–Language Pathologist in my hometown public schools. Long ago Mr. B. believed in me and therefore I believed in myself. That is the lesson I have tried to instill in my students for 32 years. I think back now and NO WAY would I stand up in front of an audience and play the Vivaldi Piccolo Concerto from memory. But I did it in high school because Mr. B. said I could. I have gone out on a limb many times since then because of that valuable lesson…The flute and piccolo my dad bought me in 8th grade and I are still together. I have played some hair raising flute parts over the years that I have thought "I can't play this!!!!" But the little voice of Mr. B. in my head said "yes you can". And voila! Bravo to the committee members and class chairs for their herculian efforts to ensure the success of this incredible event! See you all soon.

Nancy Gibson Wargo
May 26, 2006

I'm looking forward to the first reunion I have ever even considered attending. The band was such an important part of all our lives. I went to Juilliard, played in wonderful professional ensembles including the Milwaukee Symphony Orchestra for 35 years, performed in Carnegie Hall, Kennedy Center, etc…in Japan, all over Europe and Cuba BUT the single best group I ever was in…handicapping for obvious differences…was the IHS Band ! Mr B was what made it all happen. High school kids are pretty much the same everywhere but we were an exceptional group. I owe my musical life to him and the 'band' experience.

John Lounsbery
May 22, 2006

I can certainly say that in my more mature years I have come to realize just what a profound influence Mr. B was in my young life and the lives of so many others. Certainly he opened the world of music to me and his wonderful work ethic, his creativity, his boundless energy and his lessons in discipline made me a better person. I was amused not so many years ago when our local university-level (advanced) concert band proudly featured such a classic as a medley of "On Top of Old Smokey" arrangements at one of its concerts; while in our high school years at IHS (more than 45 years ago) we tackled George Washington Bridge, Death and Transfiguration and Marriage of Figaro (this at a frenetic tempo, as I remember). Aren't we the lucky ones?

Margaret Musgrave Bennett
May 17, 2006

What a wonderful surprise to hear about the band reunion! Like all of you I have very fond memories of IHS band and Mr. B. I have been involved in education most of my life, first as a teacher and then as a school administrator and I have had the opportunity to meet many outstanding teachers. I believe that Mr. B. is one of the best! He inspired me to love music, love the French horn, and understand how good organizations are so dependent on good leaders. Often at seminars we are asked to tell about a good teacher we had and then a poor one. Well Mr. B. always comes to mind and I get to rave about my experience in my high school band...Remember all of the wonderful music we played! Yes, I do still play the horn once in awhile!

Sally Henderson Hallenbeck
May 11, 2006

Hi to everybody from the IHS band! I remember those rehearsals with Mr B 7th period every day. The time just seemed to fly by, even though the day had dragged waiting for band. It was wonderful to do the marching and we all sounded fantastic when we came inside for concert band after the football season. What a fantastic time we had. I have often thought how important that experience was in the development of my future. Did any other IHS Band alum go on into ethnomusicology? That was my path. I took up the study of Indian village folk music and have been working on this since 1974. I've written a few books--and also have three sons...see you all in June!

Helen Myers
April 27, 2006

I like the advice Mr. B. wrote to me in my Sr. yearbook, which I've quoted to others over the years, (and will write in a card to him,) "Work hard, have fun and continue to seek the things in life that are beautiful." !! Pretty good!!

Barbara Darling
March 7, 2006

Reflection by Bruce Musgrave, Class of 1965

Where Are They Now?

Elsewhere in this history the claim that the IHS Band was a perfect democracy has been amply illustrated. For one-man-one-vote, we need look no farther than the opening formation of any marching band show, when each band member's marching execution stands exactly equal in importance to every other band member's role in creating the net effect. The free-enterprise system and its implicit meritocracy have their clear analogues in the fair-market competitive conventions by which the concert band members earned and maintained their seats in the organization. And democratic inclusiveness and pluralism are abundantly manifest in the make-up of the IHS band, embracing as it did students from every geographical section of Ithaca, all its socio-economic classes, and the full range of diverse IHS students across all dimensions, with the possible exceptions of those with low energy, low ambition, and low desire. But surely the test of any democratic institution is what it does and the attainments of the citizens that arise from it. So where are all those band members today, what have they done, and how do those attainments connect to their days in the band?

Forty or fifty years following their participation in the IHS Band, alums have fanned out across the fifty states and quite a few foreign countries. They include prominent governmental officials, and a statesman of major national authority at the President's right hand. Among them are clergy, practitioners of many of the trades, farmers, career military officers, and major entrepreneurs of every stripe. A great many of them became physicians and attorneys, and a disproportionately large share of them became teachers of a broad range of subjects and at diverse age levels. Many professional musicians arose from their ranks, including some dozen who played conspicuous roles in major symphony orchestras, an equal number of non-orchestral professional musicians, several high school and college band directors, music scholars at various levels, and a double handful of highly influential instrumental pedagogues, several of whom rose to the first rank of national and even international music teachers. One very common fate was for them to become educational administrators at the secondary, collegiate, and university levels, and one of them coordinates student access to the arts at one of America's leading universities.

A remarkable number of them eventually married fellow band members, to whom they remained married at a rate nearly double the national average over that time span. A few of those IHS band couples were so fortunate as to see their own children go on to become IHS band members themselves. When so many of them reappeared in the hills of Danby in late June of 2006 for what several of them independently referred to as "the only reunion of any kind I ever actually wanted to attend," the impression that they had retained their idealism, enthusiasm, and energy was inescapable. And what had become of the *adults*, drawn together by Frank Battisti half a century earlier, who had so expertly fueled the quests of those adolescent seekers?

Of all the gifts Frank Battsti brought to this enterprise, among the subtlest was his knack for finding other adults—both mentors of and acolytes to him—to join him in the vital work of providing the formative experiences on which the members of the IHS band so thrived.

Jack Graves—who had been Frank Battisti's own band director and then became his boss, first as head band director, then as assistant principal, and eventually as long-time principal of Ithaca High—appeared to many of those at the reunion to be the least changed person in the room. In 2006, he was nearly indistinguishable in appearance from the man they knew in the '50s and '60s, his mind was every bit as sharp as ever, and his wit was just as deft and appealing as it had been decades early. His post-Ithaca years had included highly effective stints as a superintendent of schools in New York and New England.

Warren Benson, every bit as influential as Jack Graves on Frank Battisiti's growth as a musician and an educator, eventually left Ithaca for a long career as a professor of composition at Rochester's Eastman School of Music. Decades later the band members were still humming his melodies, reciting his poems, and drawing on his wisdom. In death he was as alive in their minds and hearts as it is possible to be.

That close friend to both Benson and Battisti, Don Sinta, the miraculous saxophone virtuoso who had come to Ithaca for a visit and stayed on in a key step in his career as a professor of saxophone at Ithaca College, eventually left Ithaca for a long and memorable career at the University of Michigan (where he succeeded his own saxophone teacher, Larry Teal). He taught yet another generation of leading saxophonists, inspired various commissioned works in his own right, and never lost one iota of his ability to mesmerize an audience with his marvelous playing—just ask those of us who heard him play at the reunion.

And what of Frank Battisti himself? Following the astounding career at Ithaca High School that has been chronicled here, he spent a short stay at the Baldwin-Wallace Conservatory of Music, and then dug in for a second memorable career at the New England Conservatory—a stint that has already given rise to one book and several doctoral dissertations in its own right. As some of us twenty-five years his junior struggle in vain to keep up with his energy, pace, ambition, and desire to share what he has seen, we couldn't be more grateful that, long ago, in the memorable words of Warren Benson, Frank Battisti decided he wasn't concerned about "making a living, but making a life." That fateful decision undeniably determined not only what he was to do and become, but also much of what all of us under his influence did and became.

POSTSCRIPT

" T he Ithaca program represented the letter and spirit of what music education should be. This was a sanctuary for what the absolute best could be regarding all the appropriate attitudes for music education. Other school band programs tried to emulate Ithaca in terms of program and philosophy, but as the ripples got further away for the source the weaker and less defined they became…eventually losing musical integrity. This program was a *very* appropriate standard for music education. " (Michael Walters, Ithaca High School Assistant Band Director, 1966-67) (Norcross, pp. 30-31)

❧ ❧

"There was a standard of excellence…I was drawn in but didn't know why…There were always kids practicing, creating, composing, experimenting with new sounds on their instruments, writing poetry, and excited in sharing this experience. I had never seen anything like this before. The program was so well organized. There was high energy and priorities." (Thomas Everett, Ithaca Public Schools Instrumental Music Teacher, 1962-67) (Norcross, p. 31)

❧ ❧

"The mature Ithaca High School Band was more than a band. It was a musical experience in which the vehicle that traveled the musical road was a band. For many of the participants this was more than a musical experience or music education, it was a life experience or life education." (Brian Norcross, author: *One Band That Took a Chance*) (Norcross, p. 110)

❧ ❧

"Music education [in the Ithaca High School Band] was comprised of purposeful instruction which promoted enlightening experiences of lasting value…indelibly transforming the lives of its students. This is the essence of music education in its most highly-evolved, idealized form." (Eugene Corporon, Director of Wind Studies, Wind Orchestra, at the University of North Texas) (Norcross, Forward, iii)

ABOUT THE AUTHORS

Frank L. Battisti

Frank L. Battisti is Conductor Emeritus of the New England Conservatory Wind Ensemble. He founded and conducted the ensemble for 30 years (1969–99). Today the NEC Wind Ensemble is recognized as one of the premiere ensembles of its kind in the United States and throughout the world. Its performances and recordings for Centaur, Albany, and Golden Crest records have earned high critical praise and accolades. Performances by the NEC Wind Ensemble have been broadcast over National Public Radio (NPR) and other classical music radio stations throughout the United States and world. Dr. Battisti was the Principal Guest Conductor of the Longy School of Music Chamber Winds from 2000–2008. He was also the founder and Music Director of the Tanglewood Institute Young Artists Wind Ensemble from 2000–2004. In 2005 he became the ensemble's Conductor Emeritus.

Dr. Battisti is responsible for commissioning and premiering over 60 works for wind ensemble by distinguished American and world composers including Warren Benson, Leslie Bassett, Robert Ceely, John Harbison, Robin Holloway, Witold Lutoslawski, William Thomas McKinley, Vincent Persichetti, Michael Colgrass, Daniel Pinkham, Gunther Schuller, Robert Selig, Ivan Tcheripnin, Sir Michael Tippett, William Kraft, Robert Ward and Alec Wilder. Critics, composers and colleagues have praised Battisti for his commitment to contemporary music and his outstanding performances.

Dr. Battisti has guest conducted numerous university, college, military, professional and high school bands and wind ensembles and served as a visiting teacher/clinician throughout the United States, England, Europe, Middle East, Africa, Scandinavia, Australia, China, Taiwan, Canada, South America, South Korea, Iceland and the former U.S.S.R.

Past President of the U.S. College Band Directors National Association (CBDNA), Battisti is also a member of the American Bandmasters Association (ABA) and founder of the National Wind Ensemble Conference, World Association of Symphonic Bands and Ensembles (WASBE), Massachusetts Youth Wind Ensemble (MYWE) and New England College Band Association (NECBA). He has also served on the Standard Award Panel of American Society for Composers, Authors and Publishers (ASCAP) and been a member of the Music Panel for the Arts Recognition and Talent Search (ARTS) for the National Foundation for Advancement of the Arts. Battisti has been an editor for various music publishing companies and is currently a consulting editor for *The Instrumentalist* magazine.

Considered one of the world's foremost authorities on wind music literature, Battisti has written many articles on wind ensemble/band literature, conducting and music education for numerous national and international professional journals and magazines (*The Instrumentalist*, *WASBE Journal*, *WINDS*, *MENC Music Journal*, etc.). He is also the author of *The 20th Century American Wind Band/Ensemble* (1995), *The Winds of Change* (2002), *On Becoming a Conductor* (2007) and co-author of *Score Study for the Wind Band Conductor* (1990) and *Lead and Inspire* (2007).

In 1986 and 1993, Dr. Battisti was a visiting fellow at Clare Hall, Cambridge University, England. He has received many awards and honors including Honorary Doctor of Music degrees from Ithaca College in 1992 and Rhode Island College in 2010, Ithaca College Alumni Association and New England Conservatory Alumni Association's Lifetime Achievement Awards in 2003 and 2008, respectively, the first Louis and Adrienne Krasner Excellence in Teaching Award from the New England Conservatory of Music in 1997, the Lowell Mason Award from the Massachusetts Music Educators Association in 1998, the New England College Band Association's Lifetime Achievement Award in 1999, Midwest International Band and Orchestra Clinic's Medal of Honor in 2001 and the National Band Directors' AWAPA in 2006.

In June 2001 Ithaca (NY) High School presented the first "Frank L. Battisti Instrumental Music Award." This award is presented annually to an Ithaca High School Band member "possessing high musicianship, a desire for excellence, creativity and enthusiasm." Dr. Battisti graduated from Ithaca High School and was its Director of Bands from 1955–67. Under his leadership the band established a reputation for being one of the best and most unique in the United States. Among its notable achievements were the commissioning and premiering of a series of 24 works by important American composers including Vincent Persichetti, Leslie Basset, Gunther Schuller, Karel Husa and Warren Benson.

Officially retired, Battisti maintains a very active guest conducting, teaching and writing career. He lives in Leverett, Massachusetts with his wife of 55 years, Charlotte.

R. Bruce Musgrave

Bruce Musgrave serves as Assistant Head of School for Academics at Palmer Trinity School in Palmetto Bay, Florida, where he also teaches a course in Advanced Placement English Language and Composition. During his forty-year career in education he has taught English and mathematics, coached 60 athletic teams for boys and girls in seven sports, and provided educational leadership as a departmental chair, director of studies, curriculum coordinator, principal, and assistant head of school. He has held positions in the public schools of Brighton, New York and State College, Pennsylvania, and at independent schools in Kamuela, Hawaii; Hilton

Head, South Carolina; Albuquerque, New Mexico; North Hollywood California; Joplin, Missouri; and Palmetto Bay, Florida.

As a member of Frank Battisti's IHS Marching and Concert Bands from 1962-65, Musgrave played the trombone and served as Drum Major and IHS Band President. He is a 1965 graduate of Ithaca High School, and he earned B.A. and M.A.T. degrees in English from Cornell University in 1970 and 1971 respectively. Born and raised in Ithaca, New York, he is the son of Robert and Mildred Musgrave. His three sisters, two of whom were also members of the Ithaca High School Band, are also career educators. His wife of forty years, Peggy Mercer Musgrave, also graduated from Ithaca High School, where she too was a member of the IHS Marching and Concert Bands.

Musgrave's professional honors include recognition as the inaugural State Teacher of the Year for Upper Schools by the South Carolina Independent Schools Association in 1986. In 1988 he was awarded the initial F. X. Slevin prize for Distinguished Teaching by Albuquerque Academy, where he was later named as the first Robert N. Philips Teaching Chair. In 1990 he was named a commissioned essayist on English instruction for the New Standards Project and the Coalition of Essential Schools, and he is a former guest columnist for the Rochester *Democrat and Chronicle's* "Concerning Children" feature. A *Cum Laude* Society member, over the years he has been awarded teaching prizes for instructional excellence by Williams College, the University of Chicago, and Southern Methodist University, all on the recommendation of former students of his who had enrolled in those institutions. His service to regional professional education organizations includes membership on ten accreditation teams. His athletic teams won six state championships in girls' tennis, and two boys' tennis state finalist trophies; his boys' soccer teams finished as state runners-up twice, one of those teams was ranked seventh in the US for a season by *USA Today*, and he coached a district-champion girls' soccer team in New York, where he also served twice as the Empire State Games Western Region Scholastic Women's Soccer Coach. He has said often that all the professional distinctions he achieved throughout his career put together were not as great an honor as being a member of the IHS Band.

APPENDICES

APPENDIX **I**   A 50th-Anniversary Concert,
May 7, 2009

A fiftieth-anniversary concert celebrating the premiere performance of IHS Band's first commissioned piece, *Night Song* by Warren Benson, was held at Ithaca High School on May 7, 2009. Mr. B conducted the world premiere of *Night Song* with the IHS Band on May 20, 1959 in Foster Hall at the "old" high school. The three-day celebration, organized by Boynton Middle School Band Director Michael Allen, included the 50th-anniversary concert, rehearsals with the Boynton Middle School and Ithaca High School Bands, a dinner and a pre-concert discussion.

Mr. B was a member of the Boynton Middle School Band (then the Boynton Junior High Band) from 1943-46 and the IHS Band from 1946-49. He graduated from IHS in 1949. In 1953 he returned to Ithaca High School to teach instrumental music lessons and two years later (1955), he became the Director of the Ithaca High School Band until 1967. When he conducted the IHS Band on Tuesday, May 5, 2009 it marked the first time he had conducted the band since he left Ithaca High School in November 1967.

The following two articles (Figures 1 and 2) about the 50th-Anniversary Celebration and Concert appeared in the April 25 and May 6, 2009 editions of *The Ithaca Journal*, respectively.

The Mayor of Ithaca, Carolyn K. Peterson, declared Thursday, May 7, 2009, Frank L. Battisti Day in Ithaca. (see Figure 3)

The concert program on May 7 featured performances by the Flumerflutes directed by Flo Flumerfelt, Boynton Middle School Concert and Symphonic Bands directed by Michael W. Allen and the Ithaca High School Concert Band directed by Nicki Zawel. Mark Fonder, Elizabeth Peterson and Mr. B were guest conductors at the concert. (see Figures 4 and 5)

Figure 1

Concert honors local musical innovator Battisti

Ithaca has long been known as a special place for music making. Students on the hills and in the city school system are known for singing, playing musical instruments, and for coming together in bands and orchestras, enriching the community and furthering their own musical abilities.

A special aspect of music making in Ithaca was innovated by Frank Battisti.

"All my life," said Battisti, "I've been interested in asking every important composer to write a piece for band or wind ensemble. Of all the things any musician who is not a composer him-

self could do, this is the most interesting."

As an example of what he meant, Battisti explained that when Serge Koussevitzky was music director of the Boston Symphony he motivated Bela Bartok to write the Concerto for Orchestra, and Battisti believed that "once he had done that, he didn't really have to do anything else the rest of his life; he had given the world something lasting."

A native Ithacan, Battisti

CAROL KAMMEN

Pieces of the Past

was born in 1931, son of Frank and Laura Battisti. The family lived on Spencer Road. Frank remembers Ithaca as a good place to grow up because "there was always something to go to or do. It was exciting to ride the streetcars up to Cornell and play pickup basketball games in Barton Hall."

He remembers, too, riding in the rumble seat of a neighbor's car out into the countryside and of huge neighborhood picnics every

summer: a "highlight social event of the year."

It was a time when children made up their own games.

"There were no little league sports," when Frank was young and the neighboring children "organized, played, referred/umpired the games we played." In addition to sports, Frank remembers fondly that "every Sunday night those of us in the neighborhood who played a musical instrument went to the home of a piano tuner who lived near by and played music together. It was great fun!"

See **BATTISTI** Page **7B**

BATTISTI

CONTINUED FROM 1B

Frank Battisti graduated from Ithaca High School in 1949 and went on to get a bachelor's degree in 1953 from Ithaca College, which had started at the end of the 19th century as the Ithaca Conservatory, a school designed to offer as good as any school of musical education in the country. Battisti received a master's degree in 1964 and an honorary doctorate in 1992.

He began his career as an instrumental teacher in the Ithaca city public schools in 1953 and became the Director of Bands at Ithaca High School in 1955.

It was as band director that Battisti began to commission new music from leading composers. In all, he was responsible for 24 new pieces of music, adding to the literature of band music, and putting the Ithaca High School band on the map with innovative and excellent musical offerings.

Some of the composers Battisti turned to were close at hand, such as Karl Husa and David Borden. Others were from around the world, and include Robert Ward, Carlos Chavez, Barney Childs, Gunther Schuller and Alex Wilder.

Battisti also brought guest soloists and conductors to play with the band and over the years he mentored hundreds of local teens. He is remembered fondly and with appreciation. One former student wrote that she felt "blessed to be a part of the concert band," and that it "has always been at the top of my list of life experiences."

At 7:30 p.m. May 7, the Ithaca High School Band will present a concert in honor of Frank Battisti, and he will be present for the event. The concert occurs on the 50th anniversary of the first work commissioned by Battisti for the high school band, a composition by Warren Benson titled, "Night Song." The concert will also be an opportunity to hear the premier of "Night Fantasy" by Greg Rudgers, and other original compositions — some by Boynton Middle School students — written especially for the occasion.

There will be a pre-concert discussion at 6 p.m. and a pre-concert recital at 6:50. This is a time for the community to enjoy the old and new, to participate in the tradition of music-making in Ithaca and also to express our appreciation for Frank Battisti's unique efforts that made the music program in Ithaca known and respected around the country.

The concert at Kulp Auditorium is free and open to the public. Don't miss it.

Figure 2

REAL-LIFE 'MUSIC MAN' RETURNS TO ITHACA HIGH SCHOOL

Above, Ithaca native Frank Battisti, 79, talks to the Ithaca High School Band about the importance of playing the quiet sections so the audience can still hear them during a rehearsal Tuesday.

Battisti, who directed the band from 1954-67, is back to celebrate the 50th anniversary of the commissioning of the work "Night Song" by Warren Benson. Battisti is in Ithaca for a week of events celebrating the anniversary and will conduct the band at 7:30 p.m. Thursday at Kulp Auditorium after a public discussion in the school library at 6 p.m.

Also on the program Thursday will be the IHS Concert Band, the Boynton Concert Band and the Boynton Symphonic Band. Battisti, pictured at left conducting "Night Song," is retired from the New England Conservatory of Music in Boston, where he taught after 1969. He now lives in Leveret, Mass, where he is studying American history while maintaining a busy music schedule.

Images by
SIMON WHEELER
Staff photos

Figure 3

City of Ithaca Proclamation

W_hereas_, you are a native son of the City of Ithaca; and

W_hereas_, you are an internationally acclaimed author and conductor; and

W_hereas_, you have continuously exposed your students to creative learning experience of lasting value ; and

W_hereas_, you have given generously of your time and expertise; and

W_hereas,_ your students have enjoyed creative and expressive opportunities, which you helped them discover; and

W_hereas_, you have demonstrated the joy and personal rewards of excellence; and

W_hereas_, under your direction the Ithaca High School Band achieved national recognition as one of the finest and most unique high school bands in the nation; and

W_hereas_, under your leadership the Ithaca High School Band became one of the truly great achievements of instrumental music in the twentieth century; and

W_hereas_, you founded national and international associations dedicated to offering generations of students and colleagues unique learning experiences; and

W_hereas_, the Ithaca Community and students in our schools are proud of your accomplishments and grateful for your willingness to share your life's work with us,

Now, _therefore, I_, CAROLYN K. PETERSON, **Mayor of the City of Ithaca,** do hereby proclaim Thursday, May 7th, 2009 as:

Frank L. Battisti Day

In the City of Ithaca

In Witness whereof I have hereto set my hand and caused the great seal of the City of Ithaca to be affixed this the 7th day of May 2009.

Carolyn K. Peterson

Carolyn K. Peterson, Mayor

Figure 4

The Ithaca City School District

Presents

50th Anniversary Concert

*****

Special Guest

Frank L. Battisti

*****

Thursday, May 7, 2009

7:30pm

Kulp Auditorium

*****

Featuring

Flumerflutes, *directed by Flo Flumerfelt*

Boynton Concert and Symphonic Bands, *directed by Michael W. Allen*

Ithaca High School Concert Band, *directed by Nicki Zawel*

*****

World Premiere of Commissioned Works by

Gregory B. Rudgers

*****

Sponsored by Hickey's Music Center and the Fine Arts Booster Group (an IPEI affiliate)

Performance Booklets provided by

Ithaca Community
Fine Arts Booster
Group

SUPPORTING THE ARTS IN THE ITHACA CITY SCHOOL DISTRICT

Figure 5

PROGRAM

Flumerflutes

The Pink Panther Suite (Theme)	Henry Mancini Arr. Amy Rice-Young

Boynton Middle School Concert Band

Triumphant Fanfare — Richard Saucedo
Dr. Mark Fonder, Guest Conductor

Circus Swing (Student Composition) — Ofer Grossman

Overture for Winds — Charles Carter
Frank L. Battisti, Guest Conductor

Emperia (Student Composition) — Jeremy Poe

Winter Fantasy (Student Composition) — Katherine Adams

Trilogy, I. In Changing Times — Bill Calhoun
Tracy Lai, Student Conductor

Boynton Middle School Symphonic Band

Air and Allegro — John Edmondson
Katherine Henderson, Student Conductor

March of the Paratroopers — Mark Williams
Noah Elman, Student Conductor

Fire and Ice (2009 World Premiere) — Gregory B. Rudgers
Elizabeth Peterson, Guest Conductor

Featured Student Soloist

Fantasie Pastorale Hongroise, Opus 26 — F. Doppler
Eleanor Bayles, Flute
Mary Ann Erickson, Piano

INTERMISSION

Ithaca High School Concert Band

Flourish for Wind Band — Ralph Vaughan Williams
Frank L. Battisti, Guest Conductor

Night Song — Warren Benson

Prelude, Siciliano and Rondo — Malcolm Arnold

Night Fantasy (2009 World Premiere) — Gregory B. Rudgers
Gregory B. Rudgers, Guest Conductor

APPENDIX **2**   Ithaca High School Band
Commissioned Works, 1955–67

(Note: Year designates the premiere date of each composition)

1959	*Night Song* by Warren Benson
1960	*Nocturne and Rumba* by Warren Benson
1961	*Serenade for Band* by Vincent Persichetti
1963	*Theme and Fantasia* by Armand Russell
	Remembrance by Warren Benson
1965	*Designs, Images and Textures* by Leslie Bassett
	Star-Edge by Warren Benson
	Six Events for 58 Players by Barney Childs
	Entertainment III by Alec Wilder
1966	*Sinfonia No. 4 for Band* by Walter Hartley
	Recuerdo by Warren Benson
	Concerto for Alto Saxophone and Band by Alec Wilder
1967	*Celebration, Op 68* by John Huggler
	Helix by Warren Benson
	All-American; Teenage; Lovesongs by David Borden
	Fiesta Processional by Robert Ward
	Turn Not Thy Face by Vincent Persichetti

The following composers were also commissioned to write pieces for the Ithaca High School Band. However, these commissions were withdrawn when Mr. B left IHS in November 1967.

Carlos Chavez
Karel Husa
Gunther Schuller
Alvin Etler
Ernst Krenek

APPENDIX **3** Ithaca High School Band Recordings,
1955–67

Ithaca High School Concert Band—Spring 1956 (LP)
Ithaca High School Concert Band—Spring 1959 (LP)
Ithaca High School Concert Band—Music for Winds—1959–60 (LP)
Ithaca High School Concert Band—Serenade for Band—1960–61 (LP)
IHS Band—1961 Fall Tour (LP)
Ithaca High School Concert Band—Spring 1962 (LP)
Ithaca High School Concert Band—1962–63 (LP)
Ithaca High School Concert Band—Remembrance—1964 Spring Concert (LP)
Ithaca High School "Little Red" Marching Band—Half-Time—Fall 1964 (LP)
Ithaca High School Concert Band—1965 IHS High School Band Festival Concert
(LP)
Ithaca High School Concert Band—Midwest Clinic Concert—December 1965
(LP)
Ithaca High School "Little Red" Marching Band—Fall 1966 (LP)
Ithaca High School Concert Band—MENC Concert—February 1967 (LP)
Ithaca High School Concert Band—A Concert of Contemporary Band Music—
1967 Spring Concert (LP)
Ithaca High School Concert Band—MENC Concert—February 1967 (LP) A Gold
Crest Honor Award Series Recording (LP)
Ithaca High School "Little Red" Marching Band—Mr. B—Fall 1967 (LP)
Ithaca High School Concert Band—Remembrance—Frank L. Battisti and the
Ithaca High School Band (2006 Reunion CD)
Ithaca High School Bands 1954–67—The Best Ever Reunion (2006 Reunion CD
& DVD)

APPENDIX **4** Resources Used in
Writing This Book

Battisti, Frank L.—Private Letters, Papers and Photographs in Battisti Archive at
Ithaca College.
Ithaca High School Marching and Concert Band LP Recordings 1955-67.
Norcross, Brian—*One Band That Took a Chance*, Meredith Music Publications,
1984.
Selmer Bandwagon (November 1965).
The Ithaca Journal (editions from 1953–67).
The Annual (Ithaca High School Yearbook), 1954–1968.